Mastering
Financial management

Palgrave Master Series

Accounting
Accounting Skills
Advanced English Language
Advanced English Literature
Advanced Pure Mathematics
Arabic
Basic Management
Biology
British Politics
Business Communication
Business Environment
C Programming
C++ Programming
Chemistry
COBOL Programming
Communication
Computing
Counselling Skills
Counselling Theory
Customer Relations
Database Design
Delphi Programming
Desktop Publishing
e-Business
Economic and Social History
Economics
Electrical Engineering
Electronics
Employee Development
English Grammar
English Language
English Literature
Fashion Buying and Merchandising
  Management
Fashion Styling
Financial Management
French
Geography
German
Global Information Systems

Globalization of Business
Human Resource Management
Information Technology
International Trade
Internet
Italian
Java
Language of Literature
Management Skills
Marketing Management
Mathematics
Microsoft Office
Microsoft Windows, Novell NetWare
  and UNIX
Modern British History
Modern European History
Modern United States History
Modern World History
Networks
Novels of Jane Austen
Organisational Behaviour
Pascal and Delphi Programming
Philosophy
Physics
Practical Criticism
Psychology
Public Relations
Shakespeare
Social Welfare
Sociology
Spanish
Statistics
Strategic Management
Systems Analysis and Design
Team Leadership
Theology
Twentieth-Century Russian History
Visual Basic
World Religions

www.palgravemasterseries.com

Palgrave Master Series
Series Standing Order ISBN 0–333–69343–4
(outside North America only)

You can receive future titles in this series as they are published by placing a standing order. Please contact your booksetter or, in case of difficulty, write to us at the address below with your name and address, the title of the series and the ISBN quoted above.

Customer Services Department, Macmillan Distribution Ltd

Houndmills, Basingstoke, Hampshire RG21 6XS, England

Mastering
Financial management

John Whiteley, FCA

Business Series Editor
Richard Pettinger

Published by
PALGRAVE MACMILLAN
Houndmills, Basingstoke, Hampshire RG21 6XS and
175 Fifth Avenue, New York, N.Y. 10010
Companies and representatives throughout the world

PALGRAVE MACMILLAN is the global academic imprint of the Palgrave
Macmillan division of St. Martin's Press, LLC and of Palgrave Macmillan Ltd.
Macmillan® is a registered trademark in the United States, United Kingdom
and other countries. Palgrave is a registered trademark in the European
Union and other countries.

ISBN 1–4039–1336–6

This book is printed on paper suitable for recycling and made from fully
managed and sustained forest sources.

A catalogue record for this book is available from the British Library.

Library of Congress Cataloging-in-Publication Data
Whiteley, John, 1943 June 27-
    Mastering financial management / John Whiteley.
        p. cm. – (Palgrave master series)
    Includes bibliographical references and index.
    ISBN 1-4039-1336-6 (paper)
    1. Business enterprises–Finance. 2. Corporations–Finance. I. Title: Financial
management. II. Title. III. Series.
HG4026.W485 2003
658.15–dc22   2003055875

10   9   8   7   6   5   4   3   2   1
13 12 11 10 09 08 07 06 05 04

Printed and bound in Great Britain by
Creative Print & Design (Wales), Ebbw Vale

Contents

**Companion website contents
(www.palgrave.com/masterseries/whiteley)**

Rewarding employees and share scheme incentives
Reporting requirements of the Companies Act 1985
Accounting Standards
Types of business insurance
Tax compliance and planning
Individual and partnership self assessment
Corporation Tax self assessment
PAYE – a summary
VAT danger areas
Stamp Duty – a summary
Bankruptcy and liquidation principles, and small claims in the County Court
Credit card trading
Self diagnosis credit control health check
Incentives for venture capital

◼▾ Preface

The financial director or manager is a key player in the management of any business or other organisation. Finance is one of the major resources which have to be managed well to ensure the success of the organisation.

In this book, I have brought together the main elements of financial management. I have dealt with the practical aspects as well as the academic ones. The book should therefore be of use to students, to those managing their own smaller businesses, and to those already in positions of some responsibility in financial management of larger organisations. I have drawn on over 25 years' experience as a practising Chartered Accountant.

The names of the businesses used in examples and exercises are fictional, and if any businesses exist bearing those names, I apologise – this is entirely unintentional, and does not imply any knowledge of those businesses.

I have enjoyed writing this book, and hope that you will enjoy – and benefit from – reading it.

JOHN WHITELEY

▼ 1 Introduction

Taking control

Finance is one of the most important resources of a business, or indeed any organisation. The management of finance is the subject of this book. The key to management of any resource is the ability to take control of it. Throughout this book, you will find slogans, to encapsulate important key ideas. Here is the first, which will be repeated in several different contexts:

▶ If you can measure it, you can control it.

The key to control, in finance as in any other area, is accurate measurement. In order to measure things accurately, certain techniques must be learnt. Those techniques form the bulk of the rest of this book. The chapters include examples, discussion questions and exercises to work through, with answers at the end of the book.

The art and craft of financial management

This subject is not simply a matter of learning techniques. Certain personal attitudes of mind and interpersonal skills must be cultivated. To a large extent, these come with experience, but it is worth pointing out some of the basic elements here.

Financial management requires an attitude of mind which can be summarised by:

▶ Take nothing for granted. Question everything.

For example, when dealing with cost accounting, it is vital to understand the nature of each individual cost element. A costing system is a model of the business as a whole. Financial managers must understand the data.

Retaining integrity

It is essential to instil confidence in those with whom you deal. In his dealings with you, a bank manager will certainly be assessing the person as much as the business. Different groups – shareholders, customers, suppliers, employees, lenders, board members – will have different expectations, which must be balanced against each other. Understanding and balancing these expectations often calls for real interpersonal skills.

Profitability is the key to business survival – without it, there will not be a business to continue. However, the moral and ethical dimension to managing finance must be cultivated, too. Honesty and integrity must come before financial gain – either personally or for the business. To retain the trust of other board members, investors, and employees, all communications must be transparently honest and open.

The long-term interest of the business – and thereby of the shareholders – should be constantly in view. Short-term decisions often conflict with the long-term prospects of the business. Any business also has a wider responsibility to the environment, to society, and to the local community. A financial manager who can manage all these aspects will earn the respect of others who matter to the organisation, and build up a reserve of goodwill, which is one of the most important assets to bring to management.

Good communication should never deteriorate into 'spin' or manipulation of the facts and figures. Too many financial scandals and frauds have been the result of deliberate misrepresentation of figures, and, hence, misleading information. In recent history, the names 'Enron' and 'Worldcom' should be enough to remind all financial managers that the ultimate goal of communicating financial information is to present the situation as it really is.

Personal relationships

Managing finance involves co-operation with shareholders, with other people in the business, with customers and suppliers, and with bank managers or other lenders.

Current wisdom is that finance directors should not just be the mileometer of the business (i.e. measuring past performance), but they should start to become the engine – driving the business. For larger businesses, and particularly for publicly quoted companies, that emphasis has a bearing on the relationship between the financial director and the chief executive. Trust and respect between these two key people is vital.

This book also touches on various non-financial areas of management. This is not accidental, or a mistake. Understanding of other areas is vital to financial management.

Developing communication skills

Financial managers must learn communication skills. In essence, this means ensuring that the listener or reader understands the same message as the financial manager wishes to convey. They must communicate with

- other managers,
- other employees,
- directors,

- investors, and
- the public.

This requires an ability to express one's self clearly in written or spoken English, as far as possible without jargon. In finance matters particularly, and especially when dealing with board members or other managers, members of the audience are often embarrassed to ask for an explanation of something not understood. They may think that they should understand it, and be embarrassed at any lack of understanding.

Here is a golden rule of communication:

▶ Never underestimate the intelligence of your audience, but never overestimate their knowledge of your specialist subject.

More than that, communication requires the ability to establish the key facts: to distinguish the relevant from the irrelevant, the material from the immaterial, the core from the peripheral. Oscar Wilde said that facts are 'seldom pure and never simple'. Facts – especially financial ones – usually need interpretation. The skilful financial manager will be able to offer meaningful comment on the implications of the choices put before the audience – whether that audience be the board of directors, other managers, or shareholders.

Timeliness is essential in presenting reports that are needed to control the business and as the basis for decision making. Many financial disasters could have been avoided if those responsible for presenting financial information had communicated it at the right time. Directors and shareholders depend on financial managers to spot potential problems and crises before they materialise.

I have written this book assuming that the reader has no prior knowledge of the subject, and tried to avoid jargon, and explain concepts simply. There is a glossary of key terms at the end of the book, and a list of websites that I hope will prove useful for further investigation. In particular, the companion website for this book gives much more information relating to the subjects covered. The website address is www.palgrave.com/masterseries/whiteley

◼ Ⓥ 2 Understanding accounts

LEARNING OUTCOMES

By the end of this chapter, you should be able to:

▶ understand the types of financial statements produced, and the needs of their users,
▶ identify the components of financial statements, and their significance,
▶ appreciate the benefits of comparisons with other figures – both internally and externally,
▶ understand the key ratios used in statistical analysis, their uses and limitations, and
▶ adapt these methods to non-profit organisations.

Introduction

This chapter explains how to interpret accounts. They are not just a set of figures on a piece of paper, without any context. A financial manager must be able to see the reality behind the figures. In this chapter we examine different types of accounts, and what they mean. Comparisons, ratios and statistical analysis are the tools which we shall start to learn to use. We also look at performance measures for non-profit organisations.

What is behind the figures?

A casual reader may look at financial statements, go straight to the bottom line to see what the profit is, and leave it at that. A more interested person might look at the turnover figures to see how the sales are going. Many people do not get further than a cursory glance because they do not understand the intricacies of the relationships between the various figures in the financial statements.

Types of accounts

Financial statements which are issued once a year for the benefit of shareholders or proprietors, and lodged with Companies House are generally called the annual accounts. These are really for external consumption. In the case of companies, they can be subject to audit, dependent on the size of the company, and they may not appear promptly after the end of the financial period (which is usually a year).

In contrast, internal financial statements, generally known as management accounts, are not intended for the general public or even shareholders. They are produced for the benefit of managers, and should be made available extremely promptly after the end of the accounting period to which they relate. The accounting period used for management accounts is usually monthly, although for some smaller businesses, it could be quarterly.

Components of accounts

Whatever type of financial statement is under consideration, it will consist of a profit and loss account and/or a balance sheet. Accountants may expand on these forms, or adapt them to suit the purpose for which they are prepared, but they are essentially variations of the same thing.

A typical set of accounts, in abbreviated form, is shown in Figure 2.1. These consist of a profit and loss account, and a balance sheet. The figures for the immediately preceding period are shown for comparison. By commonly accepted convention, these comparative figures are shown on the right hand side of the current figures.

Profit and loss account

This account is always stated to be for a period, which is usually, but not always, a year.

Income

The profit and loss account shows the gross income, also known as turnover. This will consist mainly of the core income, whether from sales of products or services, or some other form. Other income from incidental sources is shown separately.

Direct costs

The direct costs (cost of sales) are deducted from the gross income to give the gross profit. As we shall see below, this gross profit figure is a key figure in the accounts. The percentage relationship of the gross profit to turnover is a key business indicator.

Overhead expenses

Overhead expenses are categorised into the different types of expense, and these categories, such as administration, property, transport, finance, and so on, are also useful in getting an insight into the business, and how it runs. The overhead expenses are deducted from the gross profit to arrive at the net profit, or net loss. The relationship of net profit to turnover is also a key business indicator.

Profit and loss account for the year ended 31st December 20xx

	Current year £million	Current year £million	Previous year £million	Previous year £million
Sales		500		450
Cost of sales		300		250
Gross profit		200		200
Other income		5		2
		205		202
Overheads		110		104
Net profit		95		98
Taxation	30		30	
Dividends	40		35	
		70		65
Retained profit		25		33

Balance sheet as at 31st December 20xx

	£million	£million	£million	£million
Fixed assets		400		350
Current assets	130		114	
Current liabilities	65		59	
Working capital		65		55
		465		405
Long-term liabilities				
Loans		80		85
Net assets		385		320
Capital				
Share capital		150		120
Share premium		10		
Profit and loss account		225		200

Figure 2.1 Specimen company accounts for the year ended 31st December 20xx

Appropriations

Appropriations of profit are deducted from the net profit (or loss). The most usual appropriations of profit are dividends and taxation, leaving a final figure expressed as retained profit (or accumulated losses). That is to say, it is the profit not paid away in taxation or in dividends to shareholders, and therefore retained in the business.

The profit and loss account, therefore, shows the result of the business activities for the period. For other 'not for profit' organisations, a similar account is prepared. However, because the organisation is not for profit, the account is called an income and expenditure account. It is highly unlikely that the income will exactly match the expenditure, so the excess of income over expenditure is called a surplus, and an excess of expenditure over income is called a deficit.

In Figure 2.1, identify the following (for both years):

(a) Turnover
(b) Total income from all sources
(c) Total appropriations

Balance sheet

The balance sheet is always stated as at a particular date, which is always the final date of the period for which the profit and loss account is prepared.

The balance sheet shows the financial position of the business at the date shown. The assets are stated, and liabilities are deducted from them, leaving the net assets of the business.

Capital

The net assets are represented by the capital of the business. In a limited company, this capital includes the share capital, and there may also be a share premium account (representing monies paid by shareholders in excess of the nominal value of the shares). The other element of capital is the accumulated reserves of the profit and loss account. There could also be other capital reserves, which are sometimes created when assets are revalued, and similar transactions.

In an unincorporated business, such as a partnership or a sole trader, the capital is made up of the capital accounts of all the proprietors, i.e. the sole trader or the partners. This capital consists of the money put into the business by the proprietors, added to their shares of profits, and from which any monies drawn out of the business are deducted.

Whatever the form of the business, the capital will always be equal to the net assets of the business.

Another way of looking at the correspondence between the net assets and the capital is to say that the capital is the sum that is invested in the business by the shareholders or proprietors. The concrete expression of that investment, in terms of assets and liabilities, is shown in more detail in the balance sheet.

Fixed assets

These are long-term assets of the business, consisting of tangible and intangible assets.

Tangible assets

These are assets which can actually be seen and touched, as the name suggests. They include things like land and buildings, plant and machinery, vehicles, and so on.

Intangible assets

These are things which do not have a physical existence – such as goodwill, patents and so on.

Depreciation

All fixed assets are subject to depreciation, which is written off the value of these assets each accounting period. This, in effect, spreads the cost of the assets over their useful lives.

Current assets

These are short-term assets which by their nature change from day to day – even from hour to hour – in the course of business. They include things like the bank balance, monies owing from debtors, stock, and expenses paid in advance.

Current liabilities

These are the short-term liabilities of the business, a counterpart to the current assets. Like them, they change from day to day in the course of business. They include such things as bank overdrafts, current instalments on hire purchase contracts or loans, monies owing to creditors, and expenses which have accrued. Current liabilities are generally recognised as those which fall due within one year of the balance sheet date.

Working capital $= CA - CL$

The difference between current assets and current liabilities (net current assets) is known as working capital. The management of this will be considered in more detail in Chapter 5. If the current liabilities are greater than the current assets, the difference is known as a working capital deficit. A working capital deficit could mean that the business is insolvent, although this is not necessarily true – particularly in businesses operating on a largely cash basis, such as retail shops. Insolvency means that the business is unable to meet its current liabilities as they become due.

Long-term liabilities

These are liabilities which are due for payment more than one year after the balance sheet date. They include things like long-term loans, and later instalments on loans and hire purchase contracts.

Net assets

This is simply the net sum of all the assets less the liabilities of the business. If the total liabilities exceed the total assets, then the business has net liabilities. It is also, of course, a sign of financial weakness, at the very least, and could indicate the financial collapse of the business.

EXERCISE 2.2

    In Figure 2.1, identify the following (both years):

    (a) Working capital (net current assets)

    (b) Total gross assets

    (c) Total capital

Comparisons

Internal comparisons

The figures do not exist on their own, independently of anything else. They are at their most useful when shown in comparison to something else. The most common comparisons are between the current and corresponding previous accounting periods, and of actual with budgeted figures.

    The comparison with the previous period will show what progress, or otherwise, has been made. The comparison of several preceding periods will show trends. Trends may be indicative of growth or decline, or they may follow cyclical patterns, which may mirror the economy of the country generally, or they may be peculiar to the specific trade or industry.

    The comparison with budget will show how far plans and targets have been achieved. We consider budgets in more detail in Chapter 4.

    Internal comparisons show the relationships of various figures to each other. These are considered in more detail in the section dealing with statistical analysis and key ratios.

━━━

EXERCISE 2.3

    What key features of the business can be gleaned from the comparison of the current year's figures in Figure 2.1 with the previous year's figures?

External comparisons

The figures and ratios can also be compared with those in competitors' financial statements. This could show that other businesses may be performing better in certain areas than your own business, or worse. Action can be taken to remedy situations which can be improved upon. The theory is that if one, or several other businesses can perform better in a certain area, then that better performance must be achievable.

    How is it possible to obtain access to competitors' accounts? All companies must file accounts with Companies House, and it is possible to search the records of other companies to look at their figures. However, the information filed at Companies House is often minimal. The requirements for accounts to comply with the Companies Act allow just the bare bones to be published. Many of the detailed figures are not in the public realm.

Many industries or business sectors have organisations which carry out surveys of key figures and ratios. To do this, they need access to figures that are not generally available at Companies House. However, most companies would not be happy at releasing details of their most sensitive and confidential figures. Therefore, the organisations which carry out these inter-business comparisons guarantee complete security and anonymity. They collate all the figures from different businesses and produce tables showing the average, median, top, middle and bottom quartiles, and so on. Each business will then also receive its own individual figures to show where it appears in the 'league table'. This enables action to be taken on those areas in which performance is low.

Always bear in mind, however, that very few, if any, consolidated accounts have similar characteristics these days, so there must be a large element of discrimination.

Statistical analysis and key ratios

By comparing different figures within the set of accounts, certain key ratios and relationships can be measured. These provide useful pointers to areas where business performance and profitability can be improved. Detailed examination of the key ratios and relationships often leads to more searching questions about various areas of business performance.

The key ratios shown here will be illustrated by reference to the specimen financial statements shown in Figure 2.2, which is an expanded form of the information given in Figure 2.1. The extra column shows the budget figures for the current year. The presentation is not in strict Companies Act format, but drawn up to illustrate the ratios.

The reference letters on each line to the right of the current year figures are used for identification in the explanations below.

Profit ratios

Gross profit percentage

The ratio of the gross profit to the sales (or turnover) is one of the most important key ratios for any business, of whatever type. It can be adapted to manufacturing, wholesale, retail, and even service businesses.

The gross profit (f) is calculated by deducting the cost of sales (e) from the sales turnover (a). The gross profit percentage is the gross profit (f) expressed as a percentage of the sales turnover (a). The formula is therefore:

$$\frac{f}{a} \times 100$$

In the example, the gross profit percentage is 40%, compared to 44.4% in the previous period and 43.6% in the budget.

This gross profit percentage can be further analysed to find out the reasons for any variations from the expected figure. There are several reasons for variations in gross profit percentage, including:

Profit and loss account

	Current year £million	Current year £million		Previous year £million	Previous year £million	Budget £million	£million
Sales		500	a		450		550
Cost of sales							
Materials	150		b	120		150	
Direct labour	100		c	80		110	
Factory costs	50		d	50		50	
		300	e		250		310
Gross profit		200	f		200		240
Other income		5			2		3
		205			202		243
Overheads							
Property	20		g	15		20	
Salaries	30		h	28		32	
Maintenance	10		i	12		12	
Administration	5		j	6		5	
Transport	10		k	11		9	
Marketing	10		l	9		10	
Depreciation	10		m	9		10	
Interest	15		n	14		15	
Total overheads		110	o		104		113
Net profit		95	p		98		130
Taxation	30		q	30		40	
Dividends	40		r	35		45	
		70			65		85
Retained profit		25	s		33		45

Balance sheet

	Current year £million	Current year £million		Previous year £million	Previous year £million	Budget £million	£million
Fixed assets		400	t		350		390
Current assets							
Stock	40		u	35		45	
Work in progress	10		v	9		10	
Debtors	60		w	55		55	
Cash and bank	20		x	15			20
	130		y	114			130
Current liabilities							
Trade creditors	40		z	37		40	
Taxes	10		aa	8		12	
HP instalments	5		ab	6		4	
Overdraft	10		ac	8		5	
	65		ad	59		61	
Working capital		65	ae		55		69
Total assets less current liabilities		465			405		459
Long-term liabilities							
Loans		80	af		85		70
Net assets		385	ag		320		389
Capital							
Share capital							
Preference shares	50		ah	50		50	
Ordinary shares	100		ai	70		82	
	150		aj	120		132	
Share premium	10		ak			20	
		160	al		120		152
Profit and loss account		225	am		200		237
Shareholders' funds		385	an		320		389

Figure 2.2 Specimen company accounts for the year ended 31st December 20xx

Sales mix: The mix of products included in the total sales may have shown a variation which could affect the overall gross profit percentage. For example, some lines may carry a higher profit mark up than others. A typical corner shop might sell tobacco products, confectionery, newspapers, and greetings cards. The mark up on tobacco would usually be much less than the mark up on greetings cards and confectionery. Thus, a change in the relative volumes of sales would affect the overall percentage.

Increased competition: Competition may force price cuts, with no corresponding cut in the cost of sales. This would adversely affect the gross profit percentage.

Increased materials cost The cost of raw materials may have risen, with little or no chance of passing these increases on to customers by increasing sales prices.

Cost of sales analysis

Since the gross profit is calculated by deducting the cost of sales from the sales turnover, it follows that the cost of sales expressed as a percentage of the sales turnover is complementary to the gross profit percentage. Thus, in the example, the current year's gross profit percentage is 40%, so the cost of sales percentage is 60%. This can be checked by calculating the cost of sales (e) as a percentage of the sales turnover (a). The formula is:

$$\frac{e}{a} \times 100$$

Where the cost of sales is made up of several items, the various components can be compared separately. Thus, in the example in Figure 2.2, the total cost of sales is £300 million, or 60% of turnover. Further analysis can be carried out to show the relative percentages of materials, direct labour, and factory costs. This would yield the following results:

	Percentage of sales		
	Current year	*Previous year*	*Budget*
Materials (b × 100/a)	30%	26.7%	27.3%
Direct labour (c × 100/a)	20%	17.8%	20%
Factory costs (d × 100/a)	10%	11.1%	9.1%

Each of these variations, particularly against the budgeted figures, can then be investigated. Most of the direct costs are variable costs – that is to say, they vary in direct proportion to the sales. Therefore, it would be expected that the percentage relationship of these items to the sales would remain constant. Thus, where there is a significant variance – as in the above example, for materials cost – the cause should be investigated. For instance, the increase could be due to a volume variance, or a cost variance, compared to both the previous year and the budgeted figure.

A volume variance means that the amount of materials used, or paid for and not used, has varied. This could be due to some malfunction in the manufacturing process, or other reasons such as wastage, loss or pilferage of materials.

A cost variance means that the same volume has cost more than either the previous year or the budgeted amount, and this should lead to steps being taken to control costs.

However, some of the direct costs may have an element of fixed cost, and this is particularly so in the case of direct labour and factory costs. These percentages may therefore be affected by the volume of sales and activity. The control issues here are therefore different from the control of items which are fully variable.

This process of cost analysis provides a good example of the principle seen in the introduction, which it is worth reiterating:

▶ If you can measure it, you can control it.

Detailed gross profit analysis

The analysis of cost of sales and of gross profit margins may also be extended to cover more complex situations with different products, departments or sales lines.

EXERCISE 2.4

High Street Motors sales consist of the following elements:

- Fuel and oil sales
- New car sales
- Second hand car sales
- Servicing and spares sales

The various items of sales and cost of sales are grouped into those categories to provide an analysis of the gross profit of each department. The analysis is illustrated in Figure 2.3. This analysis can be used to highlight areas in which the performance of the departments can be compared with each other for the current year, with the previous year's figures and with the budgeted figures.

What issues might be raised from this analysis?

Net profit percentage

This is a similar calculation to the gross profit percentage. However, it measures the net profit before tax and dividends or other distributions (line p in Figure 2.2) as a percentage of the sales. The formula is:

$$\frac{p}{a} \times 100$$

In this case, the figure is 19%, compared with the previous year's percentage of 21.8%, and the budgeted figure of 23.6%. This percentage can vary much more than the gross profit percentage.

Total figures

	Current year £million	£million	Previous year £million	£million	Budget £million	£million
Sales		600		610		660
Cost of sales						
Materials	370		360		398	
Direct labour	78		75		75	
Direct costs	21		22		22	
		469		457		495
Gross profit		131		153		165
Gross profit percentage		21.8		25.1		25.0

Fuel sales

	Current year £million	£million	Previous year £million	£million	Budget £million	£million
Sales		200		180		210
Cost of sales						
Materials	185		165		185	
Direct labour	3		3		3	
Direct costs	2		2		3	
		190		170		191
Gross profit		10		10		19
Gross profit percentage		5.0		5.6		9.0

New car sales

	Current year £million	£million	Previous year £million	£million	Budget £million	£million
Sales		200		200		220
Cost of sales						
Materials	100		95		110	
Direct labour	6		6		5	
Direct costs	5		5		5	
		111		106		120
Gross profit		89		94		100
Gross profit percentage		44.5		47.0		45.5

Second hand car sales

	Current year £million	£million	Previous year £million	£million	Budget £million	£million
Sales		80		120		100
Cost of sales						
Materials	60		80		75	
Direct labour	4		6		5	
Direct costs	4		5		4	
		68		91		84
Gross profit		12		29		16
Gross profit percentage		15.0		24.2		16.0

Servicing and spares sales

	Current year £million	£million	Previous year £million	£million	Budget £million	£million
Sales		120		110		130
Cost of sales						
Materials	25		20		28	
Direct labour	65		60		62	
Direct costs	10		10		10	
		100		90		100
Gross profit		20		20		30
Gross profit percentage		16.7		18.2		23.1

Figure 2.3 High Street Motors analysis of figures

> Why should the net profit percentage be subject to wider variation than the gross profit percentage?

The net profit percentage shows how much of each pound's worth of sales remains as profit after all expenses. However, tax has to be taken out of this figure and dividends or distributions can only be made out of net profit.

Overheads percentage analysis

As we have seen, the net profit percentage can vary greatly because of the many different overhead expenses. Measuring each overhead expense as a percentage of sales can also be used to indicate possible areas of control. Thus, in Figure 2.2, the comparative overheads percentage analysis would produce:

Overheads	Current year	Previous year	Budget
	% of sales	% of sales	% of sales
Property	4	3.3	3.6
Salaries	6	6.2	5.8
Maintenance	2	2.7	2.2
Administration	1	1.3	0.9
Transport	2	2.4	1.6
Marketing	2	2	1.8
Depreciation	2	2	1.8
Interest	3	3.1	2.7
Total overheads	22	23.1	20.5

The reasons for all variations should be explained. These explanations can lead to further examination of individual items making up each category of overheads.

It is not just the unfavourable variations that require explanation.

EXAMPLE 2.1

> Within the category of administration costs, the amount spent on insurance shows a favourable comparison to the budgeted figure. This should be examined to consider whether all aspects of the business are adequately insured. The insurance cost could be too low because the business does not have adequate cover. The amount of cover for each risk should be reviewed regularly, and the comparative costs of covering the risks should be reviewed at regular intervals to ensure value for money.

The nature of overheads

The nature of each type of overhead expense should also be borne in mind when seeking explanations of variances. Some expenses, such as advertising or marketing, may have a budgeted cap, and the department responsible has a certain budget within which it must work. Any overspend on budgeted items such as this must be carefully investigated, to see if any breach has occurred in internal controls.

Most overheads are fixed by their nature – that is, they are not directly variable in relation to sales. However, some overheads do have a variable element as well as a fixed element. For example, administrative salaries may well be fixed up to a certain point. However, if there is a large expansion in operations, more administrative staff may be necessary. The same may be true of distribution and transport costs. The salaries of sales staff often include a fixed element of salary, and an element of commission based on sales.

Return on capital employed (ROCE)

This is the net profit (before interest, tax and dividends) expressed as a percentage of the total capital employed in the business. Thus, it includes equity capital and loan capital. This ratio therefore measures the total returns to all suppliers of long-term finance, whether by loans or by equity capital.

In Figure 2.2, the formula is:

$$\frac{\text{Net profit plus interest} \times 100}{\text{Shareholders' capital plus long-term loans}}$$

or:

$$\frac{(p + n) \times 100}{(an + af)}$$

This calculation produces a figure of 23.7% for the current year, compared to 27.7% the previous year, and 31.6% budgeted.

Return on investment

This is sometimes known as 'return on shareholders' funds', and is thus distinct from the ROCE. This is expressed as the percentage of net profit to shareholders' funds.

- The definition of net profit is the profit before tax and dividends.
- The definition of shareholders' funds is the equity capital plus reserves. Thus, it excludes loan capital, and therefore the result of this calculation is greatly affected by the gearing (see below).

In Figure 2.2, the formula is:

$$\frac{\text{Net profit} \times 100}{\text{Shareholders' capital}}$$

or:

$$\frac{p \times 100}{an}$$

This calculation produces a figure of 24.7% as the return on shareholders' funds for the current year. However, this has declined from 30.6% the previous year, and the budgeted figure was 33.4%. Clearly some explanation is needed.

The significance of 'return on investment' and 'return on capital employed'

The return on investment, when considered in conjunction with other ratios, such as interest cover and dividend cover, is a key indicator to analysts and investors who might be considering investing in the business. The main point of investing in a business is to earn a regular income from it. The rate of return on the money invested is therefore of vital interest to the general investing public. It is therefore of vital importance to those managing the finances of the business.

Liquidity ratios

Current ratio

This is one of the key ratios in measuring liquidity. Liquidity can be closely allied to working capital, and the management of working capital is discussed in Chapter 5. The current ratio is simply the relationship between current assets and current liabilities. It is normally expressed as the ratio of current assets to current liabilities.

The current ratio calculation will arrive at a figure greater or less than one. If the current assets are greater than the current liabilities, the result will exceed one. If the current liabilities exceed the current assets, the result will be less than one.

In Figure 2.2, the calculation is:

$$\frac{\text{Current assets}}{\text{Current liabilities}}$$

or:

$$\frac{y}{ad}$$

The result of this is 2, meaning that the current assets are double the current liabilities. The previous year's ratio was 1.93. However, it was budgeted to have increased to 2.13.

If this ratio yields a figure of less than one, it might indicate some degree of illiquidity. However, some businesses, such as supermarkets, do manage to operate on a low ratio. This ratio is of the first importance, and trends must be monitored regularly.

Quick ratio

This is sometimes known as the 'acid test' ratio. The stock is excluded from the current assets, and the quick ratio is therefore a measure of the immediately available monies, compared with current liabilities.

This calculation will always result in a lower figure than the current ratio. However, the important aspect of this ratio is the trend. This ratio also gives a more sharply defined test of liquidity and solvency.

In Figure 2.2, this formula is:

$$\frac{\text{Current assets less stock and work in progress}}{\text{Current liabilities}}$$

or:

$$\frac{y - (u + v)}{ad}$$

The result of this is 1.23, compared to 1.18 the previous year, and a budgeted ratio of 1.23.

Activity ratios

These ratios cover the activities of the business and show the efficiency of the controls in various aspects of the business, such as stock turnover, and credit control.

Debtor days

This measures the debts outstanding on the sales ledger against the annual sales to give a figure showing the number of days' sales which are outstanding at any one point. In Figure 2.2, the calculation (assuming that the whole of the debtors are sales ledger debtors) is:

$$\frac{\text{Sales ledger debtors} \times 365}{\text{Annual sales}}$$

or:

$$\frac{w \times 365}{a}$$

The result is 43.8. Thus, at the balance sheet date, there are 44 days' sales outstanding (to the nearest day). The previous year's figure was 45 days, and the budgeted figure was 36 days. This measure only shows the picture at one specific date. To get a better picture, the same calculation could be carried out at different dates, and regularly throughout the year to show trends, and whether the situation is improving or declining.

Creditor days

In a similar way to debtor days, this measures how much credit is being taken from suppliers. This must be calculated from the trade creditors figure (z in Figure 2.2) compared to the total purchase ledger items in the year (which is not shown in Figure 2.2), and multiplied by 365. Although not shown in these accounts, the total purchase ledger items can be calculated by addition of the monthly totals in the purchase day book. Once again, this only shows the position at a specific date. The same calculation could also be carried out at different dates, and regularly throughout the year.

Trends are important, and a lengthening trend could show that the business is starting to exceed its normal authorised trade terms with its suppliers. If this were allowed to continue, it could endanger working relationships with suppliers, and lead to shortages of vital supplies. The whole production cycle could be disrupted, with a serious effect on the viability of the business.

Stock turnover

This measures the number of times that stock is turned over during the year. It is measured by dividing the cost of materials used by the closing stock and work in progress figure. In Figure 2.2, this calculation is:

$$\frac{\text{Cost of materials}}{\text{Stock and work in progress}}$$

or:

$$\frac{b}{u + v}$$

The result of this calculation is 3 times in the current year, 2.7 times in the previous year, and budgeted 2.7 times. In general, the higher the stock turnover figure, the better the stock control procedures.

This method is sometimes refined if the level of stock varies greatly during the year. The refinement is to use the average level of stock carried throughout the year, as the basis of comparison. This can be found by averaging out the opening stock and work in progress and the closing stock and work in progress. Thus, in Figure 2.2, the figure to use would be the average of the previous year's figures and the current year's figures, which gives 47 million instead of 50 million. This yields a stock turnover figure of 3.2 times.

If the stock records give monthly stock and work in progress figures, it is also possible to use the average of the twelve months' figures, to give an even more accurate stock turnover. This exercise can then be carried out on a 'rolling year' basis. This means that, every month, the average figure used is that of the preceding twelve months, and the stock turnover is calculated on the cost of materials over the previous twelve months.

Any adverse trends in this figure (i.e. if the stock turnover trend is decreasing) could point to dangers of stock deterioration, wastage, pilferage, or obsolescence.

There can be no absolute guide to ideal stock turnover figures. The figures vary greatly from one business to another. Manufacturing businesses, for example, generally turn stock over more slowly than retail businesses. Even different types of retail business turn stock over at different rates. Fashion retailers for instance would carry larger volumes of stock than fast food outlets or fresh food retailers.

Asset turnover

This is a calculation, or rather a series of calculations, to show how much sales are generated by the assets in use. Thus, the asset figures used can be the fixed assets, the total gross assets, or the net assets. Once again, these figures are best seen as comparisons with previous periods, to recognise trends. In general, they point to the efficiency of asset management and use.

Fixed asset turnover

In Figure 2.2, the fixed asset turnover can be calculated by the formula:

$$\frac{\text{Turnover}}{\text{Total fixed assets}}$$

or:

$$\frac{a}{t}$$

This shows £500 million of turnover generated by £400 million of fixed assets – a ratio of 1.25, compared to 1.28 the previous year, and compared to the budgeted figure of 1.41. This means that every £1 of fixed assets generates £1.25 of sales for the current year, £1.28 of sales the previous year, and £1.41 of budgeted sales. This can be broken down further, and the turnover applied to different types of fixed assets.

The comparisons for fixed asset turnover can be distorted when there is significant investment in new assets in a year.

Gross asset turnover

In Figure 2.2, the gross asset turnover can be calculated by the formula:

$$\frac{\text{Turnover}}{\text{Total fixed assets plus total current assets}}$$

or:

$$\frac{a}{t+y}$$

This gives a ratio of 0.95, compared to 0.97 the previous year, and a budget of 1.06.

Net asset turnover

In Figure 2.2, the net asset turnover can be calculated by the formula:

$$\frac{\text{Turnover}}{\text{Net assets}}$$

or:

$$\frac{a}{ag}$$

This shows a ratio of 1.30 the current year, 1.40 the previous year, and a budget of 1.41.

Capital ratios

Total liabilities to total assets

An important figure in the balance sheet is the net assets (ag in Figure 2.2). This gives the actual figure represented by the shareholders' funds. The details show how it is split between assets and liabilities, and the breakdown between long-term assets and liabilities and short-term assets and liabilities.

Another useful index is the ratio between total liabilities and total assets. In Figure 2.2, this is calculated by the formula:

$$\frac{\text{Current liabilities plus long-term liabilities}}{\text{Fixed assets plus current assets}}$$

or:

$$\frac{ad + af}{t + y}$$

In the example, the ratio is 0.27, compared to 0.31 the previous year, and a budget of 0.25.

This can also be broken down to the short-term and long-term ratios of liabilities against assets. This is calculated for short-term figures by:

$$\frac{\text{Current liabilities}}{\text{Current assets}}$$

or:

$$\frac{ad}{y}$$

and for long-term figures by:

$$\frac{\text{Long-term liabilities}}{\text{Fixed assets}}$$

or:

$$\frac{af}{t}$$

The short-term ratio figure is therefore 0.5 for the current year and 0.5 for the previous year, with a budget figure of 0.47. (This is the reverse of the current ratio above). The long-term figure is 0.2 for the current year, 0.24 for the previous year, and 0.18 budgeted.

Gearing

Gearing represents the relationship of loan capital to total capital. If a company has long-term loans of £800,000, and equity capital of £200,000, the total capital is £1,000,000. The percentage of loans to total capital is 80%. In general terms, anything above 50% is considered a high gearing, although each case must be considered on its own merit.

In Figure 2.2, the calculation is:

$$\frac{\text{Long-term liabilities} \times 100}{\text{Long-term liabilities plus shareholders' funds}}$$

or:

$$\frac{\text{af} \times 100}{\text{af} + \text{an}}$$

This calculation reveals a gearing of 18%.

Gearing is considered in further detail in Chapter 10, where it will be seen that high gearing is more risky for equity investors. A crucial factor in a high-geared company is interest cover.

Interest cover

This is a particular measure of one specific item of overhead – interest paid on loans. It shows how the interest paid relates to the profit. In Figure 2.2, the calculation is:

$$\frac{\text{Net profit}}{\text{Interest}}$$

or:

$$\frac{\text{p}}{\text{n}}$$

This calculation shows interest cover of 6 times, compared to 6.8 times the previous year, and a budgeted figure of 8.5 times.

This figure becomes significant if profits drop. If a business has a low interest cover, any drop in profits means that after interest is paid, the amount available for distribution as dividends is much lower. This is more pronounced in businesses which are highly geared.

Performance measures for non-profit organisations

The methods described above relate primarily to businesses which exist to make profits. Non-profit organisations (NPOs), such as charities, public bodies, housing associations, schools, hospitals, and so on, have different objects, and need different performance measures.

These organisations are no less accountable than businesses, although they are accountable to different people.

EXERCISE 2.6

What measures do you think are appropriate to NPOs?

NPOs must develop their own performance measures, to reflect their own missions or purposes. There are four steps to developing performance measures:

1. Identify clearly and precisely the organisation's purpose and aims.
2. Find quantitative, measurable indicators. (Remember, if you can measure it, you can control it.)
3. Develop the indicators. This involves managers from the organisation identifying and developing indicators which are relevant to the purpose, and effectively measure the achievement of the purpose and aims.
4. Implement the measurement system. This impacts on reporting systems, and evaluation of the results. Once up and running, the system is likely to go through refinements and changes.

Various schemes have been implemented to measure performance. Exhibits 2.1 and 2.2 describe two.

Exhibit 2.1

The four-pronged measure

- *Input measures.* These quantify the level of inputs into projects or aims. These inputs can be financial and non-financial (for example, the time put into them).
- *Output measures.* These measure the outputs, and are more frequently in non-financial terms. Thus, a university may measure its outputs by the number of students who graduate in a particular year, or a shelter for the homeless may measure the number of people housed.
- *Outcome measures.* These measure how well aims have been met, and they are also largely non-financial. For instance, a project in a third world country to teach adults to read may measure its outcome by the increasing (or otherwise) trend in literacy rates over a period of time.
- *Efficiency measures.* These compare the input measures with the output and the outcome measures to gauge the efficiency of the organisation in achieving its aims.

Exhibit 2.2

At-a-Glance

This scheme was developed by a financial manager of a Registered Social Landlord (previously known as a Housing Association). The purpose is to present in one easy to grasp chart, measures to monitor the performance of the organisation compared to the aims of the governing body.

The governing body is the Housing Corporation, which lists three aims for Registered Social Landlords:

1. The organisation should be properly managed.
2. The organisation should be financially viable.
3. The organisation should be properly governed.

A series of ten measurement criteria were developed using the four steps outlined above. Several of these involved non-financial measurements, for which appropriate measurements had to be refined. These measures related to the three aims, as follows:

1. *Proper management*
   - Tenant satisfaction
   - Voids and letting performance
   - Rent arrears
   - Maintenance response
   - Staff sickness
   - Staff turnover
2. *Viability*
   - Budget control
   - Cash management
   - Loan covenants
3. *Governance*
   - Various governance criteria

The monthly results of these measures are displayed graphically by a 'radar' chart (see Figure 2.4), divided into red, amber, and green areas. The red area is nearest the middle (a 'bull's eye'), then amber and the green ring is the outer area. Divisions are roughly one-third each. These areas denoted the degree of achievement – the red area denoting the greatest need for corrective action.

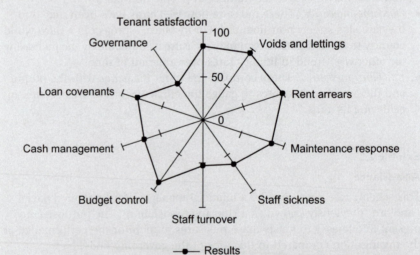

Figure 2.4   At-a-Glance chart

Now, management and the board can readily grasp what action is needed on a regular basis.

Difficulties in achieving performance measures

In practice, achieving relevant performance measures is more difficult for NPOs than for commercial businesses for the reasons given below.

Non-financial measures

A typical factor in non-profit organisations is that performance measures include much non-financial data. In practice, this requires ingenuity to devise a system of measuring things which are often intangible – such as the satisfaction of end receivers of the organisation's activities. Inevitably, these measures have to be constantly refined as they are used.

Difficulties of identification

Difficulties arise from the problem of identifying the roles. Who, for instance, owns the organisation? And who is the 'customer'?

Management attitudes

When managing non-profit organisations, it is easy to adopt extreme risk aversion and other attitudes which inhibit the implementation of new ideas. 'Commercial' attitudes can be considered inappropriate to the organisation, and the development of new performance measures is inhibited.

Additionally, members of the governing boards must be encouraged to adopt an incisive, questioning attitude which ensures that standards are not allowed to slip.

Summary

Financial accounts, cost accounts and management accounts are the raw material of financial control and management. Understanding them is a key to the effective management of the finances of any organisation.

The figures in the accounts reflect what is actually going on in an organisation. An informed reader of accounts can gain insights into how the organisation works, where its shortcomings lie, how its results have been affected by changes in policy, changes in circumstances, and many other areas.

Here is a key principle:

> ▶ Figures in accounts are not just numbers on a piece of paper. They represent something substantive – something that has happened in the real world. Discovering what they mean is a vital tool in exercising financial control.

Therefore, understanding financial statements is an indispensable tool in financial management. However, it is not enough simply to look at the accounts and understand what they mean. Understanding must be followed by action, and that action is the essence of financial management.

Experience is also important in exercising control. When financial directors or managers have been working in the same business for some time, experience of the business will enable them to spot trends or anomalies in the figures – it becomes a kind of instinct.

EXAMPLE 2.2

- An analysis of the activity ratios may show that the quick ratio has been steady for the last six months. In itself, this may appear satisfactory.
- However, over the same period, the debtor days have increased, from 36 days six months ago to 39 days at present.
- This could indicate that something is slipping in the sales ledger department – perhaps the control procedures are becoming more lax.
- Procedures should be reviewed. Are they being applied consistently? Have there been staff changes in the sales ledger department which affect the credit control procedures? Are new customers being accepted without the proper controls?
- An examination of the aged debtors lists for each month may show specific problems. Do the figures show a gradual increase month by month, or is there a sudden increase in one month, which should be examined more carefully?
- Is any particular debtor or group of debtors showing delinquent behaviour, such as unauthorised extensions of their credit period? If so, has anyone contacted them? Are current orders on hold while the problem is sorted out?

However, even the most experienced financial managers can often overlook problems or solutions which another, less experienced, person may suggest. Therefore, it is vital to remain open to any and all suggestions. Very often, something pointed out by a person from a different department can also enlighten a problem and lead to a successful course of action. Financial managers must be prepared to listen to non-financial managers, and other employees lower down the line.

ASSIGNMENT

The financial statements of O.T.T. Ltd (a privately owned company), are summarised in Figure 2.5.

Comment on what these figures suggest, and what action or enquiries you would make after examining them.

SUGGESTIONS

Profit ratios
The turnover has increased by over 28% – a significant increase. Further, the gross profit rate has increased from 40% to just over 42%. The net profit has increased by over 60%, and the net profit rate has increased from 18.8% to 23.5%. The return on capital has increased from 58% to 76%.

These indicators would appear to indicate a healthy state of affairs.

Profit and loss account

	Current year £000	£000	Previous year £000	£000
Turnover		4,500		3,500
Cost of sales				
Materials	1,800		1,500	
Direct labour	500		400	
Factory costs	300		200	
		2,600		2,100
Gross profit		1,900		1,400
Other income		10		5
		1,910		1,405
Overheads				
Property	100		90	
Salaries	150		120	
Maintenance and repairs	75		60	
Administration	35		32	
Transport	80		63	
Marketing	80		40	
Depreciation	80		100	
Interest	250		240	
Total overheads		850		745
Net profit		1,060		660
Taxation	210		130	
Dividends	600		200	
		810		330
Retained profit		250		330

Balance sheet

Fixed assets		1,200		1,250
Current assets				
Stock	600		400	
Work in progress	60		30	
Debtors	1,500		800	
Bank and cash	5		50	
	2,165		1,280	
Current liabilities				
Trade creditors	800		400	
Other creditors	120		50	
Dividends and tax	310		150	
Bank overdraft	600		0	
	1,830		600	
Working capital		335		680
		1,535		1,930
Long-term liabilities		155		800
Net assets		1,380		1,130
Represented by:				
Capital				
Ordinary shares		1,000		1,000
Profit and loss account		380		130
		1,380		1,130

Figure 2.5   O.T.T. Ltd: Financial statements for the year ended 31st December 20xx

However, the overheads should be examined in more detail, and the following questions asked:

- While turnover has increased by over 28%, overheads have only increased by 14%. Is the infrastructure of the company keeping pace with the rapid growth of turnover?
- As the company is a privately owned company, how much are the owners taking out of the company, as directors' salaries and as dividends? The salaries increased by £30,000, and the dividends increased by £400,000. Are the owners, in their capacities as directors and shareholders, taking too much money out of the company, given the need of the company to retain cash to finance its rapid growth?
- The administration costs only increased by £3,000 over the previous year, when the turnover had increased by £1 million. Does this indicate that the administration of the company will be struggling to keep up with the increased business? Further questions need to be asked.
- The retained profit is £250,000, which is less than the previous year. It could be argued that the company needs to retain more profit when its turnover is expanding so rapidly.

Liquidity ratios

The current ratio has gone from 2.1 the previous year to 1.2. Although in itself the ratio is still not bad, the decline is a warning sign.

The quick ratio also shows a dramatic change, from 1.4 to 0.8.

The company had money in the bank the previous year, but this year there is a significant overdraft. This should be considered in conjunction with the extra dividend taken out of the company, and the reduction in long-term loan considered in the capital ratios below.

Activity ratios

The debtor days were 83 the previous year – a figure which could be considered as less than satisfactory. It meant that debts were outstanding an average of nearly three months. However, that figure has worsened to 121 days – nearly four months, suggesting that credit control procedures have become more lax.

The creditor days were 97 the previous year, and have lengthened to 162 days. Frankly, we must ask how the creditors have allowed this to happen. Are the worsening debtor days being compensated by taking more credit from suppliers? Is this credit being taken unauthorised by the suppliers? If so, could it lead to problems in obtaining further supplies of materials.

The stock turned over 3.75 times the previous year, but only 3 times the current year. This further decline begins to suggest a pattern of deterioration in the activity ratios.

The fixed asset turnover has, however, increased from 2.8 to 3.75, and there has been a similar, though smaller, increase in net asset turnover. Although this might appear to be a good sign, caution should be applied, since the actual total of fixed assets has decreased, because more has been written off in depreciation than has been spent on new assets. The question must be asked, 'Does the company need more investment in new assets to sustain the increase in turnover?'.

Capital ratios

The gearing ratio has decreased considerably. The ratio of long-term debt to total debt and capital has decreased from 41% to 10%, which would appear to be a favourable indicator. Once again, however, we must ask questions. The balance sheet shows that a large amount of long-term debt has been repaid, but it has been largely replaced by a bank overdraft. The interest charge in the profit and loss account is a substantial burden on profits, and replacing long-term finance with short-term finance must be questioned in a time of rapid expansion.

Summary

Although the company does not appear to be in financial trouble at present, we must seriously question whether it is overtrading. The financial control of the company must be tightened if it is to avoid getting into difficulties. This must include a responsible attitude by the owners of the company in retaining sufficient money in the company, rather than taking out too much.

■ ▼ 3 Financial reporting
▼

LEARNING OUTCOMES

By the end of this chapter you should:

▶ have an appreciation of the reporting requirements of businesses and companies, both external and internal,
▶ understand the basic accounting conventions,
▶ appreciate how to present reports and figures effectively, and
▶ select which graphic reporting methods are appropriate to the information.

Introduction

In this chapter we study the basics of reporting on the financial information, introducing you to the types of external and internal reports which are a function of the finance department of any business. Finally, we look at the effective presentation of reports and figures, including the use of graphical displays.

Reporting – external and internal

External reporting requirements

The periodic published accounts (which limited companies have to file at Companies House), represent the external reporting requirements of a business. Any member of the public can inspect and obtain copies of accounts filed at Companies House. Other parties, such as tax inspectors, may also be interested in the accounts of incorporated or unincorporated businesses.

Limited companies, partnerships and sole traders, must prepare accounts from which to compile their self-assessment tax returns, sent to the Inland Revenue. These accounts are not examined in every case, but the Inland Revenue examine a proportion of business accounts every year.

The Inland Revenue can also examine any aspect of the accounts in connection with PAYE audits. Although the PAYE investigation is initially concerned with the deductions made from employees, and the payment of that money to the Inland Revenue, those examinations can involve many areas of the business.

Customs and Excise, which administers VAT, also has the right to examine business accounts, and they arrange regular inspection visits.

Either the Inland Revenue or the Customs and Excise can extend their enquiries into the accounting records of the business as well as the final accounts.

Basic accounting conventions

All external accounts of a business are expected to comply with certain basic accounting principles.

Accruals basis

This principle is that all income and expenditure should be matched to the period covered by the accounts, irrespective of when the actual payment or receipt occurred.

Historic cost

Business assets are normally shown at their original cost, less depreciation where applicable. In times of significant inflation, these original costs (known as historic costs) bear no relation to current costs or values. However, the historic cost probably provides the most objective measure to use in accounts.

Revaluation

There may be a desire to adjust the historic costs to current costs to try to bring into account the effects of inflation. In that case, adjustments can be made by revaluing certain assets – generally the long-term (or fixed) assets. There are still controversies about the best way to do this, but, if it is done, it requires some adjustment to be made to the equity of the business, by creating a revaluation reserve.

Materiality

Materiality means disregarding items which are insignificant in relation to the accounts as a whole. This is clearly dependent on the size of the business. What is immaterial to British Telecom may not be immaterial to a partnership of two people running a corner shop. The degree of materiality is shown in the way accounts are presented. Figures may be rounded to the nearest pound, or to the nearest million pounds.

Prudence

This concept can be summarised as 'erring on the safe side'. Thus, losses are recognised in the accounts as soon as they are reasonably foreseeable, whilst profits are only recognised in the accounts when they are actually realised.

DISCUSSION QUESTION 3.1

Why is prudence important for financial management?

Prudence requires provisions to be made in the accounts for losses or expenses which are foreseeable, but uncertain. If, for example, there is a court case pending at the date of the balance sheet, of which the outcome is uncertain, it is prudent to make a provision for the costs of the case if the decision should go against the business.

Provisions are commonly made for bad debts and discounts on sales ledger debts. It is usually not known exactly which customers will default on payment of their debts, but experience will suggest that a certain percentage of all debts will prove to be bad. Therefore, it is valid to make a general provision for bad and doubtful debts as a percentage of all outstanding debts.

Similarly, it is not known how many and which customers will take advantage of any prompt payment discounts. However, experience again suggests that a certain percentage will do so, and it is valid to make a general provision for this by way of extra deduction from profits, and corresponding reduction of the debtors figure in the balance sheet.

Consistency

It is expected that the accounts of a business will be consistent in their treatment of transactions – both within the accounting period and between one accounting period and another. This enables readers of the accounts to make proper and reasonable comparisons, on which judgements may be based.

Occasionally, however, a change in the treatment of transactions in the accounts is necessary. When this occurs, the reason for the change in treatment must be explained, and also there should be a note explaining the effect on the accounts of this change, and how the accounts of the previous year or period might have been affected if the change were implemented then. This enables a proper comparison to be made.

Going concern

This principle means that the accounts are prepared on the basis that the business will continue to carry on its business for the foreseeable future.

If a business is not a going concern, the assets must be included at their knock-down value – that is, what they could be reasonably expected to produce at auction. The inevitable losses produced by this must be shown in full.

Substance over form

This concept means that if the 'form' of a transaction suggests one thing, but the substance of the transaction is different, the substance must be reflected in the accounts. This is an 'anti-avoidance' principle. A typical example is of assets which are leased rather than owned. If the lease is really a means of financing the purchase of the asset, it must be shown as an asset, and the liability created by the lease finance shown as a balance sheet liability. This is discussed further in Chapter 10.

Official requirements

In addition to the above conventions, the accounts of limited companies must comply with the reporting requirements of the Companies Act, and the officially published Accounting Standards (see the companion website).

Internal reporting

External reports are usually published annually or half-yearly, and they can sometimes take several weeks to prepare. They are often then subject to audit, and therefore, it may be some while after the end of the accounting period that they appear.

Internal reports are needed for various purposes within the business, and are not published. They are used mainly for management purposes, and are therefore generally called management accounts. Because these accounts are needed for making management decisions, they are prepared much more frequently – generally monthly, but sometimes even more frequently than that. They are also needed promptly.

While management figures should obviously be as accurate as possible, the degree of promptness is often an overriding factor. A common saying is this:

> ▶ It is better to have management figures that are on time but only 95% accurate than to have them 100% accurate but a fortnight late.

These reports are tailored to specific needs, and they can be produced in a wide variety of formats. They are produced for many levels of management and for different departments or functions. They can be regular reports, or specific one-off reports, such as an analysis of a particular project. They are therefore concerned not just with reporting the past, but for present control and future forecasts.

Break-even analysis

Break-even analysis is one example of internal reporting. It is a technique for discovering what volume of sales must be achieved for the business to meet all its costs before making a profit. This can be applied to the business as a whole, or to divisions or departments.

This analysis requires a classification of the costs into fixed and variable. Fixed costs are those which the business will incur regardless of the volume of sales. Variable costs are those directly related to the items sold.

What are the variable and fixed costs of:

- a retail shop?
- a manufacturing business?

Some costs might include an element of fixed cost and an element of variable cost. These items need further analysis to break them down into the variable element and the fixed element.

A typical break-even analysis can be shown as a graph.

EXAMPLE 3.1

Suppose that a business sells one item only, that the selling price of each item is £10, the variable costs are £7, giving a direct (gross) profit of £3 on each article sold. If the fixed costs are £30,000, how many items must be sold to break even? Figure 3.1 shows how this is represented in a graph. The break-even point is shown where the sales line intersects the total costs line. This occurs at a sales volume of 10,000. The graph also shows the total profit or loss for any volume of sales as the difference between the sales line and the total costs line.

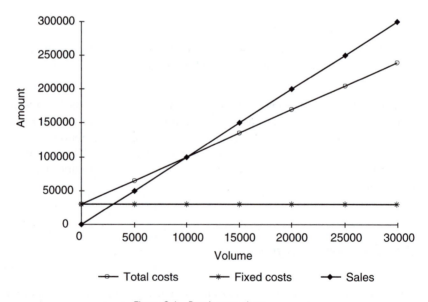

Figure 3.1 Break-even chart

This is a simplified example, and the answer could have been worked out quite simply from the numbers given for the example. However, this type of graph can be used for more complex examples.

EXAMPLE 3.2

In order to achieve a volume of 10,000 sales, the fixed costs would have to increase to £50,000, and to achieve a volume of 20,000 sales, the fixed costs would have to increase to £70,000. Suppose further that, as a result of these extra fixed costs, the variable costs of each article would reduce to £6 if sales exceed 10,000 volume, and to £5 if sales exceed 20,000 volume. Also, in order to achieve more than 10,000 volume sales, the price would need to be reduced to £9 per item, and to achieve more than 20,000 volume sales, the price would have to be reduced to £7.50. Here the answer is not obvious at first sight, and further use of a graph is needed. Figure 3.2 shows this graph.

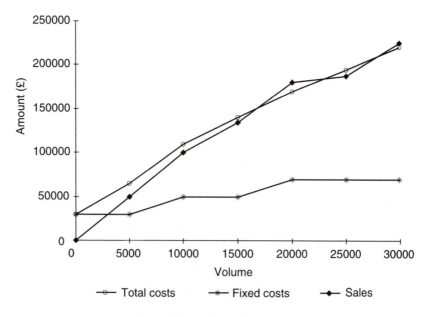

Figure 3.2   Breakeven chart

The result here shows that the profile is quite different. There are three points of intersection of the sales and total costs, at volumes of about 17,000, 23,000, and 28,000. These are points at which break-even occurs. There are intermediate points where the net result is a profit or a loss, that is, where the sales line is above or below the total costs line.

So far, the graph has been shown with only one item being produced and sold. This method can be further complicated when there are several different products involved. Separate break-even charts can be prepared for each product, with fixed expenses being allocated between the different products. The overall break-even chart is then constructed by aggregating all the individual ones. This type of chart can show which products are profitable, and which are not.

However, the exercise would have to be re-calculated if any particular product were discontinued and taken out of the analysis, because there would have to be a new allocation of fixed expenses, so that they are all absorbed into this process.

Marginal cost analysis

The concept of marginal cost is one in common use. This relates to the additional cost which would be incurred to increase sales or production by a given amount. This analysis can easily be carried out by the application of the break-even analysis and graph. Example 3.2 illustrates this principle. For production up to 10,000 items, the marginal cost of each additional unit is equal to the variable cost, that is, the materials and the direct labour. However, above 10,000 items, the marginal cost increases by the £20,000 additional fixed costs, offset by the reduction in variable costs due to economies of scale. Similar principles apply when the volume reaches 20,000 units.

The construction of the graph in Figure 3.2 illustrates this process and enables the marginal costs to be plotted.

Effective presentation of figures

Words and figures

As we have seen, financial managers should be good communicators. Unless a financial manager can get across ideas or reasons for recommendations, much of his work will be fruitless. The use of words, oral or written, is at least as important as the ability to produce figures.

In some reports, it may be useful to 'relegate' the figures to an appendix. The inclusion of a table or column of figures can interrupt the flow of an argument or presentation of facts. Putting all the figures in appendices can make a report clearer, as long as there is adequate reference to the appendices in the body of the text.

There can be no one solution which fits every report. Each report must be judged on its own merits, and designed appropriately, bearing in mind the background of the readers.

Using significant figures

Large company accounts round figures to the nearest million. This avoids long strings of numbers, and makes the figures easier to understand. When reporting verbally, it is usually more effective to tell someone that they made 'almost £370,000 profit' rather than to say that they made '£368,799 profit'. The rounding off level depends of course on the size of the enterprise.

Highlighting

Reports are sometimes presented as a dense block of rows and columns of figures. Even when the description of the figures is clearly shown, their significance may not be obvious at first sight. Even without any words, however, figures can be presented in ways which highlight the important features.

EXAMPLE 3.5

Figure 3.3 shows the overhead expenses of three branches of a firm. It is perfectly valid, but it is a solid block of figures. To get any more meaningful information, the figures would have to be examined and more work done on them. Figure 3.4 shows the same figures, with items which are more than 10% over budget highlighted. This immediately shows the items which need to be examined further. Highlighting could be done on any other basis – say, all items which were under budget.

	London branch		Leeds branch		Glasgow branch	
	Actual	Budget	Actual	Budget	Actual	Budget
Salaries	34685	30000	25684	27000	37786	38000
National Insurance	4162	3600	3082	3240	4434	4560
TOTAL	38847	33600	28766	30240	42220	42560
Rent and rates	17893	14000	12364	12300	18256	18500
Insurance	2689	2800	1687	1700	3120	3100
Light and heat	5986	5500	4837	4700	6135	6300
Repairs	686	1500	5900	1000	523	1500
TOTAL	27254	23800	24788	19700	28034	29400
Equipment maintenance	1525	1500	2543	1300	1856	1900
Equipment hire	1200	1200	1000	100	1200	1200
TOTAL	2725	2700	3543	1400	3056	3100
Printing and stationery	1586	1400	1234	1100	1867	1950
Advertising	450	400	899	600	965	600
Telephone	1432	1450	1323	1200	1963	1750
Postage	986	800	565	650	866	890
Professional fees	2534	2200	1852	1900	2132	2400
Sundries	865	750	653	600	743	750
TOTAL	7853	7000	6526	6050	8536	8340
Bank charges	869	500	768	860	637	500
Bank interest	345	400	864	750	653	700
Loan interest	1689	1500	1325	1300	1453	1450
Credit card charges	1897	1300	1659	1400	1863	1600
TOTAL	4800	3700	4616	4310	4606	4250
GRAND TOTAL	81479	70800	68239	61700	86452	87650

Figure 3.3 Overheads comparison for year ended 31st December 20xx

	London branch		Leeds branch		Glasgow branch	
	Actual	Budget	Actual	Budget	Actual	Budget
Salaries	34685	30000	25684	27000	37786	38000
National Insurance	4162	3600	3082	3240	4434	4560
TOTAL	38847	33600	28766	30240	42220	42560
Rent and rates	17893	14000	12364	12300	18256	18500
Insurance	2689	2800	1687	1700	3120	3100
Light and heat	5986	5500	4837	4700	6135	6300
Repairs	686	1500	5900	1000	523	1500
TOTAL	27254	23800	24788	19700	28034	29400
Equipment maintenance	1525	1500	2543	1300	1856	1900
Equipment hire	1200	1200	1000	100	1200	1200
TOTAL	2725	2700	3543	1400	3056	3100
Printing and stationery	1586	1400	1234	1100	1867	1950
Advertising	450	400	899	600	965	600
Telephone	1432	1450	1323	1200	1963	1750
Postage	986	800	565	650	866	890
Professional fees	2534	2200	1852	1900	2132	2400
Sundries	865	750	653	600	743	750
TOTAL	7853	7000	6526	6050	8536	8340
Bank charges	869	500	768	860	637	500
Bank interest	345	400	864	750	653	700
Loan interest	1689	1500	1325	1300	1453	1450
Credit card charges	1897	1300	1659	1400	1863	1600
TOTAL	4800	3700	4616	4310	4606	4250
GRAND TOTAL	81479	70800	68239	61700	86452	87650

Figure 3.4   Overheads comparison for year ended 31st December 20xx
with highlighting

Graphic reporting

It is said that a picture is worth a thousand words. Much financial information can be presented graphically, as well as, or instead of, in figures. Statutory reports must be presented in the right format, and comply with various regulations. However, in addition, other information can be presented. Many large companies produce their annual report and accounts in glossy formats, replete with photographs of the company's business at work, with charts and graphs to emphasise the importance of certain key figures.

Graphic presentation can be used also for internal reports. We saw in the section about break-even analysis, how a line chart (or graph) can be the best way of presenting analysis. Charts are used in conjunction with other figures shown in more conventional form.

Line charts (graphs)

These are perhaps the most recognisable and easily understood type of chart. We saw their use in break-even analysis. Figures 3.1 and 3.2 showed three lines on each chart, and the important thing was the relationship between them. Single line charts can also be effective – displayed, say, on the wall of an office or workshop, they can be an incentive to achieve targets.

Bar charts

Figure 3.5 gives an illustration of a bar chart. This shows the comparisons of the actual overheads of each branch with the budget for each branch. This type of chart serves best for comparisons between different elements.

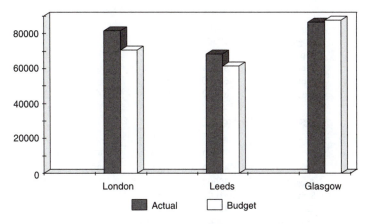

Figure 3.5 Overheads budget comparison

Pie charts

These are useful for showing the proportions of a total represented by each constituent part. Figure 3.6 shows the breakdown of the total overheads for the London branch between the different categories of overheads.

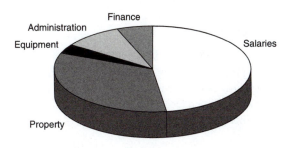

Figure 3.6 London branch overheads

ASSIGNMENT

From the data in Figure 3.7, decide which form of graphic representation is best suited to show the following, then prepare the appropriate form of graph or chart for each one:

(a) The month by month debtors figures, showing the trend.
(b) The actual debtors figures each month compared with the forecast figures.
(c) The proportions of debtors analysed by age at July and December 20xx, for comparison.

What do these figures tell you about the debtors, and how do the graphs and charts emphasise the findings?

	Actual	Forecast
July	60000	55000
August	60500	55000
September	61000	54000
October	61000	54000
November	62000	54500
December	65000	54000

Age analysis of debtors

	up to 1 month	1–2 months	2–3 months	over 3 months
July	40000	15000	30000	2000
August	40000	14000	4000	2500
September	41000	14000	3500	2500
October	40500	13000	4000	3500
November	40000	13500	4000	4500
December	39000	15000	6000	5000

Figure 3.7   Sample data – debtors summary and analysis for the six months ended 31st December 20xx

SUGGESTION

The appropriate charts are:

(a) Line chart (graph) – see Figure 3.8
(b) Bar chart – see Figure 3.9
(c) Pie charts – see Figures 3.10 and 3.11

The figures represent a gradually worsening debtors position. The amounts owing are gradually increasing month by month, and are also increasing compared to the forecasts. The age analysis comparison shows that the age profile of the debts has deteriorated between July and December, and there is a much higher proportion of older debts outstanding at December.

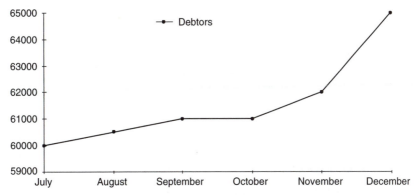

Figure 3.8 Debtors, July to December

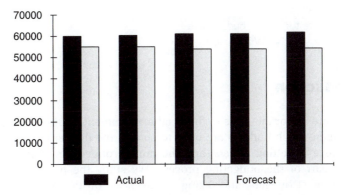

Figure 3.9 Actual and forecast debtors, July to December

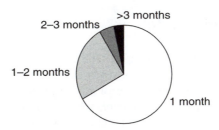

Figure 3.10 Age analysis of debts, July

Figure 3.11 Age analysis of debts, December

◼ ⱴ **4** The budgeting process

LEARNING OUTCOMES

By the end of this chapter, you should be able to:

▶ appreciate the value of budgeting to a business, and understand the budgeting cycle,
▶ piece together a budget, and
▶ carry out a SWOT analysis.

Introduction

Budgets are important tools in financial management. In this chapter, we study the ways in which budgets are used to control the finances of a business. The importance of setting targets, and the human dimension of motivation is an integral part of the budgeting process. We study the process of monitoring results against budgets, and taking action based on the comparison of actual results to budgeted results, and look at another related tool – SWOT analysis.

The budgeting cycle

Budgeting is all about controlling. There is no point in carrying out complex budgetary processes if they do not result in effective control over the financial aspect of the business. A common error made by small businesses is to prepare a plan and budget – perhaps for the bank, when requesting finance – then put it in a drawer and forget it. Budgets can incur a significant cost. If they are forgotten as soon as they are formulated, they are worse than useless.

The budgeting process consists of several steps, and does not just happen once a year – it is a continuous cycle. The process can be visualised as in Figure 4.1.

Making plans

The first essential step is to formulate plans which provide a financial model of the way the business will run. This involves obtaining reliable estimates from all departments of sales, production, costs, overheads, capital expenditure, and

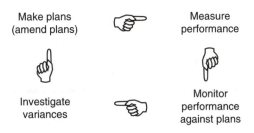

| Make plans (amend plans) | | Measure performance |
| Investigate variances | | Monitor performance against plans |

Figure 4.1 The budgeting process

so on. Budgets are first prepared covering each department of the business individually, then amalgamated into an overall budget. A budget co-ordinator or committee is often responsible for bringing it together.

Budgets can also be prepared for new projects or ventures, as well as for existing core business. Budgets and plans for existing businesses start from the basis of the existing figures – what happened last year, and how might that be altered by new data etc? A budget for a new venture starts with no previous data – this is known as zero-based budgeting. The plans are not guided by past history, but start from scratch.

The concept of zero-based budgeting can be extended to planning and budgeting for an existing business. It allows management to ask basic questions, such as 'Do we really need to manufacture the same goods in the same way as at present, in the same premises?'.

In most circumstances, the key figure for the operating budget is the sales forecast, which the sales department traditionally makes optimistic. Attention must be given to judging its practicality and realism. The nature of the forecast sales must be taken into account. For example, if the sales department forecasts quite realistically a large volume of one-off or short-term sales, management cannot base a long-term expansion of productive capacity on that forecast.

The human dimension

Plans and budgets must be understood and agreed by the people whose job it is to meet those budgets. This is why budgeting is most effective when the plans are prepared from the bottom-up rather than from the top-down. Failure to get plans agreed means that those who should be aiming to meet the budgets actually see them as an obstruction, rather than a tool for control. The budget is therefore broken down into sections which come under the control of individual managers of departments. Thus, it is vital to involve these managers in the process of formulating the plans. To make the plans effective, managers should:

- agree their budget targets,
- believe that their targets are achievable,
- receive their budgets in a form relevant to their work, and
- receive training in understanding the budgets and their place in the wider overall purpose.

Motivation

With the above criteria for effective planning, budgets can be an excellent tool for motivating managers and others to improve performance. Budgets can be the basis for awarding bonuses. If this is the case, care must be taken to ensure that budgets are not set so that they can be beaten and a bonus ensured. It is an unhealthy sign if budgets are always beaten. However, consistently setting budgets at a level too high to be met, is a disincentive to better performance.

Managers of cost-centres or profit-centres will 'fight their own corner' to protect their patch, and get what they see as their fair share of resources. Managers must be enabled to see the whole picture – not just their own corner, but how they contribute to the strategy of the business as a whole.

Measuring performance

We have already seen the key concept:

▶ If you can measure it, you can control it.

Accurate measurement of achievement is vital for the control process.

Information gleaned from the book keeping records usually provides the measurement needed for control. However, in some cases, other information is needed. For instance, production is usually measured in terms of the number of items produced, rather than the money value attaching to those items. The production manager controls the actual production of goods, not the price at which they are sold. Therefore, he needs to know the actual number of items produced, not the monetary value.

Similarly, the sales department is responsible for getting orders. Their measure is the orders received. If for any reason production has not been able to satisfy those orders, and the sales are not made, that is not the responsibility of the sales department.

Each department and profit centre should therefore have a system for recording actual achievement so that it can be compared to the budget.

The figures needed for these purposes should be produced regularly and promptly. For effective control, the figures should not be produced less than monthly, and in some cases weekly or fortnightly figures could be called for. To be effective, the figures must also be available promptly.

▶ Control is effective when it is instigated immediately.

Service businesses

Businesses selling services have different financial measures for their output. Many businesses also sell a combination of goods and services.

Service businesses cannot store up their services, as a manufacturing business can produce and stockpile its products. For example, a hotel which has empty rooms cannot store up those rooms for future use. If they are empty for one night, that night's income is lost for ever.

Thus, different performance measures have to be devised. In the case of hotels, for example, the key measure is the occupancy rate. This means comparing the actual number of bed-nights' accommodation that have been sold with the maximum possible if every bed were occupied every night.

Monitoring performance

Once accurate figures are produced they can be compared to the budget. A simple budget comparison report should be produced for each cost centre, profit centre or department. For example, a typical part of a report for factory costs might look like Figure 4.2.

The report should be the responsibility of the person most nearly responsible for meeting the budget figures. That person is the best qualified to make comments, particularly in explaining variances. The manager responsible for meeting the budget should not feel that he is being hit over the head with the budget report, nor that it is just another piece of useless paperwork. It should be seen as a tool for improving performance. If that improvement can be linked to a bonus or incentive, it maximises its usefulness.

Investigating variances

Variances from budgeted figures must be investigated, so that action may be taken to control costs and income. The budget report illustrated in Figure 4.2 gives the variances and the comments of the person preparing it. These

Budget report	Department	Date	Period	Prepared by: . . . .
Cost items	Budget	Actual	Variance	Comments
Machine operators' wages	£10,000	£12,000	+ £2,000	Excessive overtime due to quality problems
Foremen's wages	£2,000	£2,400	+ £400	Holiday cover overtime
Machinery repairs	£1,000	£500	– £500	New machinery resulted in lower repairs cost
Power supply	£2,000	£2,200	+ £200	Additional operating time due to quality problems

Figure 4.2 Budget report

comments may explain the variance, or further investigation may be needed. Once a satisfactory explanation has been established, action can be determined.

It is important to prioritise the figures needing investigation. This could be done by highlighting all variances over a certain amount – for instance, anything more than 10% over budget gets investigated first.

It is not just the budget over-runs that need investigating. Sometimes if a cost is below budget, the reason might bring to light some underlying cause which affects the rest of the business. For instance, the light, heat and power cost in a factory might be below budget because there has been a breakdown of machinery, causing production to grind to a halt.

The reasons for variances may or may not lead to any action being taken. There may be alternative courses of action.

EXAMPLE 4.1

> The budget comparison report shows that the cost of the raw material for manufacture of an item shows a considerable increase as a percentage of the selling price. This raw material is bought from one supplier, who has raised his prices. Further investigation is needed. Why has the supplier raised the price of his supply? If the price has been raised ahead of his competition, consideration should be given to switching suppliers. However, the price increase may be general, due to a lack of world supply. In this case, switching to a new supplier is of no use, since all suppliers will be raising their prices. In this case, the decision to be taken is whether the increase in costs can be absorbed or whether it can be passed on to customers.

Amending plans

Action can only be taken when:

- the actual figures and achievements have been measured,
- and compared against budget,
- and the reason for any variances ascertained.

For instance, in Example 4.1, if the price increase is passed on to customers, the budgets need to be amended for the revised selling price, which will affect sales, and the revised buying price of the raw material, which will affect raw materials cost. The gross profit margin may or may not be the same as previously, and the original plan may have to be amended. If there is some basic flaw in the original plans and budget figures, it is obvious that they have to be amended.

However, other things outside the control of the business change, and these could affect the operation of the business. For example, when the foot and mouth epidemic hit the UK in 2001, many businesses besides agriculture were seriously affected. Businesses manufacturing farm machinery, hotels and other tourist related businesses were badly affected, and had to amend their plans and budgets.

The amended plans and budgets then replace the original ones, and the whole cycle starts again.

Time scale

Most budgets and plans are made for a year. This is the most readily appreciable time scale, and one that fits in most nearly with accounting information. The yearly figures can be broken down to monthly or quarterly figures which can then be regularly monitored.

However, it is often necessary to look further ahead, and make long-term plans – say for the next three, five, or even ten years. These extended periods cannot be planned for and budgeted in such detail as a twelve month period. These budgets adopt a more 'broad brush' approach.

Objectives and goals

In making long-term plans, the objectives and goals of the business must be examined, to see how they fit into long-term plans. The objectives of a business do not just have a financial aspect. They include many non-financial aspects, such as the type of market which the business is aiming for.

EXAMPLE 4.2

> The business may aim for the 'pile 'em high, sell 'em cheap' end of the market, or for the high value, lower volume end of the market. Both can be successful, but they translate into quite different financial models.

The way in which objectives are met can be quite different. For example, the part of the world where the business operates dictates whether production is labour-intensive or highly mechanised.

All these circumstances translate differently into the financial plans and budgets. The long-term objectives when laid out over an extended period of, say five years, point to items such as the timing of major capital investment in premises or plant and machinery.

Product or service life cycle

The implications of the phases of a product or service life cycle are important. This applies to existing activities and any proposed new activities. The market for any product or service generally has four distinct phases, as shown in Figure 4.3.

1.	*Introduction*	This is generally associated with low sales, and high initial costs – therefore not very profitable.
2.	*Growth*	New suppliers of the product or service emerge into the market – greater competition is experienced.
3.	*Maturity*	The suppliers start to make better profits. Relatively few new suppliers are coming into the market.
4.	*Decline*	No new suppliers are coming into the market, but those already established in the market can continue to make profits, until the demand has completely dried up.

Figure 4.3 Product life cycle

Thus, a business will achieve the greatest overall return if it gets into the market as near as possible to the beginning of the life cycle. Any new venture may well incur high development costs. Therefore, it is best to develop new products or services when there are existing income streams from other products or services. A business will be less vulnerable to fluctuating market demand if it has a range of products or services in different phases of the market life cycle.

SWOT analysis

When working out the details of how the objectives will be achieved over the long-term, a SWOT analysis shows the Strengths, Weaknesses, Opportunities and Threats of the business.

The strengths and weaknesses are internal to the business, and therefore much more controllable. The opportunities and threats are external to the business, and therefore less controllable. All of these elements – strengths, weaknesses, opportunities and threats, can be related to several areas of the

Internal factors – Strengths and Weaknesses

Sales

- What patterns are emerging? Does the past record indicate any shift in demand for the products or services of the business? What is the profitability of different sales lines? Is any different mix of product and service indicated?
- Is there any customer feedback on the quality of products and services?
- What is the most convenient way of increasing sales? Figure 4.5 shows the four methods of increasing sales. The business must decide which of these is the most appropriate.

Customers

- Is the customer base changing?
- What are the real needs of the target group of customers?
- Can the business provide any other product or service to add value to the customers' businesses or private lives?

Competitors

- How do competitors' pricing structures compare?
- What special promotions do they carry out?
- Is their advertising enticing away any of the business's customers?
- What are their reputations in the market-place?
- How easy or difficult is it for any new competitors to break into the market?

Supplies

- How secure are supplies of raw materials, and other essentials?
- Are they dependent on world supply levels?
- Is there more than one supplier for each major item?

Figure 4.4 Questions to ask in a SWOT analysis

Figure 4.4 continued

Management and administration

- Is there any shortage of staff or skills in any individual area?
- Are training facilities adequate?
- Are there any key employees without obvious successors?
- Would any planned changes create shortages of staff or skills?
- Would the organisational structure need changing?

Premises and equipment

- Will additional resources need to be made available? If so, when and where?
- Are the current premises suitable for any planned new activity?
- What finance will any new premises or equipment require?

Financial resources

- Is the current activity adequately financed, or is there a shortage?
- What are the options for financing expansion?
- Can the management of working capital be improved in any area (see Chapter 5)?

External factors – Opportunities and Threats

Social factors

- There are always complex demographic, social and cultural forces at work in any society. How is the business affected by these influences? The effects could be felt in sales demand, in the availability of labour, or in the general economic forces.

Technology

- What changes in technology are making the most impact on business in general currently?
- Which changes affect this business, and how?
- Technological changes are occurring with ever greater speed, and these can have a fundamental impact on many areas of business. They can change demand, create demand for new products or services, and affect the way business works – in production, in communications, and in managing cash and capital.

The economy

- Many facets of the economy can affect the business – inflation, wage rates, legislation, tax rates, interest rates, foreign currency exchange rates.

Political factors

- Political stability can never be guaranteed – and this applies to some countries more than others. Could any political or legal changes affect the business?

Competition

- What is the size and influence of major competitors?
- What are their strengths and weaknesses, threats and opportunities?
- How easy is it for customers of the business to obtain substitutes for the business's products or services?

The market

- What is the size of the overall market in which the business sells its products or services?
- Is that market expanding or contracting?
- What is the size of the business's market share?
- Is that share expanding or contracting?
- Are any businesses in this market merging or forming alliances?

There are only four ways a business may increase its sales, derived from the following matrix:

New products or services	New customers
Existing products or services	Existing customers

▶ **Increase sales of existing products or services to existing customers**. This is the least risky – it does not involve going into new markets or developing new products or services. However, it can prove to be the least profitable in the long term.

▶ **Sell new products or services to existing customers.** This incurs development costs for new products or services. However, new products or services may be made to mesh in with existing ones, and the relationships with existing customers can help promote new products or services.

▶ **Find new markets and customers for existing products or services.** This incurs marketing costs and sales efforts to reach new markets. If new markets are found overseas, the initial costs may be high, and special attention must be paid to sales ledger and debt collection procedures.

▶ **Sell new products or services in new markets and to new customers.** This involves the greatest cost and risk. Development costs for new products and services are combined with initial costs of marketing, promotion and sales efforts.

Figure 4.5   The four methods of increasing sales

business functions. Vital questions must be asked. A SWOT analysis must be searching and probing. Figure 4.4 shows some of the questions that should be asked, and Figure 4.5 gives four methods for answering one of them: 'What is the most convenient way of increasing sales?'.

The bottom line

Budgets are only useful if they assist in controlling and planning the business. If they only tell the management what happened last month, they are like the annual accounts which serve that purpose for the last year. Budgets must contribute to effective action. Further, budgets may be said to provide incentives to managers to perform. However, they must be seen to encourage performance in absolute terms. It is not just performing to the budget which matters, but optimising profits and value.

Targets

Budgets are more about the future than about past performance. Thus, budgeting must be integrated with the other key management areas of the business. Much current thinking tends towards setting targets which are not expressed in monetary terms, but in measurable terms which are relevant and important to the business as a whole and to particular areas of management, or departments of the business.

This approach means that many of the targets are set by non-financial managers. Financial managers must be able to understand their language, and work in other terms than money figures. Managers must be able to identify the measurement criteria which are really important to the business, and financial managers must co-operate with them in identifying and quantifying those measures.

This approach has enabled many companies – including very large businesses – to do away with the majority of the detailed information in the budget process. This enables budgets to be prepared, and, perhaps more importantly, monitored much more quickly.

ASSIGNMENT 1

From the data in Figure 2.2 (p. 11), assume a further year has passed, and present a budget in the same form as the final column, using the following information:

Adjustments to 'Current year' column

Profit and loss account

Sales	Increase 5%
Cost of sales	
Materials	Increase 4%
Direct labour	Increase 6%
Factory costs	Increase 8%
Other income	No change
Overheads	
All items other than depreciation	Increase 6%
Depreciation	Calculate at 25% of the last closing balance of plant and machinery adjusted for purchases of items (see below)
Taxation	Calculate at 32% of net profit
Dividends	Calculate at 40% of net profit before tax

Balance sheet

Fixed assets	The brought forward figure includes land and property £350 million, and plant and equipment £50 million. Additional plant and machinery to be purchased £10 million. No assets sold or scrapped
Current assets	
Stock and work in progress	Decrease 10%
Debtors	Decrease 5%
Cash and bank	See note below
Current liabilities:	
Trade creditors	No change
Taxes	Increase 10%
HP instalments	Reduce to zero
Overdraft	Reduce to £5 million
Long-term liabilities	
Loans	Increase by £5 million
Share capital and premium	No change

Special note: Cash and bank balances

This figure will be the balancing figure after calculating all the other figures. What will be the figure for cash and bank in the budgeted balance sheet?

All figures to be rounded to the nearest £million.

ANSWER

The final figures and workings are shown in Figure 4.6.

Profit and loss account

	Current year £million	£million	New budget changes	Result £million	£million
Sales		500	inc. 5%		525
Cost of sales					
Materials	150		inc. 4%	156	
Direct labour	100		inc. 6%	106	
Factory costs	50		inc. 8%	54	
		300			316
Gross profit		200			209
Other income		5	unchanged		5
		205			214
Overheads					
Property	20		inc. 6%	21	
Salaries	30		inc. 6%	32	
Maintenance	10		inc. 6%	11	
Administration	5		inc. 6%	5	
Transport	10		inc. 6%	11	
Marketing	10		inc. 6%	11	
Depreciation	10		see calc.	15	
Interest	15		inc. 6%	16	
Total overheads		110			122
Net profit		95			92
Taxation	30		32% of profit	29	
Dividends	40		40% of profit	37	
		70			66
Retained profit		25			26
Balance sheet					
Fixed assets		400	see calc.		395
Current assets					
Stock	40		dec. 10%	36	
Work in progress	10		dec. 10%	9	
Debtors	60		dec. 5%	57	
Cash and bank	20		balancing	55	
	130			157	
Current liabilities					
Trade creditors	40		unchanged	40	
Taxes	10		inc. 10%	11	
HP instalments	5		zero	0	
Overdraft	10		red. to £5 m	5	
	65			56	
Working capital		65			101
		465			496
Long-term liabilities					
Loans		80	inc. £5 m		85
Net assets		385			411

Figure 4.6 Specimen Company new budget

Figure 4.6 continued

	Current year £million	£million	New budget changes	Result £million	£million
Capital					
Share capital					
Preference shares	50		unchanged	50	
Ordinary shares	100		unchanged	100	
	150			150	
Share premium	10		unchanged	10	
		160			160
Profit and loss account		225	see calc.		251
Shareholders' funds		385			411

Special calculations

Depreciation and fixed assets

	Total fixed assets £million	Land and property £million	Plant and machinery £million
Fixed assets brought forward	400	350	50
Assets purchased			10
			60
Depreciation			15
Balance carried forward	395	350	45

Profit and loss account	
Balance brought forward	225
Retained profit for year	26
	251

ASSIGNMENT 2

Figure 4.7 shows the comparison of the actual performance of the Supa-Dupa Widget Company Ltd against its budget. The company manufactures three main items – standard widgets, supa widgets, and giant widgets. Drawing on these comparisons, report to the board of directors on the areas to be investigated, and areas where any remedial action is indicated.

Include in your answer a variance analysis, and comment on wastage.

SUGGESTIONS

The variance analysis is shown in Figure 4.8. This shows the areas in which quantity variances and price/cost variances have occurred. These variances should be commented on where significant to the board.

Figure 4.9 shows the raw material usage and wastage. The wastage is more than budgeted, and this could point to an area in which management needs to exert more control.

Figure 4.10 shows a similar summary of labour usage. There is a shortfall here, suggesting some idle time. This indicates a further area which should be looked into. Were machinery breakdowns the cause? This could be corroborated by the increase in repairs cost in the overheads. However, the idle time could be due to other causes, such as inadequate work scheduling, leading to bottlenecks, or materials not being available at the right time. Further investigation is needed.

Figure 4.11 shows the absorption of factory overheads compared to the budgeted figures.

Further investigation should be made into the overhead expenses which show fairly consistent increases compared to budget. The most significant in percentage terms is the increase in repairs cost. A more detailed comparison of the constituent figures of each overhead item is required.

		Actual		Budget	
		Quantity	*£000*	*Quantity*	*£000*
Sales	Standard	38,000	580	40,000	600
	Supa	21,000	810	20,000	800
	Giant	4,900	480	5,000	500
			1,870		1,900
Direct costs					
Raw materials used		tons		tons	
	Rubber	49,000	95	50,000	100
	Steel	11,000	220	10,000	200
	Wood	42,000	155	40,000	150
	Glass	20,000	48	20,000	50
			518		500
Labour			305		300
Factory overheads			148		150
Machinery depreciation			48		50
Total direct costs			1,019		1,000
Gross profit			851		900
Overhead expenses					
Salaries			105		100
Property expenses			28		25
Repairs			15		10
Transport			28		25
Administration			44		40
Finance			52		50
Depreciation			52		50
			324		300
Net profit			527		600

Figure 4.7 Supa-Dupa Widget Company Ltd: Profit and loss account for the year ended 31st December

Figure 4.7 continued

Further data	Actual Quantity	£000	Budget Quantity	£000
Standard widgets				
Sale price	38,000	15.26	40,000	15.00
Costs				
Raw materials per item				
Rubber	0.7 tons		0.71 tons	
Steel	0.12 tons		0.12 tons	
Wood	0.6 tons		0.55 tons	
Glass	0.3 tons		0.3 tons	
Labour per item	0.86 hours		0.85 hours	
Factory overheads per item	£2.31		£2.30	
Supa widgets				
Sale price	21,000	38.57	20,000	40.00
Costs				
Raw materials per item				
Rubber	0.8 tons		0.82 tons	
Steel	0.15 tons		0.16 tons	
Wood	0.68 tons		0.7 tons	
Glass	0.3 tons		0.3 tons	
Labour per item	1.05 hours		1 hour	
Factory overheads per item	£2.32		£2.31	
Giant widgets				
Sale price	4,900	97.96	5,000	100.00
Costs				
Raw materials per item				
Rubber	0.95 tons		0.98 tons	
Steel	0.5 tons		0.38 tons	
Wood	0.8 tons		0.75 tons	
Glass	0.3 tons		0.3 tons	
Labour per item	1.2 hours		1.2 hours	
Factory overheads per item	£2.36		£2.35	
Labour cost	£5 per hour		£5 per hour	
Raw materials cost	per ton			
Rubber	1.94		2.00	
Steel	20.00		20.00	
Wood	3.69		3.75	
Glass	2.40		2.50	

Standard widgets

		Actual	
	Quantity	Price	
Sales	38,000	£15.26	580,000

		Budget	
	Quantity	Price	
	40,000	£15.00	600,000

Difference			−20,000

The adverse sales variance is −£20,000. This is due to an adverse quantity variance of £30,000 offset by a favourable price variance of £10,000.

				Actual
Costs		Tons	Cost	
Raw materials	Rubber	26,600	51,604	
	Steel	4,560	91,200	
	Wood	22,800	84,132	
	Glass	11,400	27,360	
			254,296	
		Hours		
Labour		32,680	163,400	
	Rate	Units		
Factory costs	2.31	38,000	87,780	
				505,476

				Budget
Costs		Tons	Cost	
Raw materials	Rubber	28,400	56,800	
	Steel	4,800	96,000	
	Wood	22,000	82,500	
	Glass	12,000	30,000	
			265,300	
		Hours		
Labour		34,000	170,000	
	Rate	Units		
Factory costs	2.30	40,000	92,000	
				527,300

Difference				−21,824

The favourable raw materials variance is £11,004. This variance can be broken down into the constituent parts for each raw material as follows:

	Quantity	Cost
Rubber	3,600	1,596
Steel	4,800	
Wood	−3,000	1,368
Glass	1,500	1,140
	6,900	4,104

The favourable labour variance is £6,600, which is all due to quantity variance.

Figure 4.8 Variance analysis

Totals	Standard	Actual Supa	Giant	Total
Raw materials	Tons	Tons	Tons	Tons
Rubber	26,600	16,800	4,655	48,055
Steel	4,560	3,150	2,450	10,160
Wood	22,800	14,280	3,920	41,000
Glass	11,400	6,300	1,470	19,170

	Standard	Budget Supa	Giant	Total
Raw materials	Tons	Tons	Tons	Tons
Rubber	28,400	16,400	4,900	49,700
Steel	4,800	3,200	1,900	9,900
Wood	22,000	14,000	3,750	39,750
Glass	12,000	6,000	1,500	19,500

Comparison of tonnage used per Figure 4.7 with usage analysed above:

		Actual	Budget
Rubber	Per Figure 4.7	49,000	50,000
	Analysed above	48,055	49,700
	Difference – wastage	945	300
Steel	Per Figure 4.7	11,000	10,000
	Analysed above	10,160	9,900
	Difference – wastage	840	100
Wood	Per Figure 4.7	42,000	40,000
	Analysed above	41,000	39,750
	Difference – wastage	1,000	250
Glass	Per Figure 4.7	20,000	20,000
	Analysed above	19,170	19,500
	Difference – wastage	830	500

Figure 4.9 Summary of raw material usage

	Standard	Actual Supa	Giant	Totals
Hours	32,680	22,050	5,880	60,610
Cost	163,400	110,250	29,400	£303,050
Figure per accounts				£305,000
Difference – labour wastage or downtime				£1,950

	Standard	Budget Supa	Giant	Totals
Hours	34,000	20,000	6,000	60,000
Cost	170,000	100,000	30,000	£300,000
Figure per accounts				£300,000
Difference – labour wastage or downtime				£0

Figure 4.10 Labour cost and usage

		Actual		
	Standard	Supa	Giant	Total
Per item	2.31	2.32	2.36	
Quantities	38,000	21,000	4,900	
Absorption	87,780	48,720	11,564	148,064

		Budget		
	Standard	Supa	Giant	Total
Per item	2.3	2.31	2.35	
Quantities	40,000	20,000	5,000	
Absorption	92,000	46,200	11,750	149,950

Figure 4.11   Factory overheads

▪ ⋈ 5 Controlling working capital

LEARNING OUTCOMES

By the end of this chapter, you should be able to:

▶ understand the nature of the key elements of working capital – stock, work in progress, debtors, and creditors, and

▶ apply the key measurement techniques to the means of control.

Introduction

In this chapter we examine one of the most important aspects of financial control – the control of working capital. We look individually at the nature of the various elements of working capital, working capital as a whole, and the ways to measure and control working capital.

What is working capital?

Any business has assets and liabilities. The total capital of the business is represented by the formula:

Total assets minus total liabilities = net assets = total capital

as shown in Figure 5.1.

Assets	500,000
Liabilities	200,000
Net assets	300,000
Capital	
Shares	100,000
Reserves	200,000
Total capital	300,000

Figure 5.1 ABC Ltd balance sheet

But total capital is not the same as working capital. To discover the working capital of a business, the assets and liabilities are broken down into long-term and short-term items. These are generally referred to by conventional names:

- long-term assets – fixed assets,
- short-term assets – current assets,
- long-term liabilities – long-term liabilities,
- short-term liabilities – current liabilities.

The division between short-term and long-term is one year. For instance, money owed to the bank, repayable within one year, is a short-term (or current) liability.

To illustrate this, we can further break down the figures from Figure 5.1 as in Figure 5.2.

Fixed assets	300,000	
Current assets	200,000	
Total assets		500,000
Long-term liabilities	120,000	
Current liabilities	80,000	
Total liabilities		200,000
Net assets		300,000

Figure 5.2

This now shows the breakdown between long-term and short-term figures. But there is a further step before we can see what working capital is. This involves grouping together the short-term items (assets and liabilities) and showing them separately from the long-term items. This is conventionally shown as in Figure 5.3.

Fixed assets		300,000
Current assets	200,000	
Current liabilities	80,000	
Working capital		120,000
		420,000
Long-term liabilities		120,000
Net assets		300,000

Figure 5.3

Working capital is £120,000 in the example above. But what does 'working capital' represent, in concrete terms?

It consists of short-term assets and liabilities, which change from day to day, even from hour to hour, in the course of business. What do these current assets and liabilities include?

Current assets

Current assets include the following, given in the order they are usually shown in a balance sheet:

1. *Stock* – raw materials. The cost of:
    - raw materials used in manufacture,
    - other items not used for production, such as cleaning materials, stationery, and so on.
2. *Work in progress.* The cost of work being carried out but uncompleted.
    - In a manufacturing business, it consists of materials in the process of being turned into finished goods,
    - In a construction business it represents building work in progress.
    - In a service business, it represents work being carried out, but not yet completed.
3. *Stock – finished goods.*
    - In a manufacturing business, it represents manufactured goods not yet sold.
    - In a trading business, wholesale or retail, it represents goods waiting to be sold.
4. *Debtors.* Money owed to the business, such as customers who have not yet paid. There are other debts owing to the business for a variety of reasons.
5. *Prepayments.* Expenses which are paid in advance (such as insurance, road fund licences, and so on). The proportion of the charge which relates to the period after the balance sheet date is known as a prepayment.
6. *Cash at bank.* The balance held in the business's bank account.
7. *Cash in hand.* The cash at the business, either in petty cash, or cash received and not yet banked.

QUESTION 5.1

Why are current assets usually shown in this order?

Current liabilities

Current liabilities include the following items, given in the order in which they are usually shown in the balance sheet.

1. *Trade creditors.* Amounts owing to suppliers of the business, for supplies of goods for manufacture or resale, goods for other expenses, or services.
2. *Other creditors.* All other amounts owing by the business, including taxes such as PAYE and VAT.
3. *Accruals.* Amounts owing, not yet billed, but which have accrued, such as telephone or electricity bills. Accruals often have to be estimated.
4. *Bank overdrafts.* Amounts owing to the bank on current account (not on loans).

5. *Loans – amounts repayable within one year.* If the amount is repayable over more than one year, then only the proportion payable within a year is included here.
6. *Other instalment loans repayable within one year.* This normally includes such things as hire purchase debts or finance lease debts. If the amount is repayable over more than one year, then only the proportion payable within a year is included here.
7. *Income in advance.* Income received in advance, and therefore part of which relates to the period after the balance sheet date, such as rent received in advance.

The cyclical nature of working capital

Working capital changes from day to day. The figure for working capital shown on the balance sheet is a 'snapshot' of the working capital at that date. To understand the true nature of working capital, it is important to grasp the working capital cycle. The typical manufacturing business has stocks of raw materials, which it converts into finished goods, sells to customers, then receives payment, and uses the money coming in to pay its creditors for more raw materials and other expenses.

At any time, money is circulating round the various phases of activity. Working capital shows a picture of that activity. The level of working capital should be controlled, but it may vary from time to time in response to external influences. These could include:

- seasonal changes,
- changes in fashions,
- interest rate changes,
- fluctuations in the general economic and trade cycle,
- changes in the industry-specific trade cycle,
- changes in market demand.

Why does working capital need to be controlled?

Cash flow – the vital element

Working capital is vital to any business. It shows the liquidity of the business. Liquidity represents cash flow, and is an important factor in the success of a business. Without good cash flow, plans are held up, and progress cannot be made. In fact, in the early stages of a new business, or in the growth stage, more businesses fail because of poor liquidity than lack of profitability.

All elements of working capital must be controlled – individually and as a whole.

Stock control

The key stock turnover ratio seen in Chapter 2 gives a broad picture. Stock control involves more detailed measurement and control of the many different lines of stock, ensuring that obsolete or damaged stock is identified, and that each stock item is at the right level.

The nature of stock

The nature of stock depends on the type of business. For example, retail businesses hold stock to sell to the public. Manufacturing and construction businesses hold stock to be made into a finished item, which will be sold either to the public or to other businesses. The level of stock as a proportion of the total assets of the business varies enormously depending on the nature of the business.

EXAMPLE 5.1

> A service-based business, such as an advertising agency, carries very little stock. A car dealership, selling new and second hand cars, could find that the stock is the largest single item on its balance sheet.

Wholesalers

Wholesale businesses must be aware of what the public is buying, and alert to the latest trends. They must have the right stock at the right time to sell to retailers. Retailers will not buy out of date stock. Wholesalers often liquidate stock, realising as much as possible – hence the many 'cheap' shops on the high streets, selling goods bought from wholesalers because they are out of date, obsolete, or otherwise unsaleable at their true price.

Retailers

Retailers must keep a constantly changing stock in front of their customers. Customers are not attracted by a display which never changes. Retailers must know their market. They must know the buying habits of their customers – whether they buy because the goods are cheap, or because the goods are high quality and reliable, for example.

Manufacturers

Manufacturers must constantly monitor the prices and availability of raw materials. They must keep enough stock to maintain their manufacturing process, while innovating, making new designs, and finding alternative materials to use in their manufacturing process. The buyer is a key person in a manufacturing business. Providing that quality is maintained, the cost of raw materials is one of the key issues.

The cost of carrying stock

The danger and cost of carrying stock can be easily recognised.

EXERCISE 5.1

> What costs and dangers can you identify in carrying stock?

However, there is also a cost and danger in holding too little stock.

EXERCISE 5.2

> What costs or dangers might there be in holding too little stock?

Stock records

A reliable system of recording stock movements is essential in any business where the level of stock is material. This system should be backed up by periodic physical checks of the quantities. A stock recording system allows control of the stock levels.

In a full stock accounting system, each item of stock will have its own record. The system will be similar in nature to a double entry book keeping system. Items coming into stock are debited and items going out are credited. A running balance shows the amount in stock at any time. This must be maintained as far as possible in real time.

Stock items are recorded in quantities, not values. These quantities may be discrete items, which can be counted, or weights, volumes, and so on for non-countable items (such as sand, cement, liquids, and so on).

Many accounting software packages provide integrated stock accounting with the normal financial accounting functions.

Stock levels

If the usage of stock is constant, the level of stock could be shown as in Figure 5.4. For each item of stock, three control levels must be determined – minimum, maximum, and re-order level.

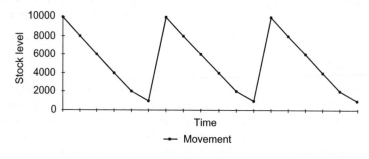

Figure 5.4   Stock levels

Stock holding costs are to a certain extent offset by ordering costs, which increase with the number of individual orders made. The ideal, or optimum, level of stock, is when ordering costs balance out holding costs, to arrive at the lowest overall cost. This is sometimes referred to as the economic order quantity (EOQ).

The formula for calculating the EOQ, is:

$$EOQ = \sqrt{\left(\frac{2 \times A \times O}{H}\right)}$$

where:

A = annual demand for the stock item
O = cost of placing one order
H = cost of holding one item of stock for one year.

However, the cost of holding one item for a year, and the cost of placing one order are somewhat esoteric, and not easy to arrive at. For all but the highest value items, it may not be practicable to use this formula. Further, it may produce a figure which takes no account of the best terms for purchasing – such as quantity discounts, and the minimum ordering quantities.

EXAMPLE 5.2

The formula gives a figure of 237 units as the EOQ, but the minimum order for the supplier is 200 units, with further orders only possible in multiples of 100. The buyer then has to decide whether to order 200 or 300. If a quantity discount applies to purchases of 500 or more, the decision would also have to be made whether to take advantage of the discount.

Minimum and maximum stock levels

For each item, the minimum and maximum stock levels must be determined, recorded and controlled.

- The maximum quantity is determined by the quantity needed for manufacture or for resale. There should be enough stock to cover manufacture or sales for a normal re-order cycle. This is dependent on the normal quantities being used or sold, and the lead time for orders (see below). The maximum level of stock will therefore determine the amount of stock to be ordered. The present level of stock is deducted from the maximum level to arrive at the order quantity. This is why stock must be recorded in real time. Making an order on the basis of out of date information can be disastrous, leading to stock levels above the maximum or below the minimum level.
- The minimum quantity is determined by the lead time and the re-order level (see below), adjusted by the 'safety cushion'.

Minimum and maximum levels should be reviewed regularly. Changing patterns of business may dictate that certain items of stock are in greater demand, or that others are in less demand, or cease to be required altogether. Changes in levels must be agreed between all the parties involved – in a manufacturing business, it is the production manager, and in a retail or wholesale business, it is the sales manager who will take responsibility for setting the levels.

Lead time

Lead time is the time it takes from ordering an item to its delivery into the stores. This has a bearing on the minimum level of stock and the re-order level. The lead time should be recorded on the stock control account.

Re-order levels

The re-order level for a particular item of stock is the level at which it needs to be re-ordered to avoid becoming out of stock, or to avoid breaching the minimum stock level.

EXERCISE 5.3

> The XYZ Company Ltd carries 'supa-widgets'. The annual demand is 156,000 items, equally spread throughout the year. The lead time from order to delivery is four weeks. The minimum stock level is 1,000. What should be the re-order level?

The re-order level should be under continuous review, to take account of changing circumstances. For example, a new supplier might be found who can deliver the goods more quickly. If the lead time shortens, the re-order level should be adjusted. In Exercise 5.3, we assumed a constant demand throughout the year. Often, demand is not evenly spread throughout the year, so the re-order levels should take this into account with seasonal adjustments.

Levels of control

The cost of stock control can be a significant cost, and the benefits of stock control have to be weighed against the cost.

In many manufacturing businesses, there are often a large number of different items of stock to be carried. It is also frequently the case that there are certain lines which account for a high proportion of the total value of stocks, but are a low proportion of the number of items of stocks carried. There are also a large number of items accounting for a low proportion of the total value of stocks. In between is another category, of an average number of items, with an average value.

This leads to levels of stock control, whereby the high value items are controlled rigorously, the middle category has a slightly lower level of control, and the high volume but low value items are subject to a much looser control. This minimises the stock control cost.

Work in progress control

The nature of work in progress

The nature of work in progress depends on the type of business. Manufacturing, construction, or service-based businesses, for example, each carry a different type of work in progress.

In a service business – for example, professional services like accountancy, work in progress consists of the time put into the job until completion, or until a billing point is reached. The invoice is raised when the job is completed. Some service businesses, such as financial advisors, or estate agents, may be remunerated by commission. In such cases, the job itself must be completed before the money is earned.

In a manufacturing business, work in progress consists of the raw materials plus the amount of work that has been carried out on them, until they become finished products.

In a construction business, work in progress consists of the construction itself in an incomplete state. Much money can be tied up in it.

Work in progress control

Money is tied up in work in progress. Raw materials and/or labour have been expended on it, and paid for, but it has to be progressed further before it is saleable.

The control of work in progress therefore consists in making sure that it is progressing according to its determined timetable. This is the domain of 'progress chasers'. They follow the progress of particular building sites, batches of production, or services rendered, and ensure that there are no unforeseen problems holding up the work in progress.

In a service business, the most common cause of hold-ups is lack of information of some sort. This could be information from the client, or from some third party. Essential to the control of work in progress in this context is good communication with whoever is holding up the flow of information. Sometimes the person responsible has not prioritised his time adequately, so that a particular job gets forgotten, or left while other less important work is done. Training is important to ensure that work is properly prioritised and progressed.

Displacement activity can also cause hold-ups. This refers to a person putting aside an important but difficult task in favour of a less important but easier one.

EXAMPLE 5.2

> Joanne, a clerk in an accountancy business occupies herself with filing and tidying the office because the next stage of the job involves contact with a known 'awkward' client, whom she is unwilling to face. The manager in charge of the job keeps chasing her to get on with the job, but she always has an excuse, and other jobs on which she is scheduled to work take precedence.
>
> The key to unlocking this type of situation is in training. The clerk must be trained to recognise priorities and to be able to handle people – even difficult people.

Another problem is that a person who has knowledge (about the process involved or the client) may be absent – perhaps ill, or on holiday – and nobody else has the required knowledge or authorisation to take up the work. There must be adequate training, and procedures in place to ensure that work can be carried out by different people as the need arises. In that connection, records must be adequately maintained. Files, for example, should have all the information necessary. The information needed to do a particular job should never be just in somebody's head.

In construction or manufacturing businesses, the most common cause of delays in work in progress is lack of the right materials at the right time. Something has not been delivered by the supplier, or the store is 'out of stock'. Another cause is breakdown of machinery or equipment. There must be adequate backup.

Delays can also occur because of the absence of a particular person. There must also be adequate training to ensure that jobs can be done by more than one person, so that bottlenecks do not occur. Integrated production planning seeks to ensure that the required materials are in place at the right time, and that other key resources such as labour and machine time are available.

Creditors

Creditors represent the 'negative' part of working capital. The current assets represent money 'tied up', whereas the creditors represent money 'released'. Just as granting credit to customers means that a business is giving them a short-term loan, so suppliers' credit is a loan received. However, this should not be taken for granted and 'milked' for all it is worth. It must be actively managed.

When first using a new supplier, the terms of business and of payment should be properly agreed. A written contract is the best way to establish a new trading relationship, covering pricing, price variations, delivery, penalties, payments terms, discounts, and so on. This is discussed in more detail in the section on credit control.

The credit limit is the amount above which credit will not be allowed. Any attempt to order new goods while the credit limit is exceeded will result in refusal of the supply. Some businesses are tempted to take more credit than the agreed terms, but a customer who consistently exceeds the payment terms could find itself out of favour. Then, when there is, say, a national shortage, or delays with delivery, the late paying customer does not get preferential treatment.

Larger businesses sometimes use their 'muscle' to squeeze unreasonable terms of trade and/or payment from smaller suppliers. This practice is coming under some pressure from The Better Payment Practice Group – an organisation including such bodies as the Institute of Credit Management and the British Chambers of Commerce – trying to promote better trading practices amongst businesses.

Good communications (both internal and external) are important at all stages of managing supplier relationships. For instance, proper stock control will ensure that goods are not ordered in excess of requirements, and that goods are ordered in good time to avoid 'out of stock' situations. Procedures should also ensure that there is no unauthorised ordering, including a cap placed on the value of any orders without special authorisation from a director or the owner of the business.

There must be good co-ordination between the various departments, so that the ordering, delivery, invoicing, and payment for the goods are properly sequenced. When delivery of goods is taken, there must be adequate checking procedures to ensure that the right quantity and quality is received – the goods tally with the supplier's delivery note and with the original order. When the invoice is received, it must be authorised, by checking against the order, the delivery note, the agreed prices, and the calculations. When all the authorisations have been carried out, the amount can be passed for payment. The business's normal payment cycle must be observed, apart from any 'special payment' cases.

Discounts

Many suppliers offer discount for early settlement. In order to discover whether it is worth taking advantage of this, it is necessary to calculate the cost of paying early and receiving the discount, or taking advantage of the normal payment terms.

EXERCISE 5.4

> XYZ Ltd buys £100,000 worth of materials from ABC Ltd during a year. ABC Ltd offers 2% discount for payment within 14 days of the invoice. The normal terms of payment are 60 days. XYZ Ltd's cost of finance is 14%. Calculate whether it is preferable to take the discount or utilise the normal payment terms.

Any query or problem with the goods or services received must be raised with the supplier as quickly as possible. Any likely delay in payment above the normal payment terms, should be discussed with the supplier(s) as quickly as possible. Early consultation can often defuse tricky situations, and promote good trading relationships. In extreme circumstances, it can avoid action by disgruntled creditors for recovery by debt collectors or the courts. Good communications can also help to retain future delivery of goods where these might be jeopardised.

Credit control

Perhaps confusingly, the control of debtors is known as credit control.

The problem

Control of stock and work in progress is within the control of the business. However, the control of debtors is outside the business's direct control. The debtors have control of the date they pay – indeed whether they pay at all.

Everyone is familiar with the sort of excuses heard for not paying on time. Excuses can vary from 'It's in the post', to 'The dog has swallowed the cheque book'.

Credit control differs from other controls. It is concerned with trying to achieve a certain pattern of behaviour by people who are outside the direct control of the business. Credit control therefore starts with the earliest event which leads to a customer of the business becoming a debtor of the business.

The cost of credit

Extending credit to customers always incurs a cost. In most businesses outside retailing, credit is recognised business practice. Credit is not an option – it is a virtual necessity.

EXERCISE 5.5

What costs are involved in extending credit to customers?

Monitoring debtors in total

We saw in Chapter 2 how the key ratio of days sales outstanding is calculated by dividing the annual sales by 365 to arrive at an average daily figure. The sales ledger total debts are then divided by this figure to give the number of days sales outstanding at any time. This should be done regularly, allowing trends to be monitored.

EXAMPLE 5.3

Annual sales year ended 31st December	£1,000,000	(a)
Sales ledger debts at 31st December	£140,000	(b)
Average daily sales (a/365)	£2,740	(c)
Number of days sales outstanding (b/c)	51 days	

The process can be refined further when the business includes different identifiable sectors operating with differing credit terms. For example, a business could have retail sales as well as credit sales. If the total sales only were analysed, the real trends in credit sales could be masked by fluctuations in retail sales. Therefore, the figures should be segregated for the different types of business, according to the credit terms, then the calculations done separately. The retail figures can be ignored for these purposes, since no period of credit is given. That will leave the credit sales analysed for a true comparison.

EXAMPLE 5.4

Annual sales year ended 31st December	£1,000,000	(a)
Made up of		
Retail sales	£ 500,000	(a1)
Credit sales	£ 500,000	(a2)
Sales ledger debts at 31st December	£ 90,000	(b)
Average daily sales (a/365)	£ 2,740	(c)
Made up of		
Retail sales (a1/365)	£ 1,370	(c1)
Credit sales (a2/365)	£ 1,370	(c2)
Number of days credit sales outstanding (b/c2)	66 days	

If the calculation had been done using total sales, the apparent outstanding days would have been 33 days.

This can be further refined if there are different sectors of the business having different credit terms, which might be the case, say, where export sales are involved. Thus if, for whatever reason, one sector of the business operates on weekly credit, and another sector on monthly credit, these two sectors can be calculated separately to give the comparisons and trends for the business as a whole and for each sector individually.

Even with this refinement, however, the picture shown is of the total debtors. In order to exert control, debtors' accounts must be controlled individually. Control starts from the beginning, when taking on a new customer.

Customer credit-worthiness evaluation

It is important to take some basic steps before doing business with another company or business. The 20/80 rule can be seen in this context. In a large enough sample, twenty per cent of the customers will cause eighty per cent of the problems, complaints and bad debts. Not all problems can be foreseen or eliminated by initial screening, but a large number can be.

Even after acceptance of a new customer, their situation should be kept under constant surveillance. Even apparently reliable and solid customers can become bad debts. Conversely, other customers who may have once been perceived high risk become less risky, and more credit-worthy.

Basic information

The first category includes full details of the identity of the prospective customer, such as:

- Name of the business/company
- Full postal address(es)
- Telephone number(s)
- Fax number(s)
- E-mail address(es)

The second set of information relates to the structure of the business:

- What is the business format (limited company, partnership, limited partnership, sole trader)?
- Who owns the business?
- Regardless of the formal ownership, who is actually running the business?
- How long has the business been in existence – in its present form, or in any previous forms (for example, a partnership may have become a limited company)?
- Are there any 'silent' or 'sleeping' partners, or other influences behind the owners/managers?
- If the business is a limited company, can the directors give any guarantees?

References

Third party verification or opinion must be obtained about the prospective customer. An independent opinion is worth more than any information obtained directly from the prospective customer. All references must be authorised by the prospective customer.

- *Trade references.* At least two other businesses in the same trade with whom the prospective customer has done business.
- *Bank reference.* Ask direct questions, such as 'Is this customer good for credit of (say) £1,500 per month?'
- *Trade opinions.* Ask around amongst competitors, or other businesses in the geographical area, the trade association, or the local Chamber of Commerce.
- *Agency references.* Agencies such as Dun and Bradstreet, Extel, and so on can often provide information.
- *Registrar of Companies.* Permission is not necessary. The company's record at Companies House is in the public domain.
- *Financial checks.* Using the principles seen in Chapter 2, examine the prospective customer's accounts to get an idea of its financial health, and look for trends. Make sure that the accounts are up to date. If companies are delinquent in filing their accounts at Companies House this is sometimes an indicator of problems.
- *The company's own staff.* Staff, particularly salesmen, often have informal knowledge – either first hand or hearsay – about other businesses. However, assess the reliability of this information before taking any action based on it.
- *A visit to the business.* A prospective customer will probably not object to a visit to their premises. Seeing things at first hand can help to gain a 'feel' for it.

When sending letters requesting references, make questions as direct as possible, and offer to reciprocate if asked. Try to find out the name of the individual to whom the request should be addressed. A stamped addressed envelope for reply is a normal courtesy. Send out all requests at the same time. Any references must be kept strictly confidential.

When looking at replies, remember that people or businesses often avoid giving an outright bad reference, and will try to suggest possible problems indirectly or in code. It is always possible that the prospective customer will have selected a trade reference by making sure that that particular supplier had always been paid on time. If possible, try to have some input into selecting a trade reference at random.

A new customer is the beginning of a new trading relationship. A business-like attitude at the beginning of this relationship establishes trust. Satisfied customers are the best source of new customers.

Establishing and enforcing credit terms

Once a customer is accepted, trading terms are established. A formal contract is useful, but not always possible. The degree of usefulness depends on the type of business, and the goods or services involved. Payment terms are not necessarily the first matter to be resolved or agreed.

If there is some dispute over other conditions (including delivery, quality, after sales service, and so on) then the payment may well be withheld or delayed. Here are some of the matters to be settled when a new customer is accepted:

- *Price.* There should be a clearly defined method of arriving at the price of the product or service. The price must be easily understood, with no possibility of misunderstanding or different interpretation. It may be:
  - a fixed price,
  - a base price with provision for a price adjustment dependent on some outside influence (such as the cost of the raw material)
  - a price to be calculated at an agreed formula, such as the time spent on services supplied.

- *Price variation.* A clause should allow for mutually agreed or predetermined price adjustment. For instance, where the price of a service is linked to the amount of time spent on the job, the hourly or other rate may be stated to be subject to adjustment annually.
- *Delivery.* The place and date of delivery should be clearly defined. This could include such normal conditions as 'ex-works', 'site delivery', 'FOB', or 'CIF'. Date(s) of delivery of the goods or services are also important, and should be clearly defined.
- *Penalties.* In some cases, it may be necessary or normal practice to agree penalty clauses. The penalties may be linked to delays, quality, performance, or any liquidated damages.
- *Payment.* The method and timing of payment should be agreed. There are several options.

  1. *Cash with order.* This should be agreed with a new customer for whom no satisfactory credit rating can be obtained. No goods will be supplied, and no work will be started until the payment is received and cleared through the bank.

2.   *Rolling deposit.* This requires the receipt of a deposit from the customer, sufficient to cover the agreed credit limit. This deposit will always remain to the credit of the customer's account, as a guarantee of future payment. Interest may or may not be paid on this deposit. This arrangement is another one which is often used until the business has enough confidence in the credit-worthiness of the customer.

3.   *Cash before delivery.* This means agreeing a down payment before starting any work or supplying any goods. The down payment should be at least enough to cover basic costs, so that the 'worst case scenario' would leave the business not bearing a loss, but at break-even. The final payment must be received before the actual delivery of the goods or service.

4.   *Cash on delivery.* This means that the goods are paid for when delivered to the agreed address. This carries the risk of non-acceptance by the recipient, and of loss or damage in transit.

5.   *Progress payments.* This method is common in the construction or civil engineering industry, but can have application elsewhere, particularly where the work to be done stretches over a long period. There is usually a down payment, followed by stage payments when the work has reached certain points. The value of the work is certified by surveyors or independent engineers, and those certificates are used as the basis for progress payments. At the completion of the work the balance of the agreed price is paid. This type of work is often the subject of penalty clauses, related to delays.

6.   *Load over load* (or *cash next delivery*). This relates to a specific type of delivery of goods where there is a regular weekly or monthly delivery, such as fuel deliveries to a petrol station. The terms are that payment for one delivery must be made before the next delivery is made.

7.   *Net 30 days.* This calls for payment within 30 days after the invoice date.

8.   *Net monthly.* This means that payment is made at the end of the month following the month in which the invoice is raised.

Credit limit

This is the amount which the business can allow on credit to the customer. It ensures that no new orders will be executed which would allow the balance owing to exceed the credit limit.

The actual level is decided by reference to the perceived risk for each customer. Once established as a customer, the credit limit should be reviewed regularly, and revised to suit altered circumstances, or to reflect growing relationship and trust.

Good communication is vital. Not only must the customer know his credit limit, but the staff – particularly the sales staff – must know it. Salespeople are always keen to get new orders – very often their salary level depends on it. However, they must be made aware of the credit limit and the current status of the customer's account. This avoids misunderstandings, and mistakes generated by over-zealous salespeople. Salespeople often have a good relationship with customers, and can encourage early settlement of outstanding accounts.

Retention of title

It is common to see some sort of 'retention of title' wording on invoices for goods, stating that the title in the goods does not pass to the buyer until payment is made. However, the effectiveness of this is limited. Once the goods have been delivered to the customer, they may be difficult to reclaim. They may have been operated on as part of a manufacturing process, or sold on to a third party.

Written contracts

Individual trade associations and the Chartered Institute of Purchasing and Supply (Tel: 01780 756777) can supply examples of standard business terms to incorporate into contracts. However, individual terms should be written in to deal with special situations.

Accelerating billing procedures

Invoices must be raised as soon as possible. If goods or services have been supplied, there should be no unnecessary delay in raising and despatching the invoice. If an invoice should have been sent at the end of April, but is delayed until the beginning of May, that could cause a further month's delay in receiving the payment.

The billing procedure is not complete until the invoice is sent to the customer. One method is to print the invoice at the same time as the delivery note. The invoice is then attached to the packaging, or sent with the driver of the delivery vehicle. The customer receives the invoice at the same time as the goods. Where this is not possible, the invoice should be sent out as soon as it has been raised. If there are authorisation procedures, there should be back-up in case of temporary absence of the person who authorises them. The price must be easily understood, with no possibility of misunderstanding or different interpretation. Use first class post to send the invoices.

For professional services, such as lawyers and accountants, the work involved for clients can often stretch over a long period. In these circumstances, in agreement with clients, interim invoices can be raised.

Obtaining payment

Sales ledger administration

Adequate administration of the sales ledger enables debts to be collected regularly and promptly. However small the business, someone must be responsible for its management and control. As the business grows, it may be possible to employ a credit controller full time.

The sales ledger shows, for each customer, the amounts of invoices charged, with credit notes and cash received credited to the account. It shows at any time the amount owing to or from that customer. The balances on each account can be listed to show the total debtors, but this list of balances does not of itself help to collect the amounts due.

Contra accounts

It sometimes happens that a customer is also a supplier, with an account in the purchase ledger as well as the sales ledger. Amounts owing to the business can be set off against monies owing by the business. The customer must agree the frequency of contras.

Monthly procedures

Procedures to control the debts should be carried out monthly at least. This includes sending a statement of account to each customer, accompanied by an appropriate letter if any part of the debt is overdue. The letters should be worded according to the time the debt has been overdue. Beyond a certain limit, the account should be marked for a personal letter or other form of contact, including the threat of further action to recover the money due.

When an account is overdue, it should be flagged, and no new orders accepted or work done for that customer until the account is settled. In smaller businesses, this instruction is often over-ridden by the owner or manager, due to a special relationship with customers.

The process of determining whether part of an account is overdue is known as 'ageing', which means allocating the balance on the account according to the amount of time it has been owing. This is done by matching payments to invoices. Payments on account are allocated on a 'first in first out' basis. In practice, this procedure of ageing the debts is carried out by most computerised book keeping systems. An example of an aged debtors list is shown in Figure 5.5.

Name	TOTAL	30 days	60 days	90 days+
A. Aardvark	1,500.00	1,500.00		
M. United	3,000.00	2,500.00	500.00	
D. Trotter	2,500.00	2,250.00		250.00
Z. Zeeble	500.00			500.00
TOTAL	£7,500.00	£6,250.00	£500.00	£750.00

Figure 5.5 Aged debtors list 31st March 20xx

The use of an aged debtors list enables problematic debtors to be identified, and efforts can be concentrated on dealing with the problem areas. If the sample is large enough, it is likely that 20% of the customers (by number) will owe 80% of the total.

Payment methods

Many debts are still settled by cheque, although there is increasing use of debit cards, credit cards, direct debits and standing orders. Apart from retail businesses relatively little cash is used.

Payment by direct debit allows the supplier to retain control of the payment process. It is particularly useful for businesses such as telephone, and utility supplies, and for public bodies such as local government, where payment is made on a regular basis, such as quarterly.

Credit card payment is extremely useful for retail businesses, or any others dealing with the general public, or where sales are made remotely by telephone or the Internet. This method of payment can be promoted as a benefit to customers. The companion website gives details of credit card trading.

Identifying valuable customers

The sales ledger can provide important information for identifying valuable customers – those who contribute the most to the business's profit. These customers can be given special treatment to ensure that they are retained and to encourage further business with them. It is likely that 80% of the business's profit comes from 20% of the customers.

Many businesses have different products or services producing different levels of profit. It is possible, by accurate analysis, to follow the transactions of high-profit products or services through to the sales ledger to identify the customers buying them. In addition, the sales ledger can easily be used to identify prompt, average, or slow payers, and which ones therefore cost the most in terms of working capital.

Using these criteria, a matrix can be produced as in Figure 5.6.

Profit element of sales			Payment
High	Average	Low	history
			Prompt
			Average
			Slow

Figure 5.6

The top left box indicates the best customers – buying high-profit items, and paying promptly. The bottom right box indicates the worst customers.

Incentivising early payment

It is one thing to expect customers always to pay their accounts on time. In practice, customers are often delinquent in settling their accounts. However, if incentives are given, customers may not need chasing to settle the account, and costs of credit control could be kept down.

Cash discounts

Discount for prompt payment is common. The invoice should show the full amount payable, with a note of the discount that may be taken, and the time limit within which it is valid.

EXAMPLE 5.5

> Invoice date 13th May. Total invoice £1000. 'Discount of 2.5% may be deducted if payment reaches us by 27th May.'

If the net amount payable after discount is stated, some customers might pay that lower amount whether or not they comply with the time limit. They may claim this was a mistake, but in fact it has been done deliberately. The customer should be left to work out the net payment after discount if paying on time.

This discount is built into the costing structure of the goods or services. In effect, if 2.5% is offered as early settlement discount, that 2.5% is first added on to the price. Customers realise that this is the case, and if they offer resistance, it is easy to explain that it is unfair for prompt payers to subsidise slow payers.

If customers take advantage of the discount even when they have not paid within the time limit, their attention must be drawn to it on the first occasion. Letting it lapse is an invitation to continue doing it. The most direct method is a telephone call to point out the error, and to remind them that the wrongly deducted discount will be included on the next statement. This can be reinforced on the next statement by highlighting it. If the customer persists, but the business does not want to risk losing the customer, a surcharge may be added to the invoice value. The ultimate sanction is to refuse any further business with the customer. Hard thinking is needed before the business retains a customer who persists in taking unjustified discount.

The cost of cash discounts

The finance cost of offering cash discounts must be calculated.

EXERCISE 5.6

> XYZ Ltd's credit sales are £1 million a year. If it were to offer a 2% discount for payment within 14 days of the invoice, what would the cost be? The normal terms of payment are 60 days, which are respected by all customers at present. XYZ Ltd's interest on its overdraft is 14%. Calculate whether it is preferable to offer the discount, assuming that 50% of the customers will take advantage of it. The company estimates that present bad debts of £5,000 a year will halve if the discount system is offered.

Issue of reminders

Another device sometimes used to incentivise early payment is to issue 'reminders for payment'. These show all the details of the goods or services supplied, but are clearly stated not to be a valid invoice for VAT purposes, and that a VAT invoice will be supplied on payment. The customer is unable to reclaim the input VAT against their VAT bill until he has paid.

Making the business invaluable

If a customer is experiencing cash flow difficulties, he will often try to apply some degree of prioritisation to his creditors, paying first those creditors seen as important. One way of remaining at the head of their queue is to make the business important or invaluable to that customer. This may mean a high degree of excellence in quality control. Trading reputation has a positive effect on credit reputation.

Businesses should do all in their power to ensure that the quality of goods is beyond question. Promises and delivery dates must be adhered to. Queries or complaints must be dealt with immediately. Sometimes it is beneficial to make some sort of compensation even when the complaint is unjustified, to enhance the company's reputation. Here is another fact of business life:

> ▶ A customer who has had a complaint satisfactorily dealt with is more loyal than a customer who has had no complaint at all.

Delinquent debtors

Despite all efforts, there are occasions when delays occur. Delays should be identified quickly and the causes dealt with.

Complaints and queries

Delays can occur through complaints or queries. Usually these are genuine, but not always. They may have been raised to gain more time while they are answered.

Therefore, make sure that there are no reasons for any complaints or queries in the invoicing procedure. Often, customers have different requirements for their own payment procedures. Try to comply with the customer's requirements. Provide as much relevant information as possible on the invoice. Items normally required include:

- full description of what is being invoiced,
- the issuing business's reference or part number, and so on of the item(s) supplied,
- quantities, weight or measurement of the item(s) supplied,
- price per unit, total price, and agreed quantity discount,
- details (if applicable) of any special pricing agreed, and by whom,
- order references from the customer,
- initials or other detail of the originating person in the customer's organisation,
- date and method of delivery of the goods,
- correct identification of the branch or department of the customer's organisation,
- if the invoice concerns services, full details of the work done, by whom, and on what dates.

It is sometimes useful to anticipate problems, by ringing the customer a few days after the invoice has been sent, to check that it has been received, and that there are no queries or complaints relating to the goods or service. This is particularly useful if the customer has complained in the past. This enquiry pre-empts any use of this tactic in the future. This approach could also be made a few days before the payment is due, to ensure that payment is in the process of being authorised.

Understanding the customer's system

Depending on the size of the customer's business, there may be many processes through which an invoice has to go before payment.

EXERCISE 5.7

What processes might hold up an invoice before payment?

If the customer is contacted about the invoice, it could be anywhere within their system. A useful ploy is for the business's invoices and statements to be brightly coloured – either the paper or the print – or to carry a prominent logo, making them immediately recognisable.

It is helpful to know the names of people dealing with the business's invoices at any stage, in particular the name of the person who authorises the payment or who writes the cheque. Write these details on the customer's sales ledger account. A good personal relationship with the right person can smooth out many problems. A person known by name is less likely to be fobbed off with a lame excuse.

Chasing procedures

Statements of the customer's account must be sent regularly and on time. Customers' systems often depend on statements to settle their accounts.

Appropriate letters should be sent with statements for overdue accounts. The computer can do the donkey-work, so that reliance is not placed on someone remembering to send a particular letter.

EXERCISE 5.8

What letters might be appropriate for various stages of overdue accounts?

Although the wording of the letters can be standardised for particular circumstances, the actual wording should be altered from time to time. The standard letter received several times loses impact.

As an alternative to the first reminder letter, coloured stickers can be used on statements, particularly in the early stages of chasing. These stickers are cheap, bright and often humorous. As with letters, however, repeated use deadens their impact.

Reminder letters should be brief and to the point. The point can often be made by judicious use of emboldened or coloured sentences or phrases. They should, of course, not constitute harassment, or be in any way offensive. As with telephone manner, 'polite but firm' is the tone to adopt.

They should always be sent out at the right time – it is just as important not to send them too early as not to delay sending them. Warning letters should always be specific – particularly about time limits for settling the account. Finally, never make an empty threat. If the final warning letter says that legal action will be taken for recovery, the papers should be prepared ready to go to the solicitor or debt collector.

An effective sanction is always to stop any further supplies to the customer until settlement of the account. The effectiveness of this depends on the importance of the business's goods or services to the customer, and their access to alternative suppliers. This sanction must be communicated to the customer and to the company's own sales staff.

When telephoning customers, all relevant details should be to hand, so that any queries can be dealt with immediately. If customers are being called regularly, a log of telephone conversations is useful so that it is known when they were last called, and who was spoken to. Be prepared for the stock replies such as 'it's in the post', and develop tactics to deal with these. If the cheque fails to arrive, or it is for a different (smaller) amount, get back to the customer to query it.

Standard telephone techniques are quickly learnt and can pay dividends. Try to maintain a 'polite but firm' attitude. Ring at different times of the day. Customers should know that the business will be persistent if they do not live up to promises.

A good alternative to telephone calls is a visit to the customer, if it is geographically possible, and if the amount warrants it. Personal presence is usually a good incentive to pay up.

A system used by some small businesses reputedly with a high degree of effectiveness is the 'one' system:

- One invoice is sent by first class post.
- One statement is sent at the end of the month, again by first class post.
- One telephone call is made if the payment is three days overdue.
- One letter is sent by recorded delivery if the payment is ten days overdue.
- One visit is made by the owner of the business if the letter receives no reply within five working days.

Charging interest on overdue accounts

Since The Late Payment of Commercial Debts (Interest) Act (1998), all businesses have the right to claim interest on overdue commercial debts. Interest may be charged at the official rate for these purposes, which is intended to compensate for the commercial rate of interest payable on bank borrowings.

It is possible to include a clause in the business contract for interest to be charged on outstanding debts, beyond the normal period of credit. This is known as contractual interest. It does not prejudice the business's right to charge interest under the above Act.

Getting outside help

The British Chambers of Commerce have established the Better Payment Practice Group to encourage British businesses to pay on time, and to help businesses with credit management. Their website is www.payontime.co.uk

Recovery of debts

When all else has failed, it becomes necessary to enforce the collection of the debt. The threat of recovery action may be enough to persuade the debtor to pay up, as long as he is persuaded that the threat will be carried out. All other avenues should be tried, and personal contact made before this final step. Take care also to ensure that there are no outstanding queries or complaints.

There are four main means of recovery: agencies, solicitors and legal proceedings, filing for liquidation or bankruptcy, and small claims in the county court.

Agencies

Debt collection agencies can be hired. Many of these operate on a 'no collection, no fee' basis. The fee is usually based on a percentage of debts recovered. Reputable agencies are registered under the Consumer Credit Act 1974, and will not engage in any underhand activities or harassment. Some agencies can also carry out overseas collections, and some may be able to trace debtors who have moved away without leaving a forwarding address.

Personal recommendation is usually a good source. A good agency should produce about a 75% success rate within one month.

Solicitors and legal proceedings

A business which receives a letter from a solicitor will usually take it seriously, and such a letter can often be effective without any further action. However, the instigating business must be willing and ready for the solicitor to proceed with any legal action for recovery. Solicitors will usually charge on a time basis for any work done, even if it ultimately results in receiving no money. A good working relationship with the solicitor is vital for this process. Some solicitors will decline to undertake this work, but many firms will do it.

Filing for liquidation or bankruptcy

Bankruptcy is the process for an individual, with the alternative of an IVA (individual voluntary agreement). Liquidation, receivership or administration are the processes for limited companies.

This is a last resort, and should not be done as an idle threat, or to 'teach a lesson'. More details are given in the companion website.

Small claims in the county court

If the debt is up to £5,000, recovery proceedings may be made through the small claims procedure. This is a relatively simple process, with a minimum of red tape. Legal representation is not necessary, costs are minimal, and if successful, they are borne by the debtor. More details are given in the companion website.

Credit insurance

It is possible to take out insurance against credit risks. This covers the risk of writing off bad debts, but not late payment. The insurance company will carry out extensive checks on credit control procedures, and the premium will be weighted according to the insurer's view of the effectiveness of the systems. Typically, the cover is up to 90% of the credit risk of bad debts.

Writing off bad debts

Sometimes, despite all the efforts, a debt proves to be uncollectable. In these circumstances the only thing to do is to write it off. The bad debt is an expense of the business, allowable against tax and VAT.

It sometimes happens that a debt previously written off as bad is later recovered. When this happens, the amount received becomes another item of income of the business. It is taxable, and VAT becomes payable on it again.

Three golden rules

There are three golden rules for credit management:

1. *Speed.* The longer a debt is outstanding, the harder it is to collect.
2. *Consistency.* A credit policy and procedures must govern every aspect of relationships with customers, and be applied consistently and at all times. Everybody in the organisation should know and abide by the policy – especially salesmen.
3. *Accuracy.* Built-in checks can help cut down errors. Inaccuracies and errors can slow up the process of getting paid.

The companion website shows a self-diagnosis health check for credit control systems, together with ten common danger signals. Any business can use these tools to improve its credit control systems.

Cash management

If the ultimate goal of the control of working capital is to turn all working capital into cash, it may be asked – why is cash management important?

Firstly, a definition. Cash in this context means money that is held either in notes and coin, or in immediately accessible funds such as a bank current account.

Every business needs a certain amount of cash to satisfy day to day commitments, and, to a certain extent, to be in a position to exploit an opportunity when it arises – prompt action may be needed, and ready cash is required to take advantage of the opportunity.

How much cash should a business keep?

There is no simple answer to this question. It varies according to several factors.

EXERCISE 5.9

What factors could influence the amount of cash a company holds?

When the level of cash holding is set, any surplus can be invested, and this is the function of treasury management (see Chapter 6). Any investment of surplus funds should ensure that a certain amount is held in readily realisable investments so that shortages of cash can be rectified.

Cash management benefits from a couple of simple financial tools. One is cash flow forecasting, and this is considered in Chapter 9. The other tool is the measurement of the operating cash cycle.

Operating cash cycle

This term refers to the time period between the cash going out for materials and expenses and the cash coming in from completed sales. In a typical manufacturing business selling goods on credit, this can be represented as shown in Figure 5.7.

This can also be calculated by the following formula:

$$O = R + W + F + D - C$$

where:

   O = operating cash cycle
   R = raw materials stock turnover days
   W = work in progress days
   F = finished goods stock turnover days
   D = debtor days
   C = creditor days

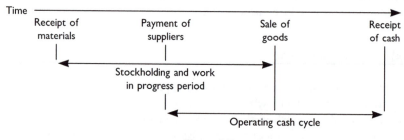

Figure 5.7

The terms were considered in Chapter 2, apart from one minor elaboration. In Chapter 2, we dealt with stock turnover, which treated stock as one global figure. In fact, stock consists of the raw materials, the work in progress, and the stock of finished goods not yet sold. For these purposes, we may add those three items together to arrive at one figure for stock, then proceed as seen in Chapter 2.

EXERCISE 5.10

Calculate the cash cycle of XYZ Ltd whose statistics are shown here for the year ended 31st December.

Extract from profit and loss account

	£	£	
Annual sales		1,200,000	(a)
Opening stock	100,000		(b)
Purchases of materials	600,000		(c)
	700,000		(d)
Closing stock	150,000		(e)
Cost of sales		550,000	(f)
Gross profit		650,000	(g)

Extract from balance sheet

	£	£	
Current assets			
Stock		150,000	(h)
Trade debtors		250,000	(i)
Cash		50,000	(j)
		450,000	(k)
Current liabilities			
Trade creditors	120,000		(l)
Other creditors	80,000		(m)
		200,000	(n)
Working capital		250,000	(o)

ASSIGNMENT

The board of XYZ Ltd, a manufacturer of potato crisps, has asked your advice on its management of working capital. Its statistics and relevant figures are summarised in Figure 5.8. What are the key areas, and what recommendations would you give the board to improve its working capital management? What further information would you seek?

Periods	January £000	February £000	March £000	April £000	May £000	June £000
Raw materials	20	21	21	24	24.5	25
Work in progress	5	6	5.8	6	6.2	6.2
Finished goods	15	16	15.5	16	16.5	17
Trade debtors	240	245	250	265	270	295
Other debtors	5	5	6	5.5	6	5
Prepayments	4	3.5	4	3.5	4	3.5
Cash	1	1.2	1	1.5	1.5	1.5
Total current assets	290	297.7	303.3	321.5	328.7	353.2
Trade creditors	35	37	40	40	40	39.5
Other creditors	5	6	6	8	8	8
Accruals	4	5	4.5	5	4.5	5
Bank overdraft	85	86	87	88	90	96
Current instalments on HP and loans	30	29	28	27	26	25
Total current liabilities	159	163	165.5	168	168.5	173.5
Working capital	131	133.7	138	153.5	160.2	179.7
Sales	120	130	135	130	130	140
Opening stock	38	40	42	42.3	46	47.2
Purchases	37	40	40	40	39.5	41
Closing stock	40	42	42.3	46	47.2	48.2
Materials cost	35	38	39.7	36.3	38.3	40
Other direct costs	25	30	31	31	30.5	32
Gross profit	60	62	64.3	62.7	61.2	68

Extract from accounts of the previous year ended 31st December

	£000	£000
Sales		1,400
Opening stock	32	
Purchases	400	
	432	
Closing stock	38	
	394	
Other direct costs	302	
		696
Gross profit		704

Working capital as at 31st December
Current assets

	£000
Stock: Raw materials	19
Work in progress	5
Finished goods	14
	38
Trade debtors	235
Other debtors	5
Prepayments	4
Cash	1
	283

Figure 5.8 XYZ Ltd working capital data

Figure 5.8 continued

Current liabilities		
Trade creditors	32	
Other creditors	5	
Accruals	4	
Bank overdraft	84	
Current instalments on HP and loans	31	
		156
Working capital		127

SUGGESTED ANSWER

It is immediately apparent that the working capital is increasing, and that at the same time, the trading results, as measured by the gross profit percentage, are declining, although turnover is increasing. The turnover for the first six months of the year is more pro rata than the previous year, and we must ask whether the sales are seasonal. (A look at the comparative monthly figures of the previous year will show seasonality, or the lack of it.) However, the trends of declining gross profit percentage and increasing working capital cause concern. The key indicator, which has no doubt prompted the board to ask for advice, is that the overdraft has gradually been increasing from £84,000 in December to £96,000 in June, even though sales are increasing.

The main causes of the increase in working capital seem to be the generally increasing levels of stock and work in progress, and trade debtors. These trends suggest that control of these items could be slipping. As the business of the company is manufacturing potato crisps, the raw materials and finished products are obviously perishable items, and that emphasises the attention that must be given to stock control. Wastage due to deterioration could be a significant item of loss.

Detailed ratios can be calculated on a month by month basis, to give the following observations.

The *stock turnover* the previous year was 11.26 times. During the six months under review, it can be analysed as follows:

	Total	Raw materials	Work in progress	Finished goods
January	10.76	21.5	84	29
February	11.1	22.2	87	30
March	11.3	22.7	84	31
April	9.86	19.3	74	28
May	9.86	18.9	75	28
June	10.06	19.4	77	29

All categories show a decline in April and May, with some recovery in June, but still not back up to the levels of the previous December. Enquiry should be made about what may have happened in those two months. The figures generally also point to a need for a tightening of stock control. How reliable are the stock figures, for example? In view of the possibility of deterioration of perishable stock, should any stock be written off?

The work in progress figures show a definite trend downwards, and the production schedules and procedures should be examined carefully.

All categories also show an increase in absolute terms, the total stock value having increased from £38,000 in December to £48,200 in June.

The *debtor days* at 31st December were 61. They then show the following pattern:

January	61 days
February	57 days
March	56 days
April	62 days
May	63 days
June	64 days

This clearly shows that, apart from an apparent improvement in February and March, the debtor days have been gradually increasing. The invoicing, sales ledger, and collection procedures should be thoroughly reviewed, and tightened as necessary. In absolute terms, the debtors have increased from £235,000 in December to £290,000 in June.

The *creditor days* at 31st December were 30. They then show the following pattern:

January	30 days
February	30 days
March	31 days
April	34 days
May	32 days
June	30 days

Apart from the slight lengthening between March and May, these figures seem to be in line with previous experience, and 30 days would seem to be a reasonable time for creditor days.

◼ ☑ 6 Financial input into management decisions

LEARNING OUTCOMES

By the end of this chapter, you should:

▶ understand and appreciate the active role to be played by the financial manager in the day-to-day decision making processes,

▶ understand and be able to apply the principles involved in the areas outlined above.

Introduction

Financial managers have a large part to play in the decisions that management has to make every day in the course of business. In this chapter we look at several of these areas:

- selling and pricing, and the related area of costing,
- risk management (including insurance, and fraud prevention),
- treasury management, and
- controls and audit.

Tax compliance and rewarding employees are further practical subjects touched upon, and reference is made to the companion website for further details.

Selling and pricing

Pricing of goods or services for sale is a key management decision. Traditionally, it has not been an area in which finance managers have been greatly involved. The marketing department usually has a far greater role.

The psychology of sales managers reveals that they will find any reason or excuse to offer a discount in order to clinch a sale. Where this is unauthorised – and particularly where it goes unchecked – the gross profit margin and the 'bottom line' suffer.

Properly used, pricing should be seen as one of many tools to achieve aims such as increasing market share or improving profitability. Pricing can, however, have far-reaching implications – the high price of new cars in the UK, bank account business charges, and petrol prices have all had a great impact on companies, on public opinion, even on the government of the day.

EXERCISE 6.1

What tools are available to use in pricing decisions?

Whatever techniques are used, pricing decisions should be made on proper evidence – they should not be taken while 'flying by the seat of one's pants'. However, sales and marketing personnel often have a gut feeling for what the market will stand. Those gut feelings should be just one amongst many tools.

The main drivers of pricing decisions can be divided into **price factors** and **cost factors**.

There are three main **price factors**:

- Pricing according to the value to the buyer. This relies on the selling business being able accurately to gauge the value buyers put on their products or services.
- Segmentation of market-place – that is, applying different pricing policies to different segments of the market.
- Long-term pricing strategies. These include such things as 'penetration pricing' to enter a new market, and pre-emptive pricing to retain market share. The long-term view is taken in order to build a permanent market for the goods or services.

The main **cost factors** are:

- Increasing volume of output to produce or improve economies of scale.
- Reducing cost of production to permit greater price flexibility.
- Emphasis on customer care and quality control. Initially, this can increase costs. In the long-term however, it should encourage increased sales.
- Realistic cost allocation methods – such as activity based costing. The direct and indirect costs of a particular item must be amenable to accurate analysis.

Cost accounting

Cost accounting (or costing) is one type of internal reporting, concerned with the determination of costs for individual units of production or output. As such, it is more readily adapted to and used by manufacturing businesses. However, the principles of cost accounting can be used for other types of business.

The cost of each product is not used as a criterion for setting prices. That is primarily a marketing decision. However, if the business knows how much each item has cost, it then knows how much, if any, profit, is made on its sale. If a particular item cannot be sold at or above cost, the decision must therefore be made on economic grounds whether to stop producing that item.

EXERCISE 6.2

What reservation can be made on the decision to stop selling a loss making item?

Costing can also be used in hypothetical situations, to determine whether there is any commercial motivation to start producing and selling a potential future product.

It is also used in break-even analyses. The measurement of costs in this way is essentially the measurement of variable costs. They are then put together with fixed costs to determine how many sales need to be achieved before the fixed costs are covered (see Chapter 3).

One of the key concepts in costing is that of the cost centre. This is the smallest unit of production for which costs can be allocated. It may be a process, or a single item, or a batch of items. The correct allocation of cost centres and the accurate recording of information is the key to meaningful costings.

Standard costing

Standard costing is a method which calculates a cost for each item of production under standard conditions. This consists of the variable costs and an allocation of fixed costs. The standard cost is fixed in advance, on the best available information at the time. When the actual figures are known, they can be compared to the standard costs. Any variances are then analysed to determine the action to be taken (if any) to rectify the situation.

EXAMPLE 6.1

The standard cost of producing a batch of 10 supa-widgets is broken down as follows:

Item	Quantity	Price per unit	Amount
Rubber	2 kg	£2.50 per kg	£5.00
Steel	1.5 kg	£3 per kg	£4.50
Labour	2 hours	£7 per hour	£14.00
Factory overheads	2 hours	£6 per hour	£12.00
Fixed costs	2 hours	£4 per hour	£8.00
TOTAL			£43.50

The actual costs have come out as follows:

Item	Quantity	Price per unit	Amount
Rubber	2.2 kg	£2.40 per kg	£ 5.28
Steel	1.45 kg	£2.95 per kg	£ 4.28
Labour	2.5 hours	£7.50 per hour	£18.75
Factory overheads	2.5 hours	£6.50 per hour	£16.25
Fixed costs	2.5 hours	£4 per hour	£10.00
TOTAL			£54.56

There has been an over-run on costing. What is the reason for this? The reason is found by analysing the variances, between price variance and volume variance. This could be done as follows (analysis of rubber variance only):

Item	Actual price	Standard price	Variance	Standard quantity	Amount
Rubber	£2.40 per kg	£2.50 per kg	– 10p per kg	2 kg	– £0.20
	Actual usage	Standard usage	Variance	Actual price	Amount
Rubber	2.2 kg	2 kg	+0.2 kg	£2.40 per kg	+£0.48

This indicates that there has been a net variance of 28p. However, the variance is due to overusage of this raw material, partly offset by a reduction in the cost of the raw material. Similar variance analyses can be carried out on the other items, and these are shown in Figure 6.1.

Item	Actual price	Standard price	Variance	Standard quantity	Amount
Steel	£2.95 per kg	£3 per kg	– 5p per kg	1.5 kg	– 7.5p
	Actual usage	Standard usage	Variance	Actual price	Amount
	1.45 kg	1.5 kg	– .05 kg	£2.95 per kg	– 14.5p
TOTAL variance					– 22p

Item	Actual price	Standard price	Variance	Standard quantity	Amount
Labour	£7.50	£7	+ 50p	2 hours	+£1
	Actual usage	Standard usage	Variance	Actual price	Amount
	2.5 hours	2 hours	+0.5 hours	£7.50	+£3.75
TOTAL variance					+£4.75

Figure 6.1 Cost variance analyses

Figure 6.1 continued

Item	Actual price	Standard price	Variance	Standard quantity	Amount
Factory overheads	£6.50	£6	+50p	2 hours	+£1
	Actual usage	Standard usage	Variance	Actual price	Amount
	2.5 hours	2 hours	+0.5 hours	£6.50	+£3.25
TOTAL variance					+£4.25

Item	Actual price	Standard price	Variance	Standard quantity	Amount
Fixed costs	£4	£4		2 hours	
	Actual usage	Standard usage	Variance	Actual price	Amount
	2.5 hours	2 hours	+0.5 hours	£4	+£2
TOTAL variance					+£2

Once variances have been established, the causes of these variances can be investigated, and remedial action taken. For example, the reason must be established for the variances in usage of the different raw materials.

EXERCISE 6.3

> What questions might be asked about the variances in raw material usage and costs?

Similarly, the reasons for the increase in cost of labour should be ascertained, and the reason for the excess time taken on the job.

Absorption costing

The basis of allocation of factory overheads and fixed costs in the above example has been the number of labour hours worked on the job. Therefore, any excess time taken on the job affects the allocation of these expenses to the cost. This basis of allocation of fixed costs in proportion to the number of direct labour hours is known as absorption costing.

However, in recent years, the use of absorption costing has been challenged. Because of greater mechanisation and automation, direct labour hours are an increasingly minor cost element.

Activity based costing (abc)

Activity based costing tries to establish in greater detail the true cost structures of cost centres – that is, processes, batches, items, and so on. It then allocates the fixed costs on a more appropriate basis than direct labour hours.

EXAMPLE 6.2

The costs of a machine processing certain constituent parts of a product may be considered in relation to the operator's time in processing that particular batch. Thus, a fairly complicated set of operations may take, say, four hours to machine a batch of 120 items. For all of this time, the operator is operating the machine. The fixed cost allocation is therefore made on the basis of four hours' direct labour, or two minutes per item. A more simple operation might only take, say, 15 minutes to machine a batch of 30 items. The fixed cost allocation on this basis would take account of the direct labour of a quarter of an hour, or only half a minute per item.

However, down time, re-tooling time, and programming time are not taken into account. If the time for re-tooling and programming were half an hour in each case, this would represent only one eighth of the time on the first, more complicated operation, but it represents double the time of the shorter operation. This factor would affect the allocation rates considerably, and, if not taken into account, could distort the true costs.

A further example relating to the comparison of smaller items with larger items might be the packing and transport or postage costs of sending out smaller orders compared with larger orders. If the packing and despatch department's costs are considered as fixed, and allocated to costs on the basis of direct labour hours, this could cause distortion of the true costs. Activity based costing would suggest that the packing and despatch department's costs be allocated as a direct cost, and the disproportionately larger amount of time spent on packing and despatching small orders would be more rationally allocated.

Throughput costing

This is another fairly recent innovation, based on the principles of activity based costing. It applies to manufacturing plants, and attempts to provide relevant cost information to management, by identifying bottlenecks in the production plant. A production plant or factory is a complicated network of operations, many of which cross each other, and use common resources. Bottlenecks occur when one particular resource is required by several processes or components. If these bottlenecks can be identified, the products and processes which use these resources can be prioritised. This is done by ranking the products or processes by the contribution they make to profit. The most valuable ones are given priority.

Risk management

All business consists in taking a series of controlled risks. Here is another key principle:

▶ There is no reward without risk

All business decisions involve weighing up the potential advantages against the potential risks incurred in going ahead. Risk cannot be completely avoided. The attitude to risk may vary at different stages of the business's existence and growth. Risks that may be acceptable in the initial start up phase may not be as acceptable when the business wishes to consolidate its position.

Further, as the business grows and develops, the incremental experience and resources at each stage will often reduce the risk inherent in its trade. The first new product launch of a business will be more risky than the fourth or fifth new product launch.

Risk does not only occur through failures. Success and growth can bring their own risks, such as overtrading. Events such as takeovers and mergers also carry a risk, particularly if the management of the acquiring company is not experienced in the business of the target company.

Financial managers may not be involved directly in all risk areas, but there are many areas where they can throw light on areas of risk management, and they should act in co-operation with other managers.

There are three basic steps in risk management:

- Identification
- Assessment
- Management

Identification

Many areas of a business are vulnerable to risk. The following key resource areas can be liable to risk. Not all businesses are at the same degree of risk in all areas, and each business must identify its own risk areas:

- *Reputation, goodwill and other intangible assets.* This area is easily over-looked, but damage to goodwill can have enduring consequences. Other intangible assets such as patents or designs can be at risk through piracy.
- *Products and services.* These can be put at risk by poor quality control, poor cost management, inadequate selling or marketing, or pirating by competitors.
- *Supplies.* The availability of the right materials and services is vital for any business. These can be at risk from poor quality or late delivery.
- *People.* People are the most valuable resource of any business. They can be at risk from inadequate health and safety procedures, inadequate management, lack of training, or poor motivation. Key employees are crucial, and should be given special attention.
- *Physical assets.* These can be destroyed or damaged by fire, flood, and other incidents.
- *Financial assets.* These can be at risk through normal business activity. Debts can go bad, foreign transactions can suffer adverse exchange rates, investments can make a loss. Fraud is another risk area.

- *Administration systems.* Production and information systems can be severely disrupted by computer failure or virus infection. Poor design and planning, poor advice, or inadequate information can also seriously affect them.
- *Funding.* Damage to public confidence in the business can threaten the availability of equity capital or loans. Protection of credit-worthiness and the ability to provide an acceptable return on capital is of primary importance.

Sources of risk

Once the vulnerable areas have been identified, the sources of risk must be identified.

Internal risk sources

Risk can come from within the business. Some of the most prominent areas are:

- *Ineffective management controls.* In extreme cases, management controls are non-existent. The business then drifts like a ship without a rudder. Without effective management controls, a business can stray into dangerous risk areas. Financial controls are amongst the most important of management controls.
- *Bad or non-existent planning.* This can lead to hold-ups in production or delivery of goods or services. The right resources must be in the right place at the right time.
- *Poor information.* Information is the key to organisation. If information is non-existent or inaccurate, serious risks can follow. For example, inaccurate information could lead to a contract being accepted which actually incurs a loss.
- *Poor quality control.* Poor quality products or services can threaten the entire business. In businesses which sell products, the quality of pre-sales and after-sales service should not be overlooked.
- *People.* People are the most valuable resource of any business. Lack of training can lead to risk. Frequent changes in the workforce mean that relatively few people build up the experience which is invaluable for efficient working. However well-trained and motivated the workforce, there is the ever-present risk of accidents, which disrupt the business and could prove disastrous.
- *Industrial disputes.* Relations with the workforce are of paramount importance. Bad industrial relations can disrupt business.
- *Machinery breakdown.* Any damage to or breakdown of machinery can seriously affect production, with consequent harm to relationships with customers waiting for orders.
- *Inherent process risk.* Some industries, such as the nuclear industry, have inherent dangers or risks attached to the process of manufacture. The construction industry has all the hazards inherent in a building site.
- *Capital investment.* Large capital investment in equipment, property, buildings, research and development, carries risks because such large investment is dependent on stable, or at least predictable market conditions and demand for a lengthy period.

External risk sources

- *Competition.* Competitors can put sales at risk, either by undercutting prices, or offering a better service. Market share is constantly the battleground of price wars. The major supermarket chains and daily newspapers are fighting a continuous battle. Industrial espionage is an ever-present risk. Patents, designs, technological developments, could all be at risk from unprincipled competitors.
- *New entrants into the market-place.* The barriers to new entrants differ greatly from one industry to another. In service industries, the barriers are lowest. New entrants only have to acquire the skills necessary to make an impact. Highly technological manufacturing businesses such as petrochemicals or pharmaceuticals have greater barriers.
- *Customers.* All businesses need customers, but they are never entirely risk-free. There is an obvious risk in having only one customer, or one main customer. In general, a greater number of customers reduces the risk element. Customers also bring the risk of defaulting on their debts.
- *Markets.* Nothing is static, and markets constantly change. Many professionals confidently predict that, in future, most businesses will earn up to 60% of their income from products or services that they did not provide five years previously. Inadequate market research can undermine the whole basis of new product or service launches. Concentration of business output in one or two markets can leave the business vulnerable to changes in demand.
- *Suppliers.* The principle of risk spreading also applies. Having too few suppliers leaves the business at risk of not being able to obtain vital supplies of its materials. The relative strengths of supplier and customer are also relevant. A small business does not have much 'clout' with a large supplier concern. If the supplier ceased production of the items, are there alternative suppliers?
- *Crime.* Fraud is an ever present and growing threat in a highly technological age. Other forms of crime are still a risk area. Crime can occur from disaffected employees, or from complete outsiders who have identified areas such as large quantities of cash that can be targeted.
- *The economy.* The national and international economy affects businesses. Interest rates, inflation, deflation, recessions, exchange rates are all part of the economic cycles affecting markets and operations.
- *Government legislation.* Policies of successive governments, such as the minimum wage, can affect businesses. Taxation policies constantly change, and the annual budget presented by the Chancellor of the Exchequer usually affects businesses. Trading overseas puts a business at risk of influence from foreign governments. Dealing with politically or economically unstable countries further increases the risk.
- *Demographic issues.* Changes in population profiles affect businesses by altering the structure of markets, or the availability of labour for the workforce.
- *Social issues.* Changes in public opinion on matters such as tobacco, alcohol, and 'green' issues can affect markets. Environmental issues are particularly

relevant as the public and other interest groups become more ready to sue companies for environmental damage.

- *Natural phenomena.* Weather conditions, flood, drought and earthquake can have an obvious primary and secondary effect on businesses. Diseases of humans and of animals can also have their effect. Often the most pressing need in this sort of case is the 'clear up' operation, and getting back to normal working as soon as possible after the event.

Assessment

With many potential areas of risk, they can seem overwhelming. However, not all risk areas are equally serious, and the next step is the assessment of risk. Assessing the risk factor means trying to measure the likelihood of the risk occurring and the impact if it should occur. Remember the principle:

▶ If you can measure it, you can control it.

When the assessment of risk is carried out, management can decide which risks need resources devoted to their management and control.

Likelihood

Some risks are uncertain by their nature, such as industrial accidents, or human or animal disease. Other risks can be susceptible to statistical probability analysis. This occurs when events are part of a natural or economic cycle, and when they occur frequently enough to rely on statistical techniques.

Some risk areas can be foreseen – if not predicted with certainty – by a combination of experience and management intuition. Experience can be shared through trade associations, chambers of commerce, and so on. Businesses are keen to share this sort of knowledge. It helps to protect their industry, and gives no individual business a competitive edge. A business can also generate its own information bank for specific risk areas – such as keeping accurate records of accidents, monitoring customer complaints, keeping a log of machinery breakdowns, and so on.

Potential impact

The direct effect of the occurrence of a risk can usually be measured in financial terms. This can include:

- the cost of replacement of whatever resource – human, material or machinery – is lost or damaged,
- the lost opportunity costs, and
- down time costs.

The indirect effects are more difficult to measure or quantify. Things like the knock-on effect of a failure of an activity in one department may be felt in other departments. The more distant from the original event, the more difficult is measurement. Effects like the ultimate impact on the business's reputation may be potential rather than realised.

Final assessment

The final assessment of risk depends on the interplay between the likelihood and the impact of a risk.

- A low likelihood and low impact event will not cause much concern. Action may not be cost effective.
- A high likelihood but low impact event causes more concern, but will be relegated on the action plan until higher profile events have been dealt with. Any action proposed must be subjected to assessment of its cost effectiveness.
- Low likelihood but high impact events are the most insidious. They include things which creep up unnoticed, and suddenly explode with lethal consequences. For example, if a drug was shown to have unexpected but damaging side effects, the potential impact could be fatal for the pharmaceutical company that developed it. These risks must be acted upon, but not necessarily as the first priority.
- High likelihood and high impact events – such as a fire or explosion at a fireworks factory – demand the most urgent action. They must be acted upon with the highest priority.

A matrix such as Figure 6.2 helps decision making.

High likelihood Low impact	High likelihood High impact
Low likelihood Low impact	Low likelihood High impact

Figure 6.2

The lowest concern would be in the bottom left corner, and the highest in the top right corner. The boundaries between the different corners are not sharp, but they merge into each other, and judgements must be made as to which are the most important. Each case must be considered on its own merits.

Management of risk

Once risk has been identified and assessed, action must be taken. Management must have agreed policies in place. These include the limits of acceptable and unacceptable risks, the structure of decision making, and the limits of authority of each level of management.

Acceptability of risk changes as the business develops, so risk management policy must be constantly reviewed. Once agreed, changes must be communicated effectively to all levels of management, and their responsibilities for risk identification and assessment agreed with them.

The obvious ways to control risk are to reduce the likelihood and potential impact of the event. Remember:

▶ Prevention is better than cure.

Minimisation of likelihood

Several steps can be taken to minimise the likelihood of the event.

- Use specialist knowledge and experience. For example, handling and transporting hazardous goods could be sub-contracted to a specialist haulage firm.
- Don't put all the eggs in one basket. This applies to customers, suppliers, and key staff. For instance, too great a reliance on one or a few customers, or seasonal sales, could be rectified by a greater emphasis on developing new markets, and reducing the seasonal nature of the trade.
- Develop information systems to warn staff of recognised or potential risks. Monitoring the situation is a continuous process. Once an event is identified there must be pre-agreed procedures to report the occurrence to the right person.
- Make physical alterations or improvements to premises, such as fire precautions, closed circuit cameras, or electronic surveillance equipment. Security systems are not always expensive. The local police crime prevention unit can often advise on systems, some of which can be linked to police response units. Insurance companies can also provide advice.
- Training of all staff on general risk issues, and specific training for staff in particular areas – such as credit control for sales ledger clerks. Employee awareness of risk is a key area in reducing the likelihood of an event.

Minimisation of impact

- *Insurance.* This is the main plank in most business's action plan for risks, and is dealt with in more detail below.
- *Contingency planning.* Plans should be on hand, and regularly reviewed, to put into place if an adverse event takes place. This sort of plan can help businesses get back to normal running as soon as possible after an event occurs. Plans should include a detailed timetable for instigating backup procedures.
- *Hedging.* This is a technique for trying to insure against adverse movements, either of currency exchange rates, or prices of raw materials, such as metals. It is dealt with in the section on treasury management.

Risk management is treated in more detail in a 'Risk Management Standard' published jointly by the Institute of Risk Management, the Association of Insurance and Risk Managers, and the National Forum for Risk Management in the Public Sector.

Insuring against risks

The principle of insurance is that of pooled risk. Many individuals and businesses pay into a pool, operated by an insurance company, and those few that suffer the insured risk receive financial compensation. In practical terms, insurance is one of those recurring expenses, and some people are tempted to ask if they could miss it out. They seem to pay in, and never make a claim. But:

> ▶ Do not ask 'Can I afford to pay it?'
> Ask instead 'Can I afford not to pay it?'

Some insurances are compulsory.

- If a business has employees, it is obliged to display an employer's liability insurance certificate.
- Certain types of business may be required to have particular types of cover under health, fire and safety regulations.
- Every road vehicle must carry at least third party insurance cover.
- If a business has a mortgage on property, the mortgage company will almost certainly require at least fire and damage insurance cover on the building.

Reviewing insurance

Insurances must always be kept under review. It is probably not a good idea to change insurance companies every year, chasing after the cheapest premiums. However, it usually pays to have a thorough insurance review every few years.

Disclosure

Contracts of insurance are of 'utmost good faith'. That means that all relevant facts should be disclosed to the insurer. Failure to do this could invalidate the policy. It is easy to overlook changes which could materially affect the risk taken on by the insurer, such as:

- a new product line,
- a new overseas market for exports,
- a change in the tenancy of buildings, or the way in which buildings are occupied,
- a change in the size of the workforce

All these could be material facts which must be disclosed. A regular review should ensure that these items are not overlooked.

The insurance industry is very sophisticated, and cover is available for every risk imaginable. The companion website gives a summary of the most important specialist areas of insurance cover. However, businesses should not be talked into taking out every new insurance product that comes along.

Level of cover

An occasional review should focus on making sure the right level of cover is in force. The level of cover is extremely important. Underinsurance can be almost as devastating as no insurance. Sometimes, the level of cover which was set some years ago, is now excessive. The level of cover is particularly important in the following types of insurance:

- *Buildings* – the rebuilding cost should be insured. (NB Rebuilding cost is not the same as market value.)
- *Stock* – the cover should be for the maximum amount of stock that could be carried at any one time.
- *Business interruption* – usual cover is for eighteen months' loss of profits based on the last annual profit figure.
- *Equipment and machinery* – cover should be for the cost of replacing machinery, and is not necessarily the same as its original cost.

Premiums

An insurance broker can survey the market to check whether better premiums are available. Bear the following in mind:

- *Uninsured excess* – the premium is reduced if the business can accept a slightly higher level of excess (that is, the claim is reduced by a fixed amount for each occurrence – for example, £1,000).
- *Discounts* – insurance companies often offer discounted premiums if the business can show that it has taken precautionary measures to reduce risk (for example, by fitting alarms or fire extinguisher sprinkling systems). Many insurers write warranties into their policies requiring at least some risk management procedures in place.
- *Frequency of premium* – it may be possible to pay the premium quarterly or monthly instead of annually.
- *Long-term agreements* – lower premiums or fixed rates may be obtained by agreeing a longer term contract with the insurance company – say, for three years.

Fraud prevention

Fraud is another area of risk management, but it is a major crime area, and is usually on the increase during a period of economic downturn or recession. A key area of financial management is fraud prevention. The old adage remains true in this area:

▶ Prevention is better than cure.

Fraud can occur at any level – from an employee trying to defraud the employer, to a business trying to defraud other parties, including the Inland Revenue or Customs and Excise, or insurance companies by bogus insurance claims. Fraud may also be aimed at investors, at company creditors, or banks.

Shareholders in private companies can be the target of fraud. If the structure of a private company is such that a minority shareholder – or even a 50% shareholder – is not involved in the day-to-day running of the company, the other owners can try to defraud the minority shareholder of value. This could arise by, for example, exceeding the normal limits for exercising prudence in preparing company accounts, making excessive provisions against assets such as work in progress or debtors, to depress profits, and justify a lower share valuation.

Then, there are always scams, by which unscrupulous operators try to extract money from businesses.

Exhibit 6.1

One scam in recent years involved the use of bogus invoices, purporting to come from directories or registers. These bogus invoices, if not subject to control procedures, would often be paid without further enquiry, and the bogus operator would quickly move on to another address. Proper authorisation procedures should uncover this fraud.

In trying to prevent fraud, management should try to enter the mind of the fraudster. The fraudster will often try to capitalise on two main factors – lack of time, and materiality. Many businesses – particularly smaller ones – do not have the time, or procedures, to deal with much detailed paperwork. The fraudster also knows that if the scam is kept to a reasonable cash figure, it may well pass unnoticed. Any amount below, say, £100 may be passed without further enquiry.

Exhibit 6.2

A service contract for maintenance of machinery or equipment may specify that up to two routine service visits are included in the annual fee, with only exceptional visits or major repairs charged separately. However, the service company actually invoices for the routine maintenance visit. The invoice-checking procedure establishes that the visit was actually made, and the invoice is passed for payment – but nobody has checked against the original contract. If this point is picked up, the service company apologises for the 'error' and cancels the invoice.

Further examples include:

- Unwarranted use of direct debit instructions – control over the payment is exercised by the supplier. Unauthorised increases in amounts collected in this way, or dates of collection, could go unnoticed by the payer.

- Unnecessarily complicated invoicing which discourages any further attempt at clarifying exactly what is being charged for.
- Allowing a due date – such as a magazine subscription renewal – to pass before any reminder is sent, while the magazine issues are still being sent.

However, many fraudsters succumb to greed. What could remain undetected if kept at a lower level becomes their downfall. For example, small amounts of goods pilfered from stock can go unnoticed for a long time – particularly if stock control procedures are lax. However, if the practice is escalated, the amounts involved excite attention, and the pilferage is discovered.

Cash fraud

Where cash is involved in the business – as in retail trading – the opportunities for fraud are always present. This can be perpetrated on the business, by an employee stealing cash; or fraud perpetrated on the Inland Revenue, by a business proprietor concealing cash transactions and evading tax.

Cash fraud is easier where there are a large number of transactions for relatively small amounts. It is also a constant concern for banking businesses and building societies, whose main business includes handling cash.

Controls should be in place where cash handling is a significant part of the business. These can include:

- moving staff handling cash to different locations without notice,
- carrying out spot checks without notice, and
- ensuring that all staff take the holidays they are entitled to. If a member of staff fails to take holidays, it is often a pointer to something going wrong.

In general, controls should ensure that, in order to carry out fraud, there should be collusion between at least two people.

Employee fraud

One particular fraud, which occurs in wages departments, is known as 'ghosting'. This involves setting up employee records for fictitious people, and the perpetrator collecting the extra wages paid. These wages can be paid either in cash, which is preferable to the perpetrator, or by diversion to a bank account. The bank account, however, always leaves a trail which can be uncovered at a later time.

Regular spot checks ensure that all employees actually exist.

Technology fraud

A major area of fraud is technology and in particular the Internet. A serious area of concern is the diversion of credit card details allowing fraudsters to use bogus credit card numbers to obtain goods or services from the Internet – or over the telephone.

Bogus businesses can also be set up online, taking orders, and accepting payment only by cheque or postal order. They accept the cash without delivering the goods, and quickly move on to a new bogus identity at a new website. This type of fraud is basically the same as the bogus invoice type seen earlier. Assured identification of any supplier to whom payment is made is vital. Some fraudsters attempt to make their website resemble that of a well-known business or brand, and thereby attract payments for non-existent goods or services. Websites can conceal foreign addresses, so it is important that the website address is 'backed up' by a real, bricks-and-mortar address (not just a postbox address).

A further area of concern in regard to the Internet and the so-called dotcom companies relates to the 'massaging' of accounts. There are many areas in which the accounts can be misrepresented. For example, Internet companies swap advertising space on their websites. No money changes hands. However, in the accounts of the companies, the equivalent amount is shown as advertising income. In other similar ways, some new dotcom companies are showing 'virtual' profits in their accounts as if they were actual, realised profits. The purpose of such misleading accounts is, of course, to attempt to attract investors' money. In addition, it was a widespread practice to pay employees and advisers in shares rather than in cash. The artificial boosting of a company's share price is a substantial fraud area.

Data protection

Ensuring the security and safety of data is a major concern. Business data can be sensitive, and leakage could be detrimental to the business. The problem arises when data is not stored in a physical form, but in electronic form, which fraudsters can then access.

Data stored electronically can also be lost. The loss of the actual information incurs time in reconstructing the lost data.

Access to data should be controlled, and adequate backup taken. Often, however, these two criteria adversely affect each other. Access can be controlled by password protection and encryption. Backup copies should be kept physically separate from the original data. Computers with sensitive information can be separated from the network and not connected to the Internet to reduce vulnerability.

The Data Protection Act 1998 provides a legal framework for the protection of data, and businesses holding certain types of data must register under this Act. Those businesses must specify how their data is protected, and allow individuals access to information held about themselves. This gives rise to problems of identification of those individuals wishing to access their information.

Reporting fraud

If a fraud is discovered, there are good reasons to report it to the police authorities, not the least being the deterrent effect on other would-be fraudsters. Reporting is one way of preventing future frauds. However, the process of reporting and investigation by the police involves considerable disruption to the normal business routine. The police need original documentation which provides them with 'best evidence'. They can, of course, provide copies or photographs of any item they retain, but it can still seriously disrupt business.

As is common, many cases of fraud involve computer records, and the police are required to seize the computerised storage medium. Again, the police can make images or copies of data, but this in itself is an extremely disruptive process.

Creating an anti-fraud culture

Steps can be taken to prevent fraud by encouraging an anti-fraud culture in the business. This can include publishing an anti-fraud policy, and taking other steps. The policy document could typically include some or all of the following items:

- What the business will do if fraud is suspected.
- What the employees should do if they suspect fraud.
- Training facilities for recognising fraud.
- The procedure for assessing fraud risk.
- IT controls should be kept strictly confidential to the IT department.
- Internal controls should be appropriate to the assessed risks.
- Active instigation of anti-fraud investigations.

Signs of weakness in systems

It is always useful to be aware of signs of weakness and by regular monitoring to eradicate them. Some signs of weakness are:

- ☹ Staff not taking holidays.
- ☹ Staff working abnormal or unusually long hours.
- ☹ Staff being paid less than the industry norm.
- ☹ Lack of separation of duties, particularly where handling cash is involved.
- ☹ Branches in remote locations not being reviewed as regularly or as rigorously as other branches.
- ☹ Unexplained variances from budget – either favourable or unfavourable.
- ☹ Clusters of transactions just below the authorisation limit.

Warning signs on the level of corporate fraud

- ☹ Substantial sales of shares by directors.
- ☹ Dominant chief executive and weak board.
- ☹ Unexpected resignations of senior executives.
- ☹ Over-elaborate corporate structure – what is it hiding?
- ☹ High incidence of transactions with related parties.
- ☹ Low standard of corporate governance compared with competitors.
- ☹ Deteriorating cash position despite profitable trading.

Tax compliance and planning

Taxation is a major area of finance affecting virtually every business and other organisation.

EXERCISE 6.4

What taxes can you identify that affect businesses?

Taxes are direct or indirect. **Direct taxes** are those levied on income (such as Income Tax and Corporation Tax). **Indirect taxes** are those levied on spending (such as Value Added Tax and Excise Duties).

The companion website gives a brief summary of tax compliance and planning principles.

Rewarding employees

Rewards generally

Rewarding employees involves setting fair rates of pay, and deciding whether any extra benefits should be paid. If any bonus schemes are proposed, they should be easily understood and seen to be fair. Perhaps the most problematic area is that of directors' remuneration. However, other employees who are seen as key personnel may also be the subject of special packages to retain their services. Details of employee rewards and incentives, including share schemes, are given in the companion website.

Treasury management

Treasury management refers to the management of cash. In particular, larger businesses have several cycles of cash – from the day-to-day working capital through to the investment of larger sums for the long or short term. It also concerns the matching of funds with their use. For example, a long-term project or fixed asset requires long-term funding. Short-term funding is more expensive and should only be used for short-term requirements.

The most usual aspect of treasury management is the management of surplus cash funds. This is obviously of most interest to businesses with large sums of cash to invest – typically seen in banks and insurance companies. However, the principles can apply to businesses of any size. There is an obvious distinction in the time scales involved. Pension funds, in particular, are investing money for long periods, and their treasury management needs are quite distinct.

Some of the ways in which funds can be invested include:

- **Deposit accounts**. These can be with banks or building societies. They earn interest, and the art of deposit investing is to obtain the best return in the time scale available.

  - *Interest rates* can be fixed or variable. They can also be stepped, that is, the rate increases according to the amount deposited. It can also be stepped by period, that is, the rate increases with each period that the deposit is left undisturbed.
  - *Interest payment and frequency.* Interest can be paid annually, quarterly or monthly. The compounding effect means that interest paid monthly actually gives a better return than if it is credited annually. Interest can be accumulated in the deposit account or paid into a current account.
  - *Notice.* Deposits can require a period of notice to withdraw the money, or allow instant access. The period of notice affects the interest rate. Withdrawals may be allowed inside the notice period, but incur a penalty. There are also term deposits, which exist for a fixed term only, usually with no withdrawal facility inside the fixed term.
  - *Certificates of deposit.* These are fixed term special deposits for higher sums, and benefit from a higher rate of interest.

- **Equity investment**. This means investing in shares of commercial companies, incurring all the risk elements associated with business. Any business must address the question of whether to invest externally in other businesses or internally by ploughing the money into its own business. In some cases, investment in other businesses represents a kind of hedging, by investing in other businesses which would perform better (perhaps through different cyclical patterns) when the investing business is not doing so well. The amount of money available determines whether investment will be managed in-house or by investing in a collective form of investment such as an investment trust.

- **Government Stocks**. These are a form of loan to the government. They have fixed redemption dates, and a nominal interest rate. A stock described as '6% Treasury Stock 2010' pays interest at 6% on the nominal value, and is redeemed in 2010. They are traded on the London Stock Exchange, and the price at which they may be bought varies with prevailing interest rates. Thus, if the nominal interest rate is 12%, and the prevailing interest rate for the equivalent date of redemption is 6%,the person buying it would expect to pay twice its nominal value. Prices are quoted with 100 representing the nominal value of the stock. Any price above that is said to be at a premium, and any price below is at a discount.

  - *Interest yield.* The yield is the actual rate of interest enjoyed by the buyer. Thus, if the nominal rate of interest of a stock is 6%, but it is bought at 120, the yield is 5%.
  - *Redemption yield.* This measures the total return over the remaining life of the stock up to maturity. Thus, if £10,000 nominal of a 6% stock is bought at 110, with ten years remaining before redemption, the price paid is £11,000.

In ten years time, it will be redeemed by the government for £10,000. There will be a loss. The redemption yield is worked out by balancing this loss against the interest received. The redemption yield in this case works out at just above 4.5%.

- **Tax incentives.** Various forms of investment offer tax incentives – in the form of exemption from income tax on the interest or dividends, and/or exemption from capital gains tax on profits made.
  - *Exemptions available to individuals.* ISAs are the most frequently used existing tax incentive, although the strict limits on the amount which may be invested limit their usefulness to businesses. Certain National Savings products carry tax exemptions, and Friendly Societies also offer limited amounts of tax-free status.
  - *Enterprise Zones.* Investments in commercial buildings within certain geographical areas can be made directly or through a property trust. Tax advantages mean that the net cost after these tax concessions can be as little as 60% of the cost of the building.
  - *Venture Capital Trusts.* Tax relief 'up front' of 20% is available for investments of up to £100,000 in approved Venture Capital Trusts. These are trusts which invest in smaller, non-quoted companies. There is also relief from Capital Gains from these. Companies may be on the 'receiving end' of these, and therefore find it easier to raise capital.
  - *Enterprise Investment Scheme.* Similar tax relief to Venture Capital Trusts is available for direct investment into smaller non-quoted companies, by investing in new shares issued by the company. Companies may also be on the 'receiving end' of these, and therefore find it easier to raise capital.

Hedging

Hedging is a term applied to techniques designed to alleviate the risk exposure arising due to timing delays and movements of prices or rates of exchange. Specifically, it can apply to foreign currency rates of exchange, prices of commodities, and equity investments.

The risk can occur because of the necessity to agree prices in advance, when the open market value, or exchange rate, can fluctuate.

EXAMPLE 6.3

A firm manufacturing widgets gets a contract to supply 50,000 to the USA in three months' time. Calculating the cost of production, overheads and shipping costs, the total cost of the products comes to £50,000. Adding the normal mark up gives a selling price of £60,000. At today's rate of exchange (assumed $1.50 = £1), that would represent $90,000. That is the price agreed. However, payment is to be made on delivery in three months' time. If the exchange rate changed from $1.50 = £1 to $1.65 = £1, the American company's $90,000 would convert to £54,545 before any commission or bank charges. This represents a significant reduction in the normal mark up, and consequent profit margin.

What can be done about this risk? On the simplest level, an additional margin could be built into the quoted price, so that the mark up is more on this type of transaction. However, this could seriously affect the competitiveness of the quote. Another possibility is to quote the price in sterling, transferring the exchange rate risk to the customer. This is not always acceptable. The main methods of hedging this risk are forward contracts, and options and derivatives.

Forward contracts

Forward contracts can be used for currency exchange rates and for commodities. The process is carried out by a forward purchase or sale of the commodity or currency, at an agreed price on an agreed date. This process eliminates all risk, but at a cost. The contracts for currency have to be made through a bank, which will charge commission. This type of contract is common, and forward prices for currencies and commodities are published. Prices are quoted for future exchanges or deliveries of the commodities at given future dates. These are not in any way a forecast of what the rates or prices might be, but based on interest rates.

However, it is obvious that rates can fluctuate in any direction. If they fluctuate in favour of Sterling, then the exporter from this country, or a buyer in this country will have gained. Therefore, if a forward contract is taken out, and the price or exchange rate fluctuates the wrong way, there will have been no benefit – in those cases it is the bank which takes the profit. Despite this possibility, many businesses still prefer to make forward contracts for the peace of mind and certainty which they give.

Options

Options eliminate the downside risk, but allow the business to retain the advantage of an improving price or exchange rate.

An option involves paying a premium for the option of dealing, in a limited quantity, commodity, currency, or security at a specified price within a certain time scale. It can be visualised as a kind of insurance policy. It gives the right (or option) to do the deal at the quoted price, but this right does not have to be exercised. The cost is called the premium. Call options give the right to buy the item at the specified price. Put options give the right to sell. Double options give the right either to buy or sell, but these options command a higher premium. The London Stock Exchange operates a traded options market in shares, in which the options themselves can be bought or sold.

Derivatives

When options are used in connection with 'real' things (like commodities and shares) rather than exchange rates, they are called derivatives. The use of derivatives is a common method of hedging commodities, and financial institutions such as banks and insurance companies dealing in shares. However, because of the fluctuations and the degree of risk, derivatives have attracted speculators hoping to make a profit on these deals. Commodity markets are highly regulated environments, and speculators must comply with rules, as well as knowing their market.

Commodities of raw materials have to be ordered a long time in advance, particularly where they are being imported. Seasonal factors and vagaries of climate can seriously affect commodity prices, and commodity futures markets grew up to give certainty of costs to manufacturers and processors of these raw materials.

These future contracts involve the right to buy the commodity at a specified time, at an agreed price. This contract does not have to be taken up, but it is an insurance policy. Speculators give the market a liquidity without which it would be difficult to operate. What makes speculation possible is the practice of buying 'on margin'. This means that in order to purchase a futures contract, only a nominal deposit of, say, 10%, has to be paid 'up front'. Thus, the potential gains are much greater for the initial outlay. However, the risks are also much greater.

Derivatives in shares require rather smaller 'margins' than commodities, and therefore attract more speculators.

Money market funds

Corporate treasurers sometimes find themselves with surpluses of cash to deposit with the bank in order to earn interest for the short term. While £10 million may be a large sum of money to a company, is much more trivial to a bank. Some of the ways of investing money in the short term are:

- bank deposit,
- commercial paper,
- collective money market funds

The interest rates are expressed as being so many percentage marks above or below the benchmark, which for these transactions is either LIBOR (London Inter Bank Offered Rate) or LIBID (London Inter Bank Deposit Rate).

Bank deposits will normally be below LIBID, but improvement on the interest rate may be had by depositing with an institution having a lower credit rating.

Commercial paper is unsecured lending to a corporate treasury, also offering a better interest rate, but at a slightly higher risk profile. This type of lending assumes that there is adequate administration and expertise to enable the proper assessment of the credit risk, and monitoring of the investment.

Collective money market funds operate as a pool for several smaller lenders to obtain better rates of interest by investing larger amounts. Even after deducting their charges, the returns can be at least as good, or slightly ahead of, LIBID rates. These funds also benefit from having the highest credit rating available. They are available in the major currencies: Sterling, US dollars, and euros.

Internal and financial controls

Internal controls have several aims:

- Ensuring adherence to management decisions and policies.
- Reducing the risk of error.
- Reducing the risk of theft or fraud.
- Safeguarding the company's assets.
- Ensuring the accuracy and completeness of financial and other records.

Non-financial controls

Not all controls are financial in nature. In certain businesses, control and security of the physical assets is extremely important, particularly where the assets are of high value and are relatively portable.

Where precious metals are concerned, for example, elaborate security measures are necessary, such as ensuring that all doors are double locked, and require two people to open them, proper authorisation of persons having access to the metals. In extreme cases, such as the use of gold in industrial processes, it is often done in hermetically sealed rooms, which are vacuum-cleaned and filtered to extract any gold dust. Clothing of personnel must also be strictly monitored.

Another important matter is physical access to the premises. Thus, key distribution is a relevant matter, as is the control of which personnel have authorised access to the premises. Leavers should of course hand in their keys.

Information technology

The following controls are appropriate:

- Regular backups must be made of all data, and stored in a separate location.
- Stand-by equipment should be available in case of mechanical failure.
- Physical access to areas holding sensitive information should be controlled – perhaps by sign-in systems or visitors' and staff badges.
- Password protection should be enabled, and the passwords should be changed regularly.
- Terminals which are left at any time, such as lunch breaks, should have logging-off procedures implemented.
- Passwords should not be left visible near the computers.
- Unauthorised computers, especially laptops, should not be brought into the computer areas.
- Access to the Internet should be strictly controlled. Adequate physical and software protection should be in place against viruses and other destructive devices.

Financial controls

Apart from cash (which usually forms only a relatively minor proportion of the total financial assets), the financial assets of a business are in an intangible form, and therefore unusually susceptible to fraud.

Internal controls should be recorded and subject to regular review. Compliance with internal controls should be regularly monitored. Integral to the internal control system is the competence of staff at all levels to carry out their duties. Regular checks should be carried out that all staff are competent and qualified for their activities. Training should be monitored and instituted where necessary.

Stock control

The nature of the business will dictate the level and type of stock held, and therefore the nature of stock controls. Stock can include:

- raw materials,
- work in progress,
- components,
- finished goods,
- consumable stores, and
- office supplies.

Some of the main controls are:

- A written system for receiving, checking, and re-ordering goods for stock.
- A named person responsible for the physical security of stocks, and precautions against theft, deterioration or misuse.
- If possible, those responsible for keeping stock records should not have direct physical access to stocks.
- Minimum, maximum and re-order levels should be recorded for each item of stock, and regularly reviewed.
- Regular reconciliations of stock records with the financial accounting records.
- A system for recording issues of goods out of stores to production.
- Adequate records for any stock in the hands of third parties.
- A named person responsible for carrying out regular physical stock checks.
- A recognised policy of authorised entry to the stores. Unauthorised entry should not be permitted.
- Regular review of stock for damage, deterioration or obsolescence.
- Scrap and waste sales recorded, and proceeds accounted for.

Ordering and purchase invoice authorisation and checking

Proper authorisation procedures must be in place for all incoming invoices, to discover and eliminate unauthorised or fraudulent invoicing.

Ordering goods should be subject to controls on:

- Requisitions from stores for replacement items – these should be within the stock control levels and re-order quantities.

- Authorisation of orders placed, including procedures to ensure that competitive quotes are obtained where appropriate.
- Purchase order forms to be kept secure, and the responsibility of a named person.

Incoming invoices should be checked and authorised for:

- Authorisation and confirmation of order. All invoices should quote an order number or reference. The person responsible for making the order should verify the amount, quality and agreed price of the order against the invoice. Any difference between the quantity or quality delivered, or price invoiced, should be investigated, and if necessary, queried with the supplier.
- Arithmetical accuracy. The invoices can include mistakes, and a simple arithmetical check can eliminate these. Any errors would require the supplier to correct and re-issue the invoice.
- Actual receipt of the goods or services. In the case of goods, there should be a delivery note confirming the actual date and quantity of goods received. This should be verified against the invoice. In the case of services, the department which has received the services should authorise the invoice. There should be regular reconciliations of goods received against goods ordered.
- Payment terms. Most invoices will be subject to the business's normal payment terms. In this case, they will go through the normal payment run on the purchase ledger at the normal dates. If special payment terms have been agreed, these must be flagged so that payment is made at the proper date.

A simple rubber stamp is often used, stamped on the invoice, and when initialled in all places, the invoice is correctly authorised. An example is shown in Figure 6.3.

Only when incoming invoices have been checked and authorised, should they be entered in the purchases ledger. Once the invoice has been entered in the purchases ledger, it can be considered as verified.

	Authorised by:
Order placed – Number	
Arithmetical accuracy	
Goods received delivery note no.	
Special payment terms	

Figure 6.3 Example of authorisation stamp for incoming invoices

Sales and debtors

This side of the administration presents many of the same features as the purchases side. However, some other features are:

- Checks on customer orders, to ensure that they are followed through to requisitions of stock, despatch of the goods, and invoicing.
- Supervision over pricing of goods on invoices.
- Supervision over discounts offered, special pricing, 'free of charge' goods, and exchanges of goods.
- A named person should have responsibility over blank invoice and credit note stationery.
- Control over despatches – an independent person should check all goods leaving the premises, and authorisation of despatches.
- Reconciliations of goods ordered, goods despatched, and goods invoiced to customers.
- Sales ledger procedures should be regularly adhered to and subject to review.
- All statements of account sent immediately to customers. No statements should be altered.
- Credit notes authorised by a named person.
- A named person responsible for authorisation of bad debts written off. The reason for any bad debts should be verifiable on file.

Separation of duties

A key element of internal control is to ensure that, as far as possible, no one employee has control of all aspects of a transaction.

EXERCISE 6.5

> What processes are involved in purchases of materials?

There is scope for the division of purchasing tasks so that no one person carries out all of them. The opportunity for manipulating the system is thereby greatly reduced, any attempt at fraud requiring collusion by at least two people.

Similarly, in the sales department, there are several different operations:

- Receiving an order from a customer
- Requisitioning the item from stock, or special manufacture
- Delivery of the goods or services
- Invoicing
- Sales ledger procedures

Even at the receipt of money, there are several stages:

- The actual receipt of the cash or cheque
- Recording it in a paying in book
- Paying it in to the bank.

All of these processes could be separated as far as possible within the staffing levels.

Some of these security concerns explain why many companies prefer to be paid by direct debit, standing order, or electronic funds transfer.

Staffing matters

Internal controls related to staff include the following:

- Are loans to employees authorised? If so, who takes advantage of them, and are any repayments overdue?
- Does the company offer any preferential rates or discounts for staff? Are these being abused?
- Do any staff not take their holidays?
- Do any staff regularly work abnormally long overtime, particularly if other staff do not do so?

Cash controls

Where cash is involved in any business, the opportunities for fraud or theft are much greater. Investigation and regular checks can uncover anomalies such as unnecessary delays between receiving cash and depositing it in the bank.

Cash controls include:

- Two people should be present when cashing up, or reconciling cash balances.
- All cash receipts should be banked intact, with no deductions for small cash payments.
- Opening the post each day should always be done by at least two people, to ensure that any incoming money is not stolen at this point.
- Lists should be kept of all money received in the post, to compare with actual bankings on a random spot check basis.
- Petty cash payments should be made from a petty cash account, under the control of a different person from the one who handles the other cash in the business.
- Petty cash should be drawn separately from the bank account, and accounted for before any further petty cash is drawn to replenish the petty cash balance.

Authorisation levels

A system should be in place to ensure that proper authorisation is applied to transactions at all levels. For instance, a secretary in the administration department could be authorised to order office stationery up to a value of, say, £50. Expenditure on a capital project of several hundreds of thousands could require the authorisation of the board, and cheque signature requirements of at least two specifically authorised people.

Cheque signatures

- It is a sound principle for all cheques to have at least two signatures, which could be any two signatures from the list of authorised signatures.
- Higher values of transaction could specify the actual signatories required.
- Blank cheques should not be pre-signed by anyone.
- Stamping or printing machines for cheque signature present their own particular and obvious problems of security. The physical security of the machine should be of the highest priority.
- Preparation of cheques should be in the hands of a non-authorised person.
- Once cheques have been signed, they should be despatched without any further delay.

Wages

The following are some wages controls:

- Employees should have written contracts.
- A named person should have authority for hiring and firing.
- A named person should authorise changes to rates of pay.
- A named person should authorise overtime carried out.
- A named person should authorise advances or loans against wages, and control their recovery.
- The system of recording hours worked, piecework, and calculation of wages should be strictly adhered to.
- Special procedures should be in place for dealing with absences and short notice departures.
- Wages should be paid to employees' bank accounts, except where cash wages are unavoidable, and authorised.
- Payment of cash wages should be supervised by a named, authorised person.
- The identity of those collecting cash wages should be verified.
- Uncollected cash wages should be the subject of specific security procedures.

Fixed assets

The following controls should be in place:

- A named person should authorise capital expenditure.
- A named person should authorise the sale or scrapping of fixed assets.
- Receipts from disposal of fixed assets should be accounted for.
- A named person should be responsible for maintaining a full register of fixed assets, including their location.
- A written policy must exist on the distinction between capital expenditure and revenue expenditure.
- The register(s) of fixed assets must be reconciled regularly with a physical check of the assets, and the financial accounts.
- The maintenance and repair log of all assets should be kept by a named person.
- There should be a written policy on the depreciation rates of all fixed assets.

Investments

The following controls should be maintained:

- A named person should authorise the purchase of investments.
- Custody of the title documents should be ensured, by a different person from the one authorising purchase.
- Physical security of title documents must be ensured, for example, in a locked, fire-proof safe or cabinet.
- A detailed investment register should be kept, and reconciled regularly to the physical check of title documents.
- Stockbrokers' notes on purchase or sale of investments should be reconciled to the title documents held and the register. Stockbrokers' charges calculations should be checked.
- Income from investments, including dividends, interest, and bonus issues, should be reconciled to the financial accounts.

Audit – external and internal

Audit is a key area of control in business finance. Companies of a certain size are obliged to have an external audit, and many large companies have internal audit departments.

External audit

External audit involves an independent person or firm (usually Chartered or Certified Accountants) making examinations to enable them to certify that the financial statements give a true and fair view of the company's transactions in the accounting period, and of the state of the company's affairs at the balance sheet date. These examinations include such things as random checking of entries in the accounting records against verifying documentation, statistical analysis of figures, verifying valuations used in the financial statements, and thorough examination of matters of principle.

External auditors are appointed by and report to the members of the company – that is, the shareholders. However, other third parties may place reliance on the auditor's report.

EXERCISE 6.6

What other parties might place reliance on the auditor's report?

Since such importance is attached to the auditor's report, it is useful to know what the report is likely to say. Auditors' reports are of two basic kinds:

1. **Unqualified,** sometimes also referred to as a 'clean' report. This means that the auditor is satisfied that the company's financial statements give a true and fair view. In itself, this is not a guarantee that there are no errors in the

financial statements, but it gives readers of the report a high degree of assurance in the integrity of the accounts.

2. **Qualified.** This indicates a reservation which the auditor may have on some aspect of the financial statements. The qualification may be relatively minor, but the wording of any qualified report should be examined carefully. For example, a qualified report may say that the financial statements give a true and fair view 'subject to . . .', followed by the areas of reservation. This may be something like a deviation from a published Financial Reporting Standard. The auditor will comment on this, and whether the deviation is appropriate to the company's business.

Other qualifications may be more serious, arising from the auditor's disagreement with the way particular items have been treated. These qualifications are likely to be signalled in the auditor's report by saying that the financial statements give a true and fair view 'except for . . .' followed by the matter of disagreement. This could arise if, for example, the auditor believed that a larger provision should be made for debts which were likely to prove irrecoverable.

A fundamental disagreement would lead the report to say that, in the auditor's opinion, the financial statements **do not** give a true and fair view. In this case, the auditor would have to explain the basis for this opinion, and the matters which led him to issue this negative report.

EXERCISE 6.7

What do you think might be the consequence of a qualified auditor's report?

It is vitally important that financial managers do all in their power to ensure that an auditor's report is unqualified.

The management of the business itself may also find certain aspects of the audit useful, such as:

- The audit can provide a further 'line of defence' against fraud and error.
- The audit can bring to light weaknesses in the internal controls of the company.
- The audit can bring to light any weaknesses in the company's accounting systems.
- The auditors can help suggest further ways to control the business.

To carry out this audit, the auditors require unfettered access to the company's records. The financial manager must ensure that all the company's records are kept in a readily understandable form and that all necessary documentation, such as invoices, contracts, and so on, is kept in a systematic filing system. The financial manager must be sufficiently aware of the business's finances to discuss relevant matters with the auditor. The audit represents a significant expense, and part of the financial manager's task is to keep the cost down as far as possible by making the audit easier. The financial manager should therefore not simply react to requests from the auditor, but be proactive in helping the auditor. Here are some of the things which could well be on the agenda of meetings between the financial management and the auditor:

- Any problems perceived since the last audit.
- A thorough review of the internal control systems.
- A review of the company's accounting policies.
- Discussion of the materiality level.
- A review of the company's present circumstances, and finances.
- Valuations of important assets.
- A review of any contingent liabilities.
- Authorisations to third parties to give information directly to the auditor.
- Details of transactions with directors.
- A review of capital raised during the accounting period.
- A timetable for the audit.
- Possible areas of doubt or disagreement which could result in a qualified audit report.

Internal audit

Internal audit departments carry out a similar function to external auditors, but they are not independent. They carry out their examinations on behalf of the management of the company. External auditors may decide that they can place a certain degree of reliance on the internal audit procedures.

Internal audit departments however also have a high profile in their duty continuously to check and monitor the effectiveness of the internal control systems. They are also involved in risk management. The Institute of Internal Auditors UK and Ireland is the official body for internal auditors, and it has defined internal audit as follows:

> ▶ Internal auditing is an independent, objective assurance and consulting activity designed to add value and improve an organisation's operations. It helps an organisation accomplish its objectives by bringing a systematic, disciplined approach to evaluate and improve the effectiveness of risk management, control and governance processes.

◼Ⓜ 7 Measures of success

LEARNING OUTCOMES

By the end of this chapter, you should:

▶ understand the terms commonly used by knowledgeable investors,
▶ know what investors would look for in investing their money,
▶ have a grasp of what to look for in judging the success or otherwise of a business, and
▶ be able to carry out an elementary appraisal of a future project.

Introduction

Performance measures were examined in Chapter 2. Here we look at the measures of success in broader terms, and what different measures are used to judge success or failure.

We start with the approach which an outsider might use to judge the success of a business before investing his money in it. We consider an alternative to traditional methods, the 'total shareholder value' approach. Then, we look at four key measures of success, before turning our attention to other, non-financial corporate values.

Finally, we look at the appraisal of future projects, which is a way of trying to assess probable future success, including the analysis of the risk element in assessing future projects.

The investment approach

One way of judging success is to look at the business from an external viewpoint. Put simply, what would a shrewd investor look for before investing money in this business? Businesses which attain the criteria which shrewd investors look for have achieved success in the market place.

Investment criteria

EXERCISE 7.1

Why do you think investors put their money into businesses?

Investment terms

It is important to understand the various terms used in thinking about the ways of investing money, and in particular the terms involved in investing in companies. Appendix 2 gives a summary of these terms. Read through this now.

Investment decisions

Investors make decisions based on the risk/reward equation. Those seeking to minimise risk will look for shares which have preferential rights, debentures, or other secured loan stocks. Those willing to take greater risk will accept ordinary shares – the rights of which are not preferential – and unsecured loan stocks. In return for the increased risk, they will expect greater returns.

Investors with sufficient money to invest will seek to spread their risks as far as possible. Their investment portfolio is likely to include investments in different market sectors, and investments with varying risk profiles.

EXERCISE 7.2

What indicators would an investor look for in a business?

Total shareholder value

Many shareholders and owners of small businesses feel that the performance shown by the bottom line of the profit and loss account and the balance sheet do not give a full picture of the value of their stake in the business. Total shareholder value is an approach which looks at the totality of what owners receive in return for their investment of capital – and of time – in the business. Thus, it includes dividends paid, capital gains, the expectation of future profits, and, if the owner works, the salary received. It could also take into account intangibles, such as the status which the owner achieves, and perhaps other benefits in kind rather than in money or money's worth.

Traditional measures

Traditional accounting figures such as the profit and loss account and balance sheet measure past performance, and therefore do not give any value or credit for future prospects. Certain accounting conventions also mean that the traditional figures do not give full significance to the true value for shareholders. These conventions include:

- *Historic costs*. Although limited revaluations are allowed, such as for land and buildings, traditional balance sheets are generally based on historic costs less depreciation. These may not reflect true current values.

- *The accruals principle.* This means that costs and revenues are matched in an accounting period, so cash flow is ignored. Cash flow statements may be added to accounts, and if so, they greatly assist in the appraisal of the value of a business.
- *Investment valuation.* Prudence is a defining convention in accounts, and investments in other businesses, subsidiaries, and in research and development, are valued ultra-conservatively. Often, this gives an unrealistic idea of their true value to the business.

Alternative measures

One alternative is to attempt to measure the generation of economic value added. This is defined as the output for any period less the real cost of all the resources consumed in the same period. The main difference between this and the traditional approach is that assets are valued at current values, and the cost of capital is brought into account.

For these purposes, capital includes loan capital. The cost of capital is calculated by considering the opportunity cost of employing that capital elsewhere.

The cost of capital is deducted from the profit before loan interest charges, but after tax. The actual interest rate to be used for cost of capital should be a weighted average of the actual cost of loans, and the notional rate to represent a fair return on equity capital.

The economic value added is therefore the value created by the business during the period, after taking into account the return due to the owners to compensate for opportunity costs of other possible investments.

This approach calls for unorthodox thinking; for example, in arriving at a current value of research and development, or treating leased assets as part of the total assets of the business, ignoring the mechanics and details of their legal ownership. If the asset is used in the business, it should be brought in at its current value.

This still only produces the economic value added for a past period. Future profits and cash flow are of course unknown. However, realistic future cash flow and profit forecasts can be converted to present values by discounting. The present value of future cash flows can be considered as the value of a business over and above its current asset values.

Cash – the ultimate measure

A company may have a high shareholder value, but ultimately, the shareholder will only be able to measure that value by cash in his hand. In other words, the only way in which shareholder value can be realised is by cash coming to the shareholder. This can be paid by way of dividends during his ownership of the shares, plus increase in the value of the shares while he holds them. For quoted companies, this poses no problem, but for unquoted companies, there must be a buyer willing to pay the price for a realistic value of the shares.

Four key measures of success

In any assessment of the success of a business, certain elements are basic. The four key financial indicators which a successful business would be expected to display are liquidity, profitability, appropriate borrowings and acceptable cash flow.

Liquidity

As a business makes profits, the value of the assets of that business increases. The key to managing for success is to ensure that the increase in assets does not occur only in long-term assets held for use in the business, such as land and property, machinery, and so on. Sufficient assets must be in liquid form to be able to pay short-term liabilities as they become due.

We saw in Chapter 2 the importance of the quick ratio. Chapter 5 dealt with the controls needed to keep liquidity healthy.

Profitability

The key to business survival and success is to make profits. Without this, money is leeching away, and the business cannot survive. The simplest measure of profitability is the bottom line of the profit and loss account. However, this measure is rather crude, and does not give insights into the business. In order to enable action to be taken, further information is needed.

In Chapter 2, we saw how various ratios and percentage analysis techniques reveal how the business is performing, and what areas could be improved. That chapter also showed the calculation of the 'return on capital employed', and the 'return on investment'. These indicate whether the business has performed better than, say, simply putting the money into a bank or building society account.

Finally, the profit and loss account should be considered in conjunction with the previous year's figures, and budgeted figures. The trend of the figures over, say, the last five years also gives useful indicators.

Borrowings

Most businesses cannot start up or expand without some form of borrowing. Chapter 10 deals with different types of borrowing in more detail. Successful management of borrowings should ensure that the type of borrowing is appropriate and matched to the purpose for which it is needed.

The long-term borrowing is compared to the equity capital employed to reveal the gearing. The significance of gearing is considered in Chapter 10. If gearing becomes too high, some equity capital may be needed to dilute the gearing ratio.

The cost of borrowings is shown as an interest charge in the profit and loss account, and a key concept is interest cover, also considered in Chapter 2.

Cash flow

The old business adage says:

▶ Cash is king.

This reflects the fact that it is possible to make a profit yet still run into cash flow problems. Cash flow must be actively managed, and Chapter 5 deals with this in some detail. A successful business is one in which the cash flow is actively managed and is not revealing any shortcomings.

Organic growth

Applying investment principles, an investor would look for organic growth in the value of the business. This means that the business does not rely primarily on acquisitions of other companies in order to grow, but that it produces real growth of its own in terms of turnover and profit.

The key indicator an investor would look for is the earnings per share, and the past record of these.

Other corporate values

Whilst this book necessarily concentrates on financial matters, there are many corporate values, which are used as measures of success, that are not just financial in nature, or as easily capable of measurement.

Corporate values are guiding principles which the organisation holds, and which are not sacrificed to short-term gain. These values are to a large extent in the custody of the top levels of management, and these people are responsible for seeing that they are maintained and communicated to all employees. The ultimate goal is to achieve a state in which the corporate values become shared values – shared between the organisation and the individuals who work there.

An organisation sharing its values with its employees usually achieves much more, and benefits are seen in greater productivity, and better staff relations. Recruitment is easier and staff retention is not so problematic. Staff feel greater job satisfaction and security. Relationships between staff in different departments and in different locations are improved. Managing change or crisis are other areas which are smoothed by shared values.

Measurement of future success

So far in this chapter we have looked at measures of success of historic performance. It is, of course, impossible to measure the success or failure of future events. However, a key area of financial management is the appraisal of possible projects or investment in machinery, plant, or other assets.

Project and investment appraisal

Certain tools and techniques can be applied to evaluate future projects and make investment decisions. The purpose is to make informed decisions when the business is faced with investing significant amounts of money in a project. These techniques enable managers to weigh up the possible future benefits (which have an element of uncertainty) against immediate costs (which are far more certain). Here are some situations for which the techniques of project appraisal are appropriate:

- Is it better to purchase a new piece of equipment, or vehicle, rather than continue to use existing, older items?
- Should the business take over or merge with another company? Would the benefits outweigh the cost of acquisition?
- Should the business produce certain components itself, or continue to buy them in from external suppliers?
- Should the business pursue the research, development and marketing of a new product or service?
- The business is faced with two or more alternative projects with roughly equivalent costs, only one of which can be undertaken. Which one should go ahead? In this case, the decision may not only involve the financial outcome, but other critical resource limitations.

The financial techniques and tools available use objective facts and figures. Even the unknown risk factors inherent in any future project can be the subject of statistical techniques. However, when all these objective facts and figures are presented for a decision, managers still apply their own subjective views of the industry and the economic environment in making a decision. To that extent it will involve 'gut feelings'.

The following are the main methods and techniques of project appraisal, which may be used individually or in combination.

Payback

This is the simplest measure of appraising a project in financial terms. It may lack some of the sophistication of other methods, but it is easily calculated and readily understood. Many businesses – even those of substantial size – use this method to appraise projects.

Payback is the measure of the length of time taken to recover the initial investment of money.

EXERCISE 7.3

> Should the business buy a new van, or continue to use the old one? The cost of the new van is £10,000. The additional costs of keeping the old van running over and above the costs of the new van are £200 per month. What is the payback period?

A marketing and advertising campaign costs £50,000. Will the extra sales generated justify the cost? The marketing director believes that the campaign will achieve extra sales of 5,000 units per month, with a profit of 50p per unit.

The measurement of payback period is relatively easily calculated, and easily understood, although certain assumptions have to be made. If cash flow is a major concern, payback time is an important factor. If this is not such a critical factor, the company may be able to look further ahead and judge the project on other measures.

However, it can also be seen that even this relatively simple measure depends on being able to forecast accurately future outcomes. In the above exercises, how certain are the additional costs of running the old van? How achievable are the marketing director's predictions of extra sales?

Despite the drawbacks, it is easy to see that the shorter the payback time, the better chance the project has of success. The size of the project affects the sophistication of the calculations. Certain day-to-day decisions involving relatively small amounts of money can probably be calculated on the back of an envelope. More complex ones would need a spreadsheet.

Average return

This is another method which is fairly simple to calculate and easy to understand. It estimates the total return over a limited period as a rate of return on the cost of the project spread over that period. Because of its limitations it is really only suitable for projects which extend over a relatively short period.

EXERCISE 7.5

Cost of project £50,000. Length of appraisal period 5 years. The forecast income from the project is:

	Year 1	Year 2	Year 3	Year 4	Year 5
Gross income	60,000	52,500	50,000	42,500	30,000
Expenses	40,000	35,000	35,000	30,000	20,000
Cash flow	20,000	17,500	15,000	12,500	10,000
Cost of project	10,000	10,000	10,000	10,000	10,000
Net cash flow	10,000	7,500	5,000	2,500	NIL

What is the average rate of return on this project?

However, the drawback of this method is seen if the pattern of the income in the above exercise were different.

Cost of project £50,000. Length of appraisal period 5 years. The forecast income from the project is as below. What is the crucial difference?

	Year 1	Year 2	Year 3	Year 4	Year 5
Gross income	30,000	42,500	50,000	52,500	60,000
Expenses	20,000	30,000	35,000	35,000	40,000
Cash flow	10,000	12,500	15,000	17,500	20,000
Cost of project	10,000	10,000	10,000	10,000	10,000
Net cash flow	NIL	2,500	5,000	7,500	10,000

The real return diminishes as the income is received later. Therefore, some more sophisticated method is required to measure the effect of the lapse of time.

Internal rate of return (IRR) and discounted cash flow (DCF)

These are methods to calculate the effective rate of return generated for the business on the original investment made in a project. The net present value (NPV) of a project can also be calculated by these techniques.

They are based on the measurement of future cash values against present cash values. They recognise that, quite apart from the uncertainty factor, money in the hand now is worth more than money in the future.

Compound interest

The measurement of the value of future money as against present money is done using compound interest. This calculation of compound interest is central to working out the IRR on a project.

EXAMPLE 7.1

If you invest £1,000 in an account paying 10% interest, at the end of one year, it will be worth £1 10. If you left it in undisturbed, after another year, it would be worth £121. This illustrates the compounding effect of interest. The interest is not simply doubled, but there is extra interest on the existing interest. The effect of this gradually increases year by year.

The effect of compound interest can be calculated by means of a formula. The formula for calculating compound interest is as follows:

$$Vn = Vp \times (1 + i)^n$$

where:

Vp is the amount of present money, i.e. now
Vn is the amount of money at the end of year n
i is the interest rate used
n is the number of years

Discounted cash flow (DCF)

This calculates the net present value (or NPV) of the project to the business now, after discounting future cash flows, using compound interest. The measurement of the difference between present money and future money is called a discount rate, and it is the 'mirror image' of the compound interest rate discussed above.

EXERCISE 7.7

What is the present value of £121 in 2 years' time, assuming a discount rate of 10%?

If the calculation is the mirror image of the compound interest calculation, then we can work out a new formula for it.

Using the same definitions as for the compound interest formula above, the formula for calculating NPV is:

$$Vp = \frac{Vn}{(1+i)^n}$$

This formula can be used to find out the present value of any given amount at any number of years into the future, at any given rate of discount. Alternatively, tables exist to give present values, and the present values of future amounts can be read from these tables. Figure 7.1 gives an abbreviated form of such a present value table, giving values up to 14% and up to 25 years, in increments of 1.

Years	1%	2%	3%	4%	5%	6%	7%
1	0.9901	0.9804	0.9709	0.9615	0.9524	0.9434	0.9346
2	0.9803	0.9612	0.9426	0.9246	0.9070	0.8900	0.8734
3	0.9706	0.9423	0.9151	0.8890	0.8638	0.8396	0.8163
4	0.9610	0.9238	0.8885	0.8548	0.8227	0.7921	0.7629
5	0.9515	0.9057	0.8626	0.8219	0.7835	0.7473	0.7130
6	0.9420	0.8880	0.8375	0.7903	0.7462	0.7050	0.6663
7	0.9327	0.8706	0.8131	0.7599	0.7107	0.6651	0.6227
8	0.9235	0.8535	0.7894	0.7307	0.6768	0.6274	0.5820
9	0.9143	0.8368	0.7664	0.7026	0.6446	0.5919	0.5439
10	0.9053	0.8203	0.7441	0.6756	0.6139	0.5584	0.5083
11	0.8963	0.8043	0.7224	0.6496	0.5847	0.5268	0.4751
12	0.8874	0.7885	0.7014	0.6246	0.5568	0.4970	0.4440
13	0.8787	0.7730	0.6810	0.6006	0.5303	0.4688	0.4150
14	0.8700	0.7579	0.6611	0.5775	0.5051	0.4423	0.3878
15	0.8613	0.7430	0.6419	0.5553	0.4810	0.4173	0.3624
16	0.8528	0.7284	0.6232	0.5339	0.4581	0.3936	0.3387
17	0.8444	0.7142	0.6050	0.5134	0.4363	0.3714	0.3166
18	0.8360	0.7002	0.5874	0.4936	0.4155	0.3503	0.2959
19	0.8277	0.6864	0.5703	0.4746	0.3957	0.3305	0.2765
20	0.8195	0.6730	0.5537	0.4564	0.3769	0.3118	0.2584
21	0.8114	0.6598	0.5375	0.4388	0.3589	0.2942	0.2415
22	0.8034	0.6468	0.5219	0.4220	0.3418	0.2775	0.2257
23	0.7954	0.6342	0.5067	0.4057	0.3256	0.2618	0.2109
24	0.7876	0.6217	0.4919	0.3901	0.3101	0.2470	0.1971
25	0.7798	0.6095	0.4776	0.3751	0.2953	0.2330	0.1842

Figure 7.1 Present value tables

Figure 7.1 continued

Years	8%	9%	10%	11%	12%	13%	14%
1	0.9259	0.9174	0.9091	0.9009	0.8929	0.885	0.8772
2	0.8573	0.8417	0.8264	0.8116	0.7972	0.7831	0.7695
3	0.7938	0.7722	0.7513	0.7312	0.7118	0.6931	0.675
4	0.7350	0.7084	0.6830	0.6587	0.6355	0.6133	0.5921
5	0.6806	0.6499	0.6209	0.5935	0.5674	0.5428	0.5194
6	0.6302	0.5963	0.5645	0.5346	0.5066	0.4803	0.4556
7	0.5835	0.5470	0.5132	0.4817	0.4523	0.4251	0.3996
8	0.5403	0.5019	0.4665	0.4339	0.4039	0.3762	0.3506
9	0.5002	0.4604	0.4241	0.3909	0.3606	0.3329	0.3075
10	0.4632	0.4224	0.3855	0.3522	0.3220	0.2946	0.2697
11	0.4289	0.3875	0.3505	0.3173	0.2875	0.2607	0.2366
12	0.3971	0.3555	0.3186	0.2858	0.2567	0.2307	0.2076
13	0.3677	0.3262	0.2897	0.2575	0.2292	0.2042	0.1821
14	0.3405	0.2992	0.2633	0.2320	0.2046	0.1807	0.1597
15	0.3152	0.2745	0.2394	0.2090	0.1827	0.1599	0.1401
16	0.2919	0.2519	0.2176	0.1883	0.1631	0.1415	0.12291
17	0.2703	0.2311	0.1978	0.1696	0.1456	0.1252	0.1078
18	0.2502	0.2120	0.1799	0.1528	0.1300	0.1108	0.0946
19	0.2317	0.1945	0.1635	0.1377	0.1161	0.0981	0.0829
20	0.2145	0.1784	0.1486	0.1240	0.1037	0.0868	0.0728
21	0.1987	0.1637	0.1351	0.1117	0.0926	0.0460	0.0388
22	0.1839	0.1502	0.1228	0.1007	0.0826	0.0258	0.0219
23	0.1703	0.1378	0.1117	0.0907	0.0738	0.0153	0.0131
24	0.1577	0.1264	0.1015	0.0817	0.0659	0.0095	0.0082
25	0.1460	0.1160	0.0923	0.0736	0.0588	0.0061	0.0054

EXERCISE 7.8

1. XYZ Ltd proposes to invest £1 million now to increase production capacity.
2. The additional sales forecast is 100,000 items per year, at a selling price of £10 each.
3. The gross profit rate is 40%, and the additional overheads are £50,000 per year.
4. There are additional marketing and promotion costs in years 1 and 2 of £50,000 each year.

What is the NPV of this project, using a discount rate of 10%?

Internal rate of return (IRR)

The next step after calculating the DCF – which in Exercise 7.8 assumed a discount rate of 10% – is to find the interest rate that will yield a zero NPV. In practice this would have to be done by iteration – that is, by constant repetition of calculations using different values as 'trial' figures. For example, in Exercise 7.8 the discount rate was 10%, which yielded a positive NPV. We could proceed by 'trying' the calculation at 20%, which gives a negative NPV, then at 15%, and gradually narrowing down the rate until the one which gives a zero NPV is found. But there is another way.

Use of spreadsheets

A simpler alternative is to use the 'function' choice on a spreadsheet. This allows the calculation of IRR and NPV at the click of a button.

Figure 7.2 shows this calculation, which has been done using the function wizard of the spreadsheet. It shows that the IRR of the project in Exercise 7.8 is 18.69%.

Now	−£1,000,000
Year 1	£300,000
Year 2	£300,000
Year 3	£350,000
Year 4	£350,000
Year 5	£350,000
Internal rate of return	18.69%

Figure 7.2 Calculation of internal rate of return

If the IRR figure for a project exceeds the cost of capital to the organisation, the result is favourable. Put another way, if the discount rate used for the DCF calculation is entered at the organisation's cost of capital, then a positive DCF is favourable, since it indicates an IRR in excess of the cost of capital.

Caveat – inflation and the risk factor

In all these calculations, it has been assumed that the future figures are known and certain. In fact, nothing in the future can ever be certain. Inflation has historically been a constant, although the rates of inflation have varied.

Business is all about risk, and there is always a risk element. We have examined risk management and insurance in Chapter 6. Here, we concentrate on the commercial risk inherent in any business venture, which has more to do with uncertainty than the specific risks seen in Chapter 6. In addition to those risks, there is the simple element of the time factor. The longer a project extends, the greater are the chances of risk factors affecting the result.

There are various methods of analysing the risk element in project or investment appraisal.

Sensitivity analysis

This technique considers the variables affecting the financial result of a project individually, to see how changes to these values would influence the outcome.

EXERCISE 7.9

What variables might affect the outcome of a project?

Sensitivity analysis takes each of these variables and compares the effect on the final outcome resulting from a variation in the expected figures. In particular, it seeks to discover what is the 'worst case' scenario for each of these variables before it reduces the outcome of the project to a negative value, using the NPV as the yardstick. It can be viewed as a break-even analysis, with which it shares many features.

These calculations are rendered easier on a spreadsheet. If a model of the project is constructed on the spreadsheet, substitute values can be entered for individual variables, to ascertain the result.

EXERCISE 7.10

Using the data in Exercise 7.8, answer the following sensitivity analysis questions:

(a) What cost of investment would reduce the NPV to zero?
(b) Assuming the sales price to be fixed, what volume of sales would reduce the NPV to zero?
(c) Assuming the sales volume to be fixed, what unit price would reduce the NPV to zero?
(d) Assuming the sales volume and price to be fixed, what gross profit rate would reduce the NPV to zero?
(e) Assuming the gross profit on sales to be fixed, what level of normal overheads (i.e. excluding the first two years' marketing and promotion) would reduce the NPV to zero?
(f) Assuming the net profit to be fixed, what additional marketing and promotion expenses in years 1 and 2 would reduce the NPV to zero?

This analysis then enables the business to discover which are the most sensitive variables in the project, that is, which ones have the least margin of safety.

EXERCISE 7.11

From Exercise 7.10, rank the variables in order of sensitivity.

Strengths and weaknesses

Sensitivity analysis directs managerial attention to the aspects of the project which are most sensitive to change. That indicates which areas need more investigation, or which could be the deciding factor in proceeding or abandoning the project.

However, it does not in itself indicate clear decisions about those variables – even the most sensitive ones. Those decisions must be made only after further investigation and groundwork. The other main weakness is that sensitivity analysis can only deal with one variable at a time. In reality, variables do not alter one at a time.

Mathematical models do exist to deal with multi-variant analysis. The statistical techniques involved in these are somewhat complex, and beyond the normal mathematical techniques of financial management studies.

Scenario analysis

This is another form of sensitivity analysis. It involves taking different variables for the project, and assigning values to them according to different scenarios. Typically, these scenarios depict:

1. The optimistic view.
2. The pessimistic view.
3. The most likely view.

These produce a range of outcomes, in the form of the NPV of the project. However, scenario analysis does not assign any probabilities to the scenarios. Obviously, the most likely view is the one expected to prevail, but the optimistic and pessimistic views give the 'top of range' and 'bottom of range' of outcomes.

Simulations

This is yet another extension of the sensitivity analysis idea. It sets out to assign probability values to the range of values assigned to the different variables. A computer is used for this technique, because it uses random selections of values, assigns these to all the different variables, then carries out multiple iterations of this process – which could run into thousands.

Probabilities and their measurement

Assigning probabilities to events is one of the most subjective areas of risk analysis. However, a degree of objectivity can be obtained. Past experience lends objectivity. A business's experience will indicate how certain events are likely to turn out. For example, when investing in new machinery or vehicles, past experience gives an indicator of how long their useful life will be, the possible events leading to down time, such as the risk of breakdowns, and the regular servicing needed. The sales department will have some idea of the market potential of the product, and the sensitivity of the market to price changes.

Past experience however is not an error-free guide. New technologies, for example, may dramatically affect the life span of machinery. Customers may react differently from their past reactions. Some subjectivity is implicit in all probability assessments.

The results of the simulations are summarised to give a range of outcomes in the form of NPV, and the distribution of the different outcomes within this range.

EXAMPLE 7.2

A simulation of 1,000 trials on random figures produces the following distribution of results in the range of NPVs between £500,000 and £1,000,000:

£500,000–£600,000	5%
£600,001–£700,000	15%
£700,001–£800,000	30%
£800,001–£900,000	40%
£900,001–£1,000,000	10%

This approach therefore gives an idea of the most likely outcome. However, it cannot be assessed simply on the results of the figures overall. The detailed results of each random trial should give an indication of the complex relationships between the variables. For this reason, in simulations, the variables are assessed in more detail than we have so far considered in relation to sensitivity analysis.

EXERCISE 7.12

Using the data in Exercise 7.8, what further breakdown of the variables could be used?

When carrying out simulations, it is important that the results are not interpreted in a mechanistic way. The results are only as good as the underlying assumptions and probabilities. In the end, human judgement must apply.

Application of risk analysis techniques

The final result of all risk analysis techniques is an estimation of how risky the project will be. When this is decided, it is recognised by adjusting the discount rate used in IRR and DCF calculations, as discussed above. The discount rate to be used in DCF calculations is therefore made up of two elements:

- The basic rate, and
- The risk premium.

The higher the risk is judged, the higher will be the risk premium.

Risk reduction

We have seen how risk analysis affects the appraisal of future projects. However, remember the key principle we have seen several times:

▶ If you can measure it, you can control it.

The value of measuring something simply to create a more accurate projection is limited. The key to management is control. Therefore, there is greater point in analysing and measuring risk if that information is used to reduce risk.

Diversification

Remember the old adage:

▶ Don't put all your eggs in one basket.

A business will reduce its risk if it has several projects in which it has invested its resources. If the reason for diversification is risk reduction, then it follows that the different projects in which a business invests should be complementary. That is to say, the risk elements should cancel each other out, as far as possible.

The technical term for this complementarity is the 'coefficient of correlation'. This can be measured, by assigning values between −1 and +1 to the correlation. A correlation of +1 indicates that two projects have exactly equal responses to the determining variables. A correlation of −1 indicates that two projects have exactly equal but opposite responses to the determining variables. A correlation of 0 indicates that there is no relationship at all between the response of two projects to the same variables. The ideal scenario for risk reduction is therefore to choose two projects as near as possible to −1 correlation.

EXAMPLE 7.3

A civil engineering company can invest in projects for building roads or building railways. If the risk element is government policy on the relative importance of roads or railways, then the risk elements would be opposite for each option, as follows:

	Project A Road building NPV	Project B Railway building NPV
Government decisions:		
Favouring roads	£25 million positive	£15 million negative
Favouring railways	£10 million negative	£20 million positive

It can be seen that if the company invests in both projects, then whatever government policy is in force, there is a net positive NPV of £10 million.

There are other risk factors which produce opposite outcomes – such as seasonal businesses. In different parts of the country or the world, seasons could operate to complement each other. Thus, a skiing business could operate in the northern hemisphere at one part of the year, and the southern hemisphere season for a different part of the year. A seasonal business could diversify into non-seasonal products or services. Another example of diversification is a company diversifying from manufacturing goods only into supplying services related to those goods as well as the goods themselves.

As the company takes on an increasing number of projects, the relative risk factor of each individual project is correspondingly less. Thus, from this point of view, it *may* be better to invest in two projects with an initial outlay of £1 million each, rather than in one project with an initial outlay of £2 million. However, each case must be looked at individually, with an eye to maximising the NPV of all projects.

A further qualifying consideration is the amount of management required for the successful operation of a wide variety of projects. Businesses generally – even conglomerates – have a 'core' business which provides their main drive and concentrates their efforts. Many businesses find that limited diversification provides the optimum benefit taking into account the management require-ments of their core business.

Caveat

The coefficient of correlation is only a *relative indicator*. It should not be allowed to dictate the choice of projects on its own. Far more important is the return on projects in absolute terms, that is, the projects with the best NPV.

Decision time

Once the calculations have been completed, and the financial manager has produced the appraisal report, the board has to make a decision – the go/no go decision. The decision will be made partly on non-financial factors, including the 'gut feeling' of the decision makers, but also on the perception of the risk element, and partly on the financial project appraisal.

Hurdle rates

To get a go-ahead decision, the project appraisal is often subjected to benchmarks or hurdle rates. These are standards which the project appraisal must meet to get the go-ahead. They can be simple, or complex, being a combination of different factors.

EXAMPLE 7.4

> The project appraisal may show a payback period of 5 years, and an IRR of 20%. The hurdle rates may be set at a payback period of not more than 4 years, and an IRR of 18%. This project has met one hurdle rate, but failed the other.

The hurdle rates are usually set by the board, in consultation with the financial department, and should be under constant review. It is usual to demand that a project meets all applicable hurdle rates, but a project could be considered if it met most of the hurdle rates and failed on one only.

The question arises, 'What is the appropriate hurdle rate to use?'. The answer could be the marginal cost of borrowing. That is to say, the cost of borrowing the next £1. However, particularly for substantial projects incurring substantial borrowing, further borrowing could upset the gearing, and the bank or other lending institution may not be happy at this. It may be more appropriate to use the weighted average cost of capital, known as WACC. This takes into account the gearing, and the cost of each type of capital – loans and equity.

EXAMPLE 7.5

	Proportion	Cost	Result
Loan capital	40%	10%	4%
Equity capital	60%	20%	12%
TOTAL	100%		
WACC			16%

In these circumstances, 16% would be a reasonable hurdle rate.

However, this calculation can be taken a step further. Supposing that the organisation could raise 95% of the project cost by loan, and the remaining 5% by equity. The calculation would then be, *for this particular project,* as in Example 7.6.

EXAMPLE 7.6

	Proportion	Cost	Result
Loan capital	95%	10%	9.5%
Equity capital	5%	20%	1%
TOTAL	100%		
WACC			10.5%

This would appear to give a lower hurdle rate for this particular project than previously. However, the size of the borrowing has to be taken into account. Suppose that the size of the loan required were such as to change the gearing to 50/50. The calculation would then be as in Example 7.7.

EXAMPLE 7.7

	Proportion	Cost	Result
Loan capital	50%	10%	5%
Equity capital	50%	20%	10%
TOTAL	100%		
WACC			15%

The WACC has now changed to 15%, which would be a more realistic hurdle rate.

Project comparison

As stated at the beginning of this section, these techniques may also be required to decide between alternative projects. The project appraisals of two or more alternative projects will be looked at side by side to decide which one gets the go-ahead. The normal criteria of payback, DCF and IRR will be compared.

Comparison of mutually exclusive projects will normally involve comparisons of projects with similar costs, if not similar incomes and periods. However, occasionally, there will be projects of differing magnitudes to compare. The comparisons could be misleading if the IRR is the only factor taken into account. A project with a greater IRR but on a smaller base would provide less money if the figures are viewed as absolutes.

EXAMPLE 7.8

	Initial cost	IRR	NPV at 15%	Payback
Project A	£500,000	19%	£110,000	4 years
Project B	£100,000	24%	£20,000	3 years

Project B has better ratings on all measurements, but, in the end, puts less into the business's coffers. As mentioned, it is unusual to have competing projects with such wide variations of initial cost, but this apparent anomaly should be borne in mind.

Another possible treatment of project comparisons of differing magnitudes is to put them side by side, and deduct the figures of the smaller one from the larger. This shows what would be the effect of choosing the larger instead of the smaller. In effect, it appraises the effect of investing the extra money in the larger project. This can also highlight significant differences compared to 'normal' methods of appraisal. Figure 7.3 shows the comparison of two such projects. The initial comparison would seem to show that project B has a greater IRR, and a shorter payback period. However, by calculating the figures on the additional project costs, Project A would be seen as preferable. The NPV is greater, and there is a positive answer to the investment of the additional money in project A.

	Project A	Project B	Difference between Project A and Project B
Costs:			
Now	−£500,000	−£125,000	−£375,000
Year 1	£140,000	£75,000	£65,000
Year 2	£150,000	£55,000	£95,000
Year 3	£175,000	£45,000	£130,000
Year 4	£240,000	£25,000	£215,000
Year 5	£250,000		£250,000
Payback	over 3 years	under 2 years	over 3 years
IRR	23%	27%	22%
NPV at 15%	£97,166	£22,337	£74,829

Figure 7.3 Project comparison

ASSIGNMENT I

Imagine you are an investor with £200,000 to invest. If you had to choose one, which of the two companies shown in Figure 7.4 would you invest your money in? Alternatively, would you spread your risks by investing in both, and if so in what proportions? What criteria have you used for your choice? Is there any further information you would like to know before making a final choice?

SUGGESTIONS

Company A has shown some organic growth, but has mainly grown by the acquisition of another business in year 3. To do this, it increased its long-term borrowings by more than the increase in equity capital, increasing the gearing. As a consequence, the interest cover has declined. Company A has a larger market capitalisation than company B. However, since the acquisition, its ratio of turnover to fixed assets has sharply declined, as has its gross profit ratio. The net profit ratio declined in years 3 and 4, but revived in year 5. The dividend yield has remained steady, and there has been a steady increase in dividends each year, but since the takeover, the dividend cover has declined. The earnings per share have shown a steady increase, but the price of the shares has increased even more, so that the price/earnings ratio has increased from 9.05 in year I to 14.3 in year 4, but then dropped back to 12.7 in year 5.

Company B has a smaller market capitalisation, but it has shown some organic growth. The dividends have been erratic, but there has been a general upward trend. Its ratio of turnover to fixed assets is better than company A's, and has stayed fairly stable, in contrast to company A's decline. Its gross profit ratio, although less than company A's, has increased slightly. It appears to have raised some money in year 4 to invest in new fixed assets, and in year 5, this seems to have resulted in a greatly increased profit. The dividend yield has varied between about 2.8% and 4%. Apart from the loss making year, the interest cover and dividend cover seem to be more than adequate, both of these better than company A. The price/earnings ratio has declined from 10.5 in year 2 to 2.78 in year 5. All other things being equal, this would seem to indicate a buying opportunity. However, further investigation would be needed into the apparent upturn in turnover and profits in year 5: is it sustainable, and does it indicate a change in the company's fortunes?

ASSIGNMENT 2

Figure 7.5 shows a project for XYZ Ltd, a manufacturer of potato crisps, to invest £500,000 in the introduction of a new product, and you have been asked to report to the board on your recommendation. The alternative is to issue a licence to another company, Gary's Crisps Ltd, to produce the product, charging a licence fee of 1% of the gross sales.

Using the techniques of IRR, DCF, payback period, and risk analysis, indicate whether you would recommend the company to go ahead with the project, or the alternative (assuming the same sales forecast for Gary's Crisps Ltd as for XYZ Ltd).

The suggested answer, with workings, is shown in Figure 7.5a.

Company A Balance sheets	Year 1 £millions	Year 2 £millions	Year 3 £millions	Year 4 £millions	Year 5 £millions
Fixed assets	1500	1600	5200	5200	5300
Current assets	250	250	400	450	460
Current liabilities	150	180	350	410	430
Working capital	100	70	50	40	30
Loan capital	550	550	3150	3100	3100
Net assets	1050	1120	2100	2140	2230
Capital					
Ordinary shares of £1	650	650	1000	1000	1000
Share premium			550	550	550
Reserves	400	470	550	590	680
	1050	1120	2100	2140	2230
Profit and loss accounts					
Turnover	3000	3250	7500	7600	8000
Gross profit	1200	1350	2750	2800	3000
Overheads – General	965	1050	2050	2100	2200
Finance	55	55	315	310	310
Net profit	180	245	385	390	490
Dividends	65	100	185	225	250
Tax	55	75	120	125	150
Increase in reserves	60	70	80	40	90
Share price	£2.50	£3.80	£4.60	£5.60	£6.25

NB In year 3, company A took over company C. Its sources of finance are reflected in the balance sheets.

Company B Balance sheets	Year 1 £millions	Year 2 £millions	Year 3 £millions	Year 4 £millions	Year 5 £millions
Fixed assets	500	550	580	700	800
Current assets	100	110	115	125	130
Current liabilities	40	60	60	75	75
Working capital	60	50	55	50	55
Loan capital	160	180	160	240	220
Net assets	400	420	475	510	635
Capital					
Ordinary shares of £1	300	300	300	310	310
Reserves	100	120	175	200	325
	400	420	475	510	635
Profit and loss accounts					
Turnover	1500	1850	1950	2050	2400
Gross profit	550	700	740	780	920
Overheads – General	540	602	624	686	690
Finance	16	18	16	24	22
Net profit (loss)	(6)	80	100	70	208
Dividends	0	35	15	13	23
Tax	0	25	30	22	60
Increase in reserves	(6)	20	55	35	125
Share price	£0.50	£2.80	£1.75	£1.45	£1.85

Figure 7.4

XYZ Ltd (potato crisp manufacturer)

Project – Introduction of a new product into the company's range.

It requires new machinery costing £400,000, with a life span of approx. 5 years, and a residual value of £5,000 at the end.

The machinery will be bought on loan, repayable over five years at the end of each year.

Initial promotion, marketing and advertising costs £100,000.

The sales department have suggested a selling price of 50p in year 1, increasing by 1p in year 2, and by 2p a year thereafter.

Direct costs estimates per item

Volume	Year 1	Year 2	Year 3	Year 4	Year 5
200,000	20p	22p	24p	27p	30p
400,000	19p	21p	23p	26p	29p
600,000	18p	20p	22p	25p	28p
800,000	17.5p	19.5p	21.5p	24.5p	27.5p
1,000,000	17p	19p	21p	24p	27p

Marketing probability estimates for sales

	Year 1	Year 2	Year 3	Year 4	Year 5
200,000				0.1	0.3
400,000	0.1	0.1		0.5	0.2
600,000	0.5	0.4	0.4	0.3	0.5
800,000	0.3	0.3	0.3	0.1	
1,000,000	0.1	0.2	0.3		

Overheads estimates

	Year 1	Year 2	Year 3	Year 4	Year 5
Existing	500,000	505,000	510,000	512,000	514,000
Additional for project	56,000	56,500	57,000	57,000	57,000
Existing turnover	**4,000,000**	**4,200,000**	**4,250,000**	**4,300,000**	**4,400,000**

Cost of capital
  10%

Cost of finance for new machinery
  12%

Figure 7.5

Sales and gross profit

Units	Sale price	Probability	Expected sales	Direct unit costs	Unit profit	Expected gross profit
Year 1						
400,000	0.50	0.1	20,000	0.19	0.31	12,400
600,000	0.50	0.5	150,000	0.18	0.32	96,000
800,000	0.50	0.3	120,000	0.175	0.325	78,000
1,000,000	0.50	0.1	50,000	0.17	0.33	33,000
			£340,000			£219,400
Project overheads						56,000
Interest on loan						48,000
Net profit						£115,400
Year 2						
400,000	0.51	0.1	20,400	0.21	0.3	12,000
600,000	0.51	0.4	122,400	0.20	0.31	74,400
800,000	0.51	0.3	122,400	0.195	0.315	75,600
1,000,000	0.51	0.2	102,000	0.19	0.32	64,000
			£367,200			£226,000
Project overheads						56,500
Interest on loan						38,400
Net profit						£131,100
Year 3						
600,000	0.53	0.4	127,200	0.22	0.31	74,400
800,000	0.53	0.3	127,200	0.215	0.315	75,600
1,000,000	0.53	0.3	159,000	0.21	0.32	96,000
			413,400			246,000
Project overheads						57,000
Interest on loan						28,800
Net profit						£160,200
Year 4						
200,000	0.55	0.1	11,000	0.27	0.28	5,600
400,000	0.55	0.5	110,000	0.26	0.29	58,000
600,000	0.55	0.3	99,000	0.25	0.3	54,000
800,000	0.55	0.1	44,000	0.245	0.305	24,400
			£264,000			£142,000
Project overheads						£57,000
Interest on loan						£19,200
Net profit						£65,800
Year 5						
200,000	0.57	0.3	34,200	0.30	0.27	16,200
400,000	0.57	0.5	114,000	0.29	0.28	56,000
600,000	0.57	0.2	68,400	0.28	0.29	34,800
			216,600			107,000
Project overheads						57,000
Interest on loan						9,600

Figure 7.5a Project calculations

Figure 7.5a continued

Payback period calculation

		Cash outflow	Cash inflow	Balance
Immediate	Machinery	400,000		– 400,000
	Initial expenditure	100,000		– 500,000
	Loan		400,000	– 100,000
Year end 1	Profit		115,400	15,400
	Loan repayment	80,000		– 64,600
Year end 2	Profit		131,100	66,500
	Loan repayment	80,000		– 13,500
Year end 3	Profit		160,200	146,700
	Loan repayment	80,000		66,700
Year end 4	Profit		65,800	132,500
	Loan repayment	80,000		52,500
Year end 5	Profit		40,400	92,900
	Loan repayment	80,000		12,900
Sale of machinery			5,000	17,900

The payback comes partway through year 3.

DCF Calculation

		Cashflow	Discount 10%	Present value
Immediate	Machinery	– 400,000	1	– 400,000
	Initial expenditure	– 100,000	1	– 100,000
	Loan	400,000	1	400,000
Year end 1	Profit	115,400	0.909	104,899
	Loan repayment	– 80,000	0.909	– 72,720
Year end 2	Profit	131,100	0.826	108,289
	Loan repayment	– 80,000	0.826	– 66,080
Year end 3	Profit	160,200	0.751	120,310
	Loan repayment	– 80,000	0.751	– 60,080
Year end 4	Profit	65,800	0.683	44,941
	Loan repayment	– 80,000	0.683	– 54,640
Year end 5	Profit	40,400	0.621	25,088
	Loan repayment	– 80,000	0.621	– 49,680
Sale of machinery		5,000	0.621	3,105
NPV				**£3,432**

IRR calculation
The NPV at 10% is £3,432.
By iteration, we can arrive at the IRR of approx. 12.5%.

Sensitivity analysis
Sales and gross profit – a variance of 0.5% would reduce the NPV to zero.
Project overheads – a variance of 1.6% would reduce the NPV to zero.
Loan interest – a variance of 2.9% (i.e. increase in the interest rate to 12.35%) would reduce the NPV to zero.

Figure 7.5a continued

Alternative

We must assume the same sales as XYZ Ltd has forecast. The calculation therefore becomes:

	Sales	Licence fee	Discount 10%	Present value
Year 1	340,000	3400	0.909	3,091
Year 2	367,200	3672	0.826	3,033
Year 3	413,400	4134	0.751	3,105
Year 4	264,000	2640	0.683	1,803
Year 5	216,600	2166	0.621	1,345
				£12,377

Conclusion

The project has a small positive NPV, but the sensitivity analysis shows a very small margin of safety. The project only looks marginally viable.

The alternative has a much greater NPV, and would seem to be the better choice.

However, there could be two drawbacks, related to the nature of this alternative.

Firstly, there is a risk element that Gary's Crisps Ltd will not achieve the sales forecast by XYZ Ltd Any failure by them to meet the sales forecast by XYZ Ltd would reduce the NPV. The risk is in someone else's hands. A possible way to reduce this risk is to set a minimum licence fee payable each year, irrespective of Gary's Crisps Ltd's sales.

The second possible drawback is perhaps more fundamental. Would handing this new product over to Gary's Crisps Ltd undermine the competitiveness of XYZ Ltd? There is the risk that Gary's Crisps Ltd would become more aggressive and start to take over some of XYZ Ltd's market share of other products.

▣ Ṿ 8 Phases of business life

LEARNING OUTCOMES

By the end of this chapter, you should be able to:

▶ give an indication of the sources of finance most appropriate to each stage of a business's life,
▶ appreciate the financial management issues involved in takeover or merger situations, and
▶ know how to cope with crisis.

Introduction

Businesses go through different stages in their life cycle. At each stage the finance needs are different, and the demands of financial management will also be different. In this chapter, we look at start up, growth, merger or takeover, and crisis management.

In relation to mergers and takeovers, the main issues examined are the valuation of shares, vulnerability and resistance to takeovers, and the purchase consideration for shares in a company that has been taken over.

Start up

Every business starts with an idea. That idea has to be developed and tested before any commercial operation can begin to produce and market the product or service. The usual stages of a start up and the finance needed are:

- *Seed finance* is needed to research a new project before the business has reached start up. This involves research and assessment of the concept – that is, whether it has commercial viability – and development of it.
- *Start up*. This stage occurs when the product or service is being developed, the business being formed into a company, and initial marketing taking place. The product or service has not yet been sold commercially.
- *Early stage*. At this stage, the product or service development is completed and further funds are needed for commercial manufacture and selling. Typically, the business is not yet making a profit.

Business angels are a common source of finance for these stages. They are wealthy individuals who are willing to make investments into a business based on their own experience and interests. Business angels usually have a particular expertise, and perhaps have retired as senior executives of major companies. Alternatively they may have sold a successful business, and wish to use the proceeds in some other constructive way. They may operate individually or in a small group.

Because of their background and the way in which they work, business angels will normally expect to be involved in the business on a 'hands on' basis. It is vital therefore that before proceeding, the important question of their compatibility with the existing management is established satisfactorily. To put it bluntly, if the business angel is going to come in and look over the shoulders of management, is he or she the sort of person with whom the management can gel?

Comparison of business angels and venture capitalists

Venture capitalists are discussed in more detail in Chapter 11. Usually the investment of business angels will be an equity investment. Their expected rate of return and fees are likely to be less than venture capitalists'. They will often invest locally and/or in a business sector in which they have experience. The capital available for investment is likely to be lower than that offered by venture capitalists, although there may be more if they act as a group. Thus it is likely that business angels can finance one stage of growth, but other sources may be needed to finance the next stage.

A business angel will want to see a proposal, although the assessment process may not be as exhaustive or formal as a venture capitalist's. There are several websites which aim to link businesses requiring capital with business angels, whose addresses can be found in Appendix 1.

Growth

Once a business has started, and expands, the management needs of the growth stage become different. Perhaps most important is the degree of financial management needed. The classic danger for growing businesses is overtrading.

Overtrading

This happens when growth puts a greater strain on the working capital requirement. This is because the growth in sales leads to increased stockholding, increased work in progress, and increased credit given to customers. These increases are typically not matched by increased credit terms from suppliers, while certain overhead expenses and direct expenses such as wages need to be paid regularly. This danger has been the downfall of many expanding businesses. The growth stage is typically profitable, but profitability without the cash flow is impotent.

Because of the danger of overtrading, the management of working capital (see Chapter 5) is of critical importance in the growth stage of a business.

However, outside finance is also often needed at the growth stage. Growth often involves the acquisition of new premises, new plant or equipment, new transport. Common growth stages and the finance requirements are:

- *Expansion.* At this stage, a business is trading profitably or breaking even. Further finance may be needed to expand the business or to develop the market, the product or the service further. Additional working capital may be needed, or finance for expansion of production facilities, or for developing the market or introducing more product ranges.
- *Mezzanine stage.* This stage is also sometimes known as the bridge stage. Bridge finance is used by companies undergoing the transition from being privately owned to going public, and possibly becoming quoted on the Stock Exchange.

Venture capitalists are often the choice for this stage. Further details are in Chapter 11.

Acquisitions, mergers and demergers

A business often reaches the stage where the management feels that, in the interests of the shareholders, the business should merge with another, or take over another business. A company may also be the target of another company's bid to take it over – that is, to acquire it. In these circumstances, the financial manager's role becomes very important – whether in the predator company or the target company.

Definitions

First, it is useful to define the various terms and jargon used.

Merger

This happens when two or more businesses of more or less equivalent size combine. There is generally broad agreement between the management of the businesses about the desirability of merging and the terms of the merger. The outcome is usually the creation of a new company to take over the businesses of the existing ones. All groups of shareholders receive a stake in the new company, pro rata to their existing shares.

Horizontal merger

This occurs when a company merges with or takes over another company in the same industry and at the same stage of the added value chain. For example, if one retail supermarket chain merges with another, this is a horizontal merger.

Vertical merger

This occurs when a company at one stage of the added value chain merges with another at a different stage. For example, if a retail supermarket chain merged with a wholesale grocer, that would be a vertical merger.

Conglomerate merger

This occurs when a company merges with another which is in a different, unrelated, business area. For example, if a retail supermarket chain merged with a motor car manufacturer, this would be a conglomerate merger.

Takeover

This term generally refers to the scenario where one company acquires control of a smaller company. The business of the smaller company is then absorbed into the business of the acquiring company. The shareholders in the smaller company may receive a cash payout for their shares, or shares in the acquiring company.

Predator company

This term describes a company launching a takeover bid for another company.

Target company

This term describes the company for which a takeover bid has been made.

Bid

This term refers to the terms of the offer by the acquiring company to take over control of the target company.

Hostile bid

This refers to a bid which is not welcome by the target company. The management of the target company may decide to contest the bid or to accept it. Contested bids often make news headlines – usually in the financial press, and occasionally in the general news.

Why do mergers and takeovers occur?

We can imagine directors of a company wishing to expand their company because of an urge to get bigger. Some mergers and takeover bids do happen because the managers or directors of the predator company have personal ambitions. If they can manage a larger company, they have greater prestige, power, and usually money. These takeover bids are more often contested than others.

However, the reality of the situation is usually that mergers or takeovers only happen when there are potential gains. Put another way, the combined businesses of the two or more companies involved should be of greater value than the sum of the companies if they continued their separate existences. In what ways might this increased value occur?

1.   Economies of scale

A larger company may be able to make economies of scale in several ways.

Lower administration costs

It often happens that when a merger or takeover occurs, there are redundancies. These often happen across the board, but it is likely that the brunt of the redundancies occur in the administration department. Larger companies can often be run by fewer administration staff than the two separate companies. This is particularly true as technological advances mean that more work can be automated. This effect is seen when banks or insurance companies merge or are taken over.

Greater bargaining power

Economies of scale can also be made in the greater bargaining muscle of a larger company. When ordering from a supplier, for example, better terms and cheaper rates can be obtained when the supplier knows that it will have regular large orders from a customer.

2.   Elimination of competition

A merger or takeover is often carried out to eliminate the element of competition. Two or more companies may agree that their competition in the same market place is counter-productive. A merger will mean that they can better exploit the market by working together. Alternatively, a large company may wish to acquire a smaller one to gain that company's share of the market to add to its own.

The larger market share can lead to economies of scale similar to those discussed above in relation to greater bargaining power. A business with a greater share of the market can often obtain better terms and profit margins than one with a smaller market share.

Caveat

When businesses gain a large proportion of the market share, particularly when this approaches a monopoly, there is less customer choice, and the increase in consumer prices often becomes counter-productive. A government body known as the Competition Commission can be invoked to consider whether a particular merger or takeover is in the public interest. If necessary, that body can veto the merger or takeover.

3.   Better use of resources

A frequent justification for a takeover is that the management team of the target company has not made the best use of the resources at its disposal, and that the new team introduced by the acquiring company can improve on their performance. This type of takeover bid is not necessarily made by a larger company against a smaller one. This often leads to a takeover battle, where the management of the target company defend their management record, and often improve their performance while the battle is going on.

4. Better use of complementary resources

This is a rationale which often applies when similar businesses merge. It may be that one company has better research and development capabilities, while the other has better marketing ideas and staff. Another example of this is when different businesses operate in the same field but in different geographical areas.

The combination of the strengths of the two or more businesses provides the impetus for the merger, and typically the management of the businesses will be favourably disposed to this type of merger.

5. Use of surplus cash funds

There may be occasions in the life of a company when it has surplus funds, without the opportunity to plough those funds back into its own business. As an alternative to investing the surplus funds in the money market or some other such account, investing the money in another company may be a viable and profitable use of surplus funds.

6. Diversification

We have seen in Chapter 6 that risk is always present in business. Some risk is inherent in the industry or business sector in which the company operates. Other risks are more specific to the company itself.

Diversification is a way of reducing risk. A merger or takeover may be seen as a way of diversifying a company's operations and therefore its exposure to risk.

EXAMPLES 8.1

1. The existing business of a company is seasonal, and a merger or takeover which takes it into another industry which is less seasonal 'smoothes out' the seasonal variations.
2. Industries and business sectors go through economic activity cycles, and merger with a company in a different industry could mean that while one business is at a 'low' in its economic cycle, the other is at a 'high'.

The financial management role

In takeover and merger bids and negotiating cycles, the role of the financial manager is crucial. The three main areas involving financial management are:

- valuation of businesses and shares,
- vulnerability and resistance to takeover bids,
- purchase consideration for a takeover.

1. Valuation of businesses and shares

From the point of view of both the predator company and the target company, the valuation of the shares is important. It is important also in a merger, where two or more similar sized companies join forces. Share valuations are also important in flotations of companies, offers of shares for sale, and liquidations.

The main methods used for valuations are those based on:

- asset values,
- analysis, and
- future cash flows.

In all cases there are difficulties of measurement. Remember the principle we saw at the outset?

▶ If you can measure it, you can control it.

EXERCISE 8.1

What difficulties can you foresee in the measurement of asset values or future cash flows?

Asset values

What methods are used to value a company's shares based on asset values?

1. Balance sheet values

This is the simplest method. There are three steps, and all the figures can be extracted from the company's latest balance sheet.

(a) Take the total gross assets.
(b) Deduct the total liabilities, to arrive at the total net assets of the company.
(c) Divide the total net assets of the company by the number of shares, to give the value of each individual share.

This method is simple, and the final figure cannot be disputed on the basis of the published balance sheet of the company.

EXERCISE 8.2

Why is this method not the final word?

---

2. Net realisable values

This method takes into account the value which the various assets would realise if they were sold off. It therefore assumes that the assets are being sold off piecemeal. It also takes into account the costs (such as auctioneer's fees) of selling off the various assets. For this reason, this method is sometimes referred to as 'break up valuation', or 'knock down valuation'.

What drawback can you see in this method?

3. Replacement values

As the name suggests, this method uses the cost of replacing all the assets in their present state. This takes into account current values, and is likely to provide a more realistic estimate of the asset values, particularly in a merger or takeover scenario.

EXERCISE 8.4

What difficulties can you see in this method?

Analytical methods

Quoted companies

Where the shares of the company involved are quoted on the Stock Exchange or any other recognised market, such as the Alternative Investment Market or the Unlisted Securities Market, the valuation of the shares may well coincide with the shares price quoted on the market. However, sometimes the market price of shares may not reflect their effective economic value in a merger or takeover. Shares in a particular company or market sector may be out of fashion or out of favour. Market sentiment can be a fickle indicator of the true worth of shares.

EXERCISE 8.5

Why may shares have a different economic value from their quoted market price?

Unquoted companies

Where a company's shares are not quoted on a recognised market, analytical methods may be used to help put a valuation on that company's shares, by comparison with similar companies which are quoted.

The first task, often the most difficult, is to try to find suitable companies with which to compare the share values.

EXERCISE 8.6

What difficulties might there be in finding a suitable match?

Valuation methods

The analytical method involves comparison of ratios, the two main ratios used being the price–earnings ratio and the dividend yield ratio.

The price–earnings ratio is calculated by dividing the market value per share by the earnings per share, and we have seen its implications in Chapter 7. A higher figure means that market sentiment views the company's prospects in a more favourable light. In order to calculate the value of shares, the equation can be rearranged so that it is the product of multiplying the target company's earnings per share by the equivalent price–earnings ratio.

EXAMPLE 8.2

Earnings of Unquoted Company Ltd are £2.50 per share. The price–earnings ratio of Comparable Company plc is 5.5 times. By multiplying these two figures, we arrive at a market value of £13.75 per share.

The dividend yield method involves expressing the gross dividend per share as a percentage of the market value per share, as seen in Chapter 7. This is obviously only possible where the market value per share is known. However, this calculation can be re-arranged to apply the dividend yield of the similar quoted company to the gross dividend per share to obtain the market value per share.

EXAMPLE 8.3

Gross dividend of Unquoted Company Ltd is 50p per share. Dividend yield of Comparable Quoted Company plc is 3.5%. By applying this yield to the gross dividend we obtain a market value of £14.28 per share.

Cash flow methods

Future dividends

This method of valuing shares is based on the future dividends which could be received from those shares. If the value were based only on the dividend to be received in the next year, it could be calculated using:

$$\text{value} = \frac{\text{next dividend}}{\text{required rate of return}}$$

However, the value of the shares should not only reflect the next dividend, but the entire stream of dividends (in fact, the entire stream of income of any sort) from the shares. As we saw in Chapter 7, net present value and discounted cash flow techniques are based on the theory that future money is not worth as much as present money, and the further into the future, the more the figure is discounted. Applying that to this method of valuing shares, we can arrive at the following formula:

$$value = \frac{Div_1}{(1+R)} + \frac{Div_2}{(1+R)^2} + \cdots \frac{Div_n}{(1+R)^n}$$

where:

Div_n = the dividend received in future period n

R = the required rate of return.

However, this model suffers from a couple of drawbacks. Firstly, the future dividends could be projected for an almost infinite number of years. However, the further in the future, the smaller the impact they have on the final result. Secondly, projection of future dividends would assume a constant rate. In reality, company dividends tend to fluctuate. Most companies would hope to be able to show a gradual increase in the rate of dividend, but fluctuations do occur in both directions.

If we could assume a constant rate of growth of dividends, the value using these methods could be reformulated as follows:

$$value = \frac{Div_1}{R - G}$$

where:

G = the constant rate of growth.

Surplus cash availability

This method is based on future cash available to lenders and shareholders. This is calculated by taking the net cash flow generated by the business (*not* the profit), after deducting payments of tax, dividends, and investment in new assets. This remaining cash is available to lenders and shareholders.

The value of the shares in this model is calculated by using the net present value and discounted cash flow techniques, with the cost of capital as the base rate. Once again, problems are encountered in forecasting future events, especially as cash flow is not only dependent on profits. This method arrives at a value of the business as a whole, and this calculated value is then divided by the total number of shares.

The formula for this calculation is similar to the original equation for future dividends, except that cash availability is substituted for dividends, and cost of capital is substituted for required rate of return.

As with future dividends, the formula can be expressed to assume a constant rate of growth of cash availability. The formula for expressing this value is:

$$value\ of\ business = \frac{cash\ availability}{CC - G}$$

where:

CC = cost of capital

G = the constant rate of growth of cash availability.

In this method, cash availability is assumed to be for lenders and shareholders. Therefore, the calculated value is for the business as a whole, but before deduction of the loan creditors and preference shareholders. Those amounts must therefore be deducted to give the amount available to ordinary shareholders.

EXERCISE 8.7

What factors might disturb the assumption of a constant rate of increase in cash availability?

Summary

The different methods of valuing shares produce different figures. It could be a useful exercise to implement all the methods to arrive at the range of valuations. Those valuations would then provide the higher and lower extremes. Those extremes would be used in negotiating figures. However, certain methods may be more appropriate than others – everything depends on the individual circumstances, and generalisations are misleading.

2. Vulnerability and resistance to takeover bids

Vulnerability

A takeover or merger affects many people and organisations – not just the target company. Shareholders, employees, suppliers, customers are all affected positively or negatively by a takeover.

Many businesses therefore pay much attention to their vulnerability to a takeover bid. Surveys have been carried out of the characteristics of businesses which have been acquired. By comparing their business statistics and key ratios with industry averages, certain characteristics have been identified to indicate vulnerability to takeover bids. These include:

- Lower than average return on capital during the four or five years preceding the takeover.
- Lower 'acid test' ratio.
- Lower current ratio.
- Lower net profit margin before and after tax.
- Higher 'growth-resource mismatch' than average.

This last category was identified in the USA by Palepu (1986). It refers to the fact that if a business has a disparity between resources and growth it will be seen as good value for acquisition. Thus, a company will represent good value if it shows:

- high growth and low resources, or
- low growth and high resources,

even though these two scenarios would seem to be contradictory. In this definition, growth is represented by sales growth, and resources by liquidity and gearing (low gearing representing high resources and vice versa).

In summary, if a business wants to reduce its vulnerability to a takeover, it should maintain good general financial health.

Resistance

Not all takeover bids are defended or resisted. Where the businesses are of similar size, the acquisition is seen as a merger rather than a takeover, and these are less frequently resisted.

Resistance may occur because the managers believe it is in their own interests, or that it is in the shareholders' interests. They may also make a defence to influence the predator company to increase its bid, and thereby increase the shareholders' wealth.

What methods of defence and resistance can be used? Some defences must by their nature be made before any takeover bid, but others can be made after a bid.

Change of status

If the company were to change its status to private limited company from public limited company, any predator company would find it more difficult to acquire shares. Private limited companies are allowed to put restrictions on the sale of shares (and for this reason, the lack of marketability makes their shares of less value than an equivalent public limited company). Such restrictions could include, for example, a clause stating that shares to be sold must first be offered to existing directors, or existing shareholders.

Establishing employee share option schemes

If employees make up a substantial proportion of the shareholders, they are more likely to resist a takeover bid, since it is more likely that their jobs will be affected. This measure will be the more effective when it has been in force for some time, and the employees have built up larger shareholdings.

Circulating shareholders

If the management wishes to resist a bid, it will often write to all shareholders promptly setting out its reasons for resisting the bid. This sometimes involves the disclosure of previously confidential information, such as future plans, forecasts, valuations of assets, new contracts and so on. Once these have been disclosed in this way, they are in the public domain.

Lessening the company's appeal

The management may take steps to make the target company less attractive to bidders. Sometimes this could involve taking steps which are in consequence not entirely in the company's highest interest. This is known as 'taking a poison pill'. This could involve selling off prime assets, tangible ones, or intangible ones such as patents, or brand names. Another term used in takeover jargon is 'the crown jewels', referring to the company's prized assets which are sold off as a defensive measure.

Another measure to make the company less attractive is to put into operation 'golden parachutes'. This refers to agreements with directors to pay large amounts to them for loss of office in the event of a takeover. It could also include such tactics as paying large sums to shareholders, thereby reducing the cash balances and increasing the gearing.

Pac-man defence

This refers to the target company making a counter-bid for the predator company. It is a difficult defence when there is a large discrepancy in the size of the predator company and the target company.

Seeking a different acquirer

This is known as the 'white knight' defence. It happens when the target company seeks some sort of merger or combination with a company it would prefer to the predator company. This could happen because of differing management styles, or a lack of clear synergy.

Predator action

The predator company may respond to the defences of the target company in several ways. It may circulate the shareholders of the target company, with its explanations or reasoning. It may overcome resistance by increasing its offer. It may even pitch its first bid deliberately low as a negotiating ploy.

The City Code on Takeovers and Mergers

The City Code protects the interests of shareholders of both the predator company and the target company by ensuring that they are given complete information to make a proper decision. In practice this means that shareholders receive an enormous quantity of literature which they do not understand and they have to rely on professional advice to interpret the information.

3. Purchase consideration

When a company wishes to buy another company's shares, it has to devise ways to pay for them. The most common ways are:

- cash,
- shares in the predator company,
- loan capital in the predator company,

or any combination of these three methods.

Cash

This is the preferred method for the target company shareholders . They receive cash, which they have the choice of re-investing or not, as they wish. They may wish to re-invest in the predator company, or in a different company, or not re-invest at all. They have complete freedom of choice. However, the receipt of cash may trigger a liability to Capital Gains Tax.

A cash offer is also the most easily understood by target company shareholders. Other offers may require sophisticated knowledge and understanding to evaluate the offer.

A cash offer may include part of the consideration in deferred form – cash payments being spread over a period of time. This may lessen the appeal of the bid to the target company shareholders.

From the point of view of the predator company, this method also means that there is no dilution of its capital. However, it does mean that the cash paid for the offer has to be financed. This can be done by:

- taking a loan,
- making a new share issue, (which would involve dilution of the capital), or
- selling off assets.

Each of these options may pose difficulties for the predator company.

Shares

This involves issuing to the target company shareholders new shares in the predator company, on some equitable basis to reflect the price to be paid. This may not be as favourable to the target company shareholders as the cash option. They may not wish to retain shares in the predator company. However, the exchange of shares in this way does not trigger a Capital Gains Tax liability.

The number of shares in the predator company given to target company shareholders is determined by the market value of the shares in each of the companies. Thus, any fluctuation in the values may seriously affect the offer. In addition, the predator company must ensure that the authorised capital of the company is adequate for the issue of the new shares. If not, special resolutions must be passed, and special forms registered at Companies House. All this could add to the cost of the takeover.

The issue of new shares also means that the capital of the predator company is diluted. There could also be a dilution of the earnings per share if the additional earnings from the acquisition of the new business are lower than the existing earnings per share.

Loan capital

This involves the issue of loan stock or debentures to the target company shareholders. This shares some of the disadvantages of the issue of shares from the point of view of the target company shareholders. However, they would not acquire any equity in the predator company, and that could be a further disincentive.

However, the loan stock issued could be convertible, so that it has the option to be converted into ordinary shares of the predator company at some future date. This could provide relative security in the early years after a takeover, with the chance to participate in the future prosperity of the merged business if it is successful.

From the point of view of the predator company, this, like the share issue, is less of a strain on cash resources. However, it does increase the gearing, and therefore the financial risk becomes greater.

Demergers

As the name suggests, demergers (also sometimes referred to as divestments) are the opposite to mergers. In a demerger, a company sells off an identifiable sector of its business operations. This may be done for several reasons.

EXERCISE 8.8

What reasons can you identify for a company wanting to sell off part of its business?

Divestments can be structured as a management buy-out or buy-in (see below), or a spin-off.

Spin-off

This occurs when the company creates a new company to take over the business operations of the part to be divested. One of the biggest in recent years was the spin-off of ICI's pharmaceutical business to a newly-formed company called Zeneca plc, which later became AstraZeneca plc.

In this structure, shareholders of the existing company are given shares in the new company in proportion to their existing holdings. The value of their shares in the original company will be adjusted by the market to take account of the spin-off.

Management buy outs and management buy ins

- *Management buy out.* This situation occurs when the existing operating management and/or investors wish to buy the whole business, a division of the business, or perhaps a product line. Specific financing is matched to this, often provided by venture capitalists. In a management buy out, shareholders must be extra vigilant. The managers involved are of course looking to secure the best deal for themselves, and this could lead them to withhold certain information from the shareholders. Shareholders often seek independent advice in these circumstances.
- *Management buy in.* This is the situation when a group of managers from outside the business wish to buy into the business and run it, or buy into a division of the existing company.

Crisis management

There are sometimes occasions when even the best business runs into difficulties. These difficulties can arise from external sources, such as a natural disaster. In recent history, the foot and mouth crisis affected many businesses in agriculture and related businesses, and also in tourism related businesses. Another external source of difficulties could be the failure of a major customer or supplier, leaving either a bad debt or a lack of vital supplies. Other difficulties can be self-inflicted.

Whatever the reason, there could be significant financial problems, which have to be managed. The first rule of crisis management is:

▶ Don't panic!

The second rule is:

▶ Don't stick your head in the sand.

A crisis will not go away. It has to be faced. Very often external help is needed from the bank or other finance source. The management must not attempt to minimise the crisis, but should set out all the facts, and suggest a way forward. The bank will be much more likely to respond positively to this open, honest approach.

Short-term measures

A crisis is usually short-term, and short-term measures are required. Once the situation has been retrieved, the short-term measures can be discarded. Here are some of the most common short-term measures that can be adopted.

Downsizing

This involves reducing the scale of operations in one form or another. The most commonly recognised form of this includes reducing the number of employees. However, there are often ways to manage without getting rid of employees.

EXERCISE 8.9

What ways can you think of to avoid having to get rid of staff?

Re-negotiating long-term contracts

Some commitments are long term, and their continued presence could be detrimental to survival of the crisis. It may be possible to persuade, say, a landlord of rented property to accept a re-negotiated contract for the rent. If the landlord can see that the only alternative to re-negotiation may be the failure of the business, and the property standing empty, success is likely.

Rationalising the supplier base

Another possibility may be to review the supplier base. Although diversification may be advantageous in many cases, it may still be better in a crisis to concentrate on fewer suppliers, buying in larger quantities. This may give the leverage to negotiate better prices and terms.

Cutting budgeted expenditure

Certain classes of overhead are subject to budget restrictions. Thus, it may be possible to reduce expenditure on, say, advertising, or research and development as a short-term measure. However, the long-term future of the business must not be endangered by short-term expediencies.

Focusing on core activities

A crisis may lead management to a radical re-think on its activities. It may take the opportunity to re-define its core activities, and consider whether any peripheral activities should be curtailed. This can lead to the realisation of surplus assets, and/or the re-direction of valuable resources, including labour, into the core activities.

This process can lead to more than a short-term measure, since the business may well find that its financial health improves by concentrating on the core activities.

Releasing locked up capital

In a crisis, many businesses find that they are able to release the capital locked up in long-term assets, or under-utilised assets.

Identifying under-used assets

Using the techniques described in Chapter 2 for comparing the ratio of sales to fixed assets, it could be possible to further refine this process, and compare the ratio of certain classes of fixed assets to the sales of particular types.

This could identify fixed assets which are being under-employed. The sale of those assets could realise some capital, without seriously affecting the sales.

Sale and leaseback

This operation involves selling assets to a leasing company, then leasing them back at a fixed rental, payable at regular intervals.

It may be possible in this way to realise the capital value of certain assets, without having to dispose of them.

Deferring non-essential capital expenditure

Certain capital expenditure may have been planned and budgeted some time in advance. A careful examination of priorities may result in suspending certain capital expenditure which is judged to be non-essential. Once again, however, the long-term future of the business should not be jeopardised.

Selling off surplus assets

A review of the business prompted by a crisis may reveal certain assets which are surplus to real needs. These could be sold off to raise some capital.

ASSIGNMENT

The board of XYZ plc, which is a retail supermarket, is considering making a takeover bid at 31st December 20xx for ABC plc, which is a food wholesaler. The board of XYZ plc believes that it can make significant savings – estimated at £5 million – if the two businesses were merged. The balance sheets and other information relating to each company are given in Figure 8.1.

You are asked to advise the board of XYZ plc on:

- The amount of and the form of the offer to be made to the members of ABC plc.
- Any possible objections that might be raised by members of ABC plc.
- The financial results of the newly-merged businesses if the bid were successful, assuming other policies remained the same, and that apart from any savings already identified, the pre-tax profits would rise by 4%. These results should include the pre-tax profit, the earnings per share, the net assets per share, the estimated share price, and the comparison of present dividend yield to expected dividend yield.
- What other factors should be considered by the board of XYZ plc?

SUGGESTED ANSWER

1. Amount of offer to be made

   The market value of ABC's shares is £1.40 per share at the latest balance sheet date. It is assumed that there are no further factors which might mean that the shares are over-priced or under-priced.

   In order to persuade the members of ABC plc to accept the offer, the amount should be pitched at a premium to the present market price. A premium of, say, 25% would give an offer price of £1.75 per share.

2. Form of offer

   A cash offer of £1.75 would require the raising of £175 million, the finance costs of which would make a significant dent in the projected savings foreseen.

   A loan stock offer would have the same effect as regards the cost of servicing the loan.

   A share offer could be made which would have to match the current value of XYZ plc's shares to the offer price. This means that XYZ plc would have to offer 70 million shares at their current market value of £2.50 to achieve the value of £175 million. Therefore the offer would have to be of 7 shares in XYZ plc for every 10 shares in ABC plc. This raises an issue which is dealt with in point 5.

3. Possible objections by shareholders in ABC plc

   The value of £1.75 per share is below the net asset value per share of ABC plc. The net assets of ABC plc are £200 million, and there are 100 million shares, making the net asset value £2 per share. From their point of view, would it not then be better to sell off the assets of the company and pocket the £2 per share? The answer to this objection is that the net asset value per share is irrelevant for these purposes. What matters is the market value per share. The market has

	XYZ plc		ABC plc	
Profit and loss accounts	£m		£m	
Sales		100		200
Pre-tax profit		8		12
Dividends paid		4		10
Balance sheets				
Fixed assets				
Freehold property		60		180
Equipment		10		50
Vehicles		5		40
		75		270
Current assets – stock	15		50	
debtors	5		50	
cash	20			
	40		100	
Current liabilities				
Trade creditors	10		60	
Other creditors	5		20	
Bank overdraft			25	
	15		105	
Working capital		25		– 5
		100		265
Long-term liabilities				
Loans		10		65
Net assets		90		200
Share capital issued				
Ordinary shares of £1 each		50		100
Reserves		40		100
		90		200
Authorised share capital		100		100
Stock market data:				
Share price of last three years				
31/12/2003	£1.50		£2.00	
31/12/2004	£2.00		£1.80	
31/12/2005	£2.50		£1.40	
Dividends paid per share				
31/12/2003	6.5p		11p	
31/12/2004	7p		11p	
31/12/2005	8p		10p	
Earnings per share				
31/12/2003	13p		8p	
31/12/2004	15p		7.5p	
31/12/2005	16p		6.7p	

Figure 8.1 Extracts from profit and loss accounts and balance sheets of XYZ plc and ABC plc for the year ended 31st December 20xx

valued the shares at less than £2 per share, and this reflects market sentiment towards the business.

The shareholders might also point to the fact that the dividends paid by XYZ plc are lower than those of ABC plc. However, the dividend record of XYZ plc shows an increasing trend, while that of ABC plc shows a declining trend. In addition, what matters is the total shareholder value. The shareholders in ABC plc will be exchanging ten shares worth £14 for seven shares worth £17.50. In addition, the calculations (see 4(d)) indicate that the expected share price after the merger would increase to £3.39, so that the new value they would have in the merged companies would be £23.73

4. (a) Results of the newly merged businesses

		£m
Profits of the existing companies – XYZ plc		8
ABC plc		12
		20
Additional savings		5
		25
Increase of 4%		1
New pre-tax profits		26

(b) Earnings per share

Pre-tax profits – as above	£26 million
New issued share capital – shares of £1 each	120 million shares
Earnings per share = 21.7p per share	

(c) Net assets per share

		£m
Total net assets – XYZ plc		90
ABC plc		200
		290
New issued share capital – shares of £1 each		120 million shares
Net assets per share = £2.42 per share		

(d) Estimated share price after the merger
New earnings per share = 21.7p per share
Existing price–earnings ratio 15.625 times
Therefore the expected new share price would be £3.39, by multiplication of these two factors.

(e) Dividend yields in XYZ plc before and after the merger

Existing dividend per share	8p
Existing share price	£2.50
Therefore existing dividend yield	3.2%
New earnings per share	21.7p
Profit retention as per current policy	50%
Therefore new dividend per share	10.85p
Therefore new dividend yield	3.2%

This means that there is no change in the dividend yield, but it is based on a higher expected share price.

5. The merger is a vertical one – the retail supermarket is merging with the food wholesaler.

The savings already identified then are probably economies of scale. There are also possible savings on other elements. The balance sheets show that ABC plc has a large value of fixed assets, including freehold property, equipment and vehicles, which could be under-utilised. The retail supermarket business may well be able to further integrate these assets into its own business, and make further savings. It could even possibly sell off surplus assets and release cash resources.

The offer in the form of shares would require a further 70 million shares to be issued. However, the company has an authorised capital of 100 million shares, of which 50 million have already been issued. Therefore, it must carry out the legal requirements to increase its authorised share capital by at least 20 million shares.

An alternative might be to issue a mixture of shares and loans to the existing shareholders of ABC plc, or convertible loan stocks. This would alter the capital structure and gearing of the company.

▪ ☑ **9** Managing bank relations

LEARNING OUTCOMES

By the end of this chapter, you should be able to:

▶ summarise the main facilities available from a bank for businesses,
▶ put yourself in the shoes of a bank manager approached with a business proposition,
▶ prepare for an interview with a bank manager, and
▶ produce an elementary business plan, including a profit projection, and cash flow forecast.

Introduction

In any business, the relationship with the business's bankers is key. In this chapter we consider the main areas in which that relationship comes into play. This involves not just the technical aspects of presentation of figures, but also the personal aspects of how to manage the relationship. However large the business may be, the bank still recognises that it is dealing with people – the managers – and they will determine how the business operates.

What does the bank have to offer?

Any business may wish to open a bank account or change its bankers. Before taking a step, management must think about priorities and what they want from the bank. For example, a new business starting up may like the idea of free banking for the first year or two. Alternatively, working capital requirements may mean that an overdraft renewable on demand is important. It could even be something as simple as the location of the branch, with accessibility to the manager who has authority to take decisions on the account.

Whatever bank is chosen, think long term. The business is entering into a long-term relationship – one which should be stable. All the homework must be done beforehand. It is always a good idea to shop around before buying something, and this applies to banking. Before opening an account, see what is available at various banks, and how they operate. Special offers may be all very well, but in a long-term relationship, a bank that understands the business and one that will help it to grow is vital.

- Free banking for the initial period (up to two years) of a new business
- Guaranteed overdrafts not repayable on demand
- Free business service reviews
- Free business planning and book-keeping software
- High interest deposit accounts
- Instant access deposit accounts
- Commercial mortgages
- Credit and debit cards
- Foreign currency accounts and international payments
- Asset finance
- Electronic banking and telephone banking
- Business insurance services
- Free appraisals of business proposals and commercial viability
- Business loans
- Loan guarantee schemes

Figure 9.1   Summary of typical business services and facilities offered by banks

Banks are extremely competitive, and it is never a good idea to let banking arrangements simply drift on without any regular review. On the other hand, it is also not a good idea to be chopping and changing the bank frequently. However, any bank manager will realise that the business is seeking the best possible service from the bank, with the greatest availability of facilities, and at the most economical cost. For instance, banking coins and notes is usually more expensive in terms of charges than banking cheques. However, this is an area where it is may be possible to negotiate lower charges. Figure 9.1 summarises the typical business services and facilities offered by banks.

How the bank manager approaches the customer

When presenting a proposal, it is useful to be able to put one's self in the shoes of the person sitting on the other side of the desk. So how does a bank manager approach a proposition? He will assess both the individual and the proposal.

The individual

Character

What is the individual's track record? If the person is an existing customer of the bank, the manager will know the track record. He will know whether overdraft limits have been exceeded, and so on.

If the person is a new customer, references are taken. The bank manager will possibly ask to see previous bank statements – and they would have to cover a consecutive period. If a new customer presents previous bank statements with a gap, there is the immediate suspicion that the gap could be an attempt to hide a problem.

Then, the bank manager will form his own opinion about the individual during discussions. Is this individual trustworthy? Does he or she answer questions openly, or is he or she guarded? Naturally, this is a personal assessment by the bank manager, but bank managers have much experience in interviewing people and assessing their characters.

Capability

The bank manager will also try to gain an idea of the person's capability to manage the business. Again, the bank manager will have much experience of judging people's competence, and if an existing customer of the bank, he will have formed some idea already.

When dealing with a new customer, the bank manager will want to investigate further. He may well want to visit the business premises, even if working from home. He will form an opinion of the quality of the product and/or service. If there are any key workers, he will want to talk to them. Once the bank manager has had a good look, he will form an opinion of the state of the business and its recent progress.

The proposal

The bank manager often uses a set procedure to assess the proposal, such as the mnemonic: PARTS. This stands for Purpose–Amount–Repayment–Terms– Security, and defines the sort of questions the bank manager will ask himself and the customer.

Purpose

- What is the money required for?
- Is the purpose reasonable, taking into account all other known facts about the business?
- Is the stated purpose likely to be hiding any other, that is, is it the *real* reason for requesting the money?

Amount

- Is the amount requested sufficient?
- Does it cover any contingencies, and all of the incidental costs connected with the proposal?
- Is the amount requested excessive?
- What is the timing?
- Will the drawdown of the funds be made in instalments?
- Is the proposal realistic in relation to the capital of the business?
- If the proposal is for purchase or construction of an asset, are the bank being asked to fund all of the asset? If not, what proportion of the asset is the bank being asked to finance?

Repayment

- How is the customer proposing to make repayments?
- Is the repayment time scale realistic?
- Is any repayment moratorium likely to be necessary?
- Has the customer produced a cash flow forecast taking into account the suggested repayments?
- What if the business hits problems – how are the repayments likely to be affected?
- Do the proposed repayments extend beyond the life of the asset?

Terms

- Does the customer understand the bank's terms in relation to interest, charges, commission, arrangement fee, and so on?
- Has the customer considered insurance cover for death, accident, or health of the proprietor(s), directors, managers, or other key personnel?

Security

- What security is available?
- Does the security carry sufficient value?
- Can the Small Firms Loan Guarantee Scheme help?

Overall

The bank manager is just as keen as the customer for the project to succeed. If successful, both parties will profit from the deal. However, the bank manager must give the proposal as rigorous an examination as possible. A bad decision can be onerous to both parties. A bank, or other lender, can probably take a loss without too much pain, but if it goes wrong, it could be catastrophic for the customer. The 'what if?' questions are extremely important.

Maintaining good relationships

The bank realises that businesses exist to make money just as much as banks do, so the relationship does not have to be one-sided. If the bank does not seem to be forthcoming, take the initiative and take steps to build a better relationship with the bank. There are a few simple guidelines to maintaining a good working relationship with the bank.

Think of the bank as a resource for the business

The bank is not the enemy to be outwitted or got the better of. The bank can and should be an active partner in helping the business grow. Many have specialist business departments which could help, say, in developing a new idea.

Provide the bank with information

Let the bank have the financial information about the business. This could mean letting them have quarterly or half-yearly accounts. Offer to meet them to explain any queries they may have.

Keep to agreements made

Make sure that the business can make repayments when they are due. Do not infringe the overdraft limit. The bank can refuse payment of cheques. This will result in a charge on the account, and could damage the business's reputation with the person to whom the cheque is paid.

No surprises!

Sometimes going over the bank overdraft limit is unavoidable, or there may be some other bad news. If this is going to happen, the bank must be told as soon as possible. Be as precise as possible – tell them how much you are going over the limit, and how long it will last. The bank is unlikely to refuse this request, and they will not then bounce any cheques.

The surprises do not have to be bad news. If the bank is not up to date with the business's progress, they may suddenly hear of ambitious expansion plans, as a complete surprise. In that case, they will not be as enthusiastic about lending money as if they had been kept up to date regularly, and knew that expansion was a possibility.

Mollify bad news

If something has gone wrong, always show what action is being taking to remedy the situation.

Demonstrate awareness

In all dealings with the bank, show that the management is commercially aware, up to date with the business's own transactions, and that control over business's finances is active.

Never rush the bank for a decision

Banks have their own timetable, and will not delay the customer unnecessarily.

Think ahead

The successful end of one negotiation is the end of that chapter, not the end of the story. Look ahead to future development, and start preparing the way for the next negotiations with the bank.

Writing winning business plans

In order to raise finance for any purpose, the lender will want to see a business plan. This can be a long or short document. The length of the plan and the amount of detail will depend on the nature of the project for which finance is required, and the amount involved. A lender will not be impressed with a plan that is either too scanty or unnecessarily elaborate.

Personal contact with the bank manager is at least as vital as the written plan.

The plan must convince the lender that management is capable, and that the plan is viable. Here are a few practical suggestions:

- Send in the documentation a few days in advance. This allows the bank manager to consider the proposal without undue rush.
- Be prepared to listen to alternative ways of restructuring the proposal.
- A meeting at the business premises could be beneficial – bank managers often like to visit customers' premises. However, make sure that interruptions are avoided.
- Be prepared for awkward questions. If there are awkward questions, do not be defensive or aggressive. Answer as openly and honestly as possible. Do not try to bluff.
- Do not accept any comments that are not understood or if there is any disagreement. Ask questions to clarify points which seem to be unclear.
- Do not agree to too much security. Work out the bank's maximum exposure to loss, and agree to that figure. If the bank asks for double that amount, it is too much.
- Try to avoid giving personal guarantees.
- Concentrate on getting the proposal accepted first, and only then move on to negotiating terms and rates.
- Be prepared to negotiate for favourable terms – do not threaten.
- Make a summary at the end of the meeting of what has been agreed. Follow it up in writing.

People

The lender must be convinced that the management of the business is trustworthy, and capable of managing the business in general and the particular project for which finance is sought. The business plan must contribute to this objective by giving enough information on the personal level.

Proposal

The lender must be convinced that the proposal is sound, and commercially viable. In addition, the lender must see how the proposal fits in with the business as a whole, and if its viability could be affected by the rest of the business. The business plan must, therefore, show that all the homework has been done, and that, as far as possible, all the 'what-ifs' have been covered.

Contents of a business plan

Every situation is unique, so there can be no hard and fast way of making a business plan which must be adhered to in every case. However, the following elements will be needed in most cases.

1. Summary

1.1 Introduction to the proposal and business plan. State clearly and simply why the money is needed, and for what it will be used. Then give a thumbnail sketch of the business in its present state – what its activities are, who runs it, and a brief summary of figures. Three figures will be sufficient here – latest annual turnover, profits, and net assets.

1.2 If the proposal and business plan are for a new business, instead of giving the details of the business in its present state, give a brief summary of what activity the business will carry on, and the projected figures for the initial period – turnover, profit and net assets.

NB This section should be brief, to give the lender a quick overview, which they can keep in their mind as an outline map.

2. The proposal

2.1 Give details of what the money is for, detailed costings of all items, and what form of finance is proposed.

2.2 Provide a detailed timetable for the acquisition of all items for which funding is sought, and a timetable for the integration of these into the business.

2.3 Provide a timetable for repayment, building in any moratorium you think may be necessary.

3. Management

3.1 Give details of the experience and qualities of the owners, directors or managers of the business.

3.2 If the proposal is for a new business, emphasise why the owner(s), directors or managers are qualified to make the new business succeed, and how they can work together.

3.3 If the proposal is such that new management expertise will be hired, give details of the profile of the person to be recruited, or the person in mind for the job.

3.4 Give details of any other specialised help or expertise available, such as business mentors, business angels and so on

3.5 If the proprietor(s), directors or managers are nearing retirement age, give details of the proposed succession, to ensure that the project or the business as a whole is not jeopardised.

4. Product and/or service

4.1 Give full details of the activities of the business. The main business could be manufacturing, selling (retail or wholesale), or service. Increasingly, many businesses have a mixture of activities which could include any combination of these three.

4.2 If there is a diversity of activities, indicate which is the main or core activity, and which are regarded as by-products or secondary activities. If, as is often the case, one activity depends on another, and neither could properly be carried out in isolation, make this clear. Try to show how the different activities are linked, and what would be the effect on one activity if the other suffered a downturn.

4.3 Indicate as fully as possible the range of products or services concerned, and the possibility for developing new products or services.

5. Marketing

5.1 Convince the lender that the business knows the market for its products or services, and that it knows its existing and/or potential customers.

5.2 Firstly, give an idea of the size of the global, national, or local market in the product or service. Even if the business does not aspire to take over the whole market, the lender must be convinced that it will be able to make some impression on it.

5.3 If the market is a growth area, state the reasons for believing this. Convincing the lender that the business is operating in a growth area will boost the chances of a successful proposal.

5.4 Next, state what sector of the market is targeted. For instance, *The Times* and the *Sun* are two different types of newspaper, aimed at different sectors of the newspaper reading market. Avoid making value judgements about any sector of the market. The *Times* reader may be different from the *Sun* reader, but neither is better or worse than the other in terms of market sector.

5.5 Specify in more detail the customer or client profile. For instance, if selling computer hardware or software, the typical customer may be small or medium sized professional businesses (for example, accountants, architects, solicitors and so on). The more specialised your product or service, the more specific is likely to be the typical customer profile.

5.6 Specify the competition. Give as much detail as possible on competitors' turnover, number of staff, geographical spread, and growth or decline in recent years.

5.7 The pricing of the product or service is also a marketing issue. Give details of the pricing structure of the products or services.

6. Sales

6.1 Convince the lender that the product or service will sell. Emphasise its USP (unique selling point).

6.2 Give details of advertising campaigns, and an idea of the advertising budget.

6.3 Give details of any special present or future promotions. Targeting promotions is particularly useful.

6.4 Give details of the sales force, saying how and where they sell.

6.5 Pricing of the product or service is most important. As shown in 4.7, this is a marketing issue as well as a sales issue. Give full details of any discounts, special offers or reductions.

7. Operational

7.1 Give details of the location, type of accommodation, and tenure of all business premises. Give details of the length of leases, outline of the terms of leases, and in particular when any rent reviews become due.

7.2 Give details of the main fixed assets of the business – tangible and intangible.

7.3 Give details of staffing levels, and experience of existing staff at all levels. If further staff will be needed for the project, give details of the expected number required, and at what levels.

7.4 Give details of insurance cover – what risks are covered, and the amount of cover.

8. Short-term, medium-term and long-term goals

8.1 Short-term – give a detailed forecast of profits and a detailed cash flow projection for a one-year period.

8.2 Medium term – give a less detailed forecast of growth and profits over the next five years, with a cash flow projection.

8.3 Long-term – give details of your vision of the future development of the business over the next five- to ten-year period.

9. Financial details

9.1 Give details of the last three years' accounts figures, showing trends.

9.2 Provide a detailed profit forecast and cash flow projection for the coming year.

10. Security

10.1 Provide full details of anything offered as security. If the business owns a freehold property, provide an up-to-date survey and/or valuation.

Cash flow forecasting

A cash flow forecast is an essential part of a business plan and borrowing proposal. It sets out for a specific period (usually one year for the short-term) the forecast receipts and payments of the business, and presents these, usually with monthly rests, in the form of a table.

CASE STUDY

This case study shows the cash flow forecast for one year of a company running a hotel – The Supa-Dupa Hotel Ltd. It is running a hotel in a resort area, where much of the trade is seasonal. In the process of trying to maximise its profit, the company plans to increase the usage of the hotel all year round. It has identified a potential market for a 'health and fitness centre', and plans to convert under-used rooms in the hotel into this centre (essentially a gym), to be opened adjacent to the hotel's swimming pool. The centre and swimming pool would then be opened to non-residents all year round. The cash flow forecast and profit projection are to accompany the business plan and proposal to the bank for the finance of this project.

The cash flow forecast is shown in Figure 9.2.

What are the processes involved in creating a cash flow forecast?

1. First, make a realistic projection of the profit and loss account for the year. This involves making assumptions about the various elements of the profit and loss account (for example, sales volume, gross profit rate, levels of overheads and rates of cost increase) and then quantifying them. This is shown in Figure 9.3.

2. The assumptions are the most critical part of the projected profit and loss account and the cash flow forecast. They must be explained in as much detail as possible. This is shown in Figure 9.4.

3. Next, make adjustments to the annual figures to arrive at the actual amounts expended during the year. This means making the accrual adjustments at the beginning and the end of the year. Non-cash items such as depreciation must also be adjusted. This is shown in Figure 9.5.

4. Next, incorporate capital items in the cash flow forecast. This includes expenditure on fixed assets, repayments of loans, or hire purchase contracts, payments of tax, and dividends. Incoming cash should also be shown, including loans received. The amounts of income and expenditure are allocated to the months in which they should become due for payment.

5. The inflowing and outflowing cash is then totalled for each month, and adjusted on the opening bank balance. The projected bank balance is then shown at the end of each month, and carried forward to the next month. The projected situation of the bank account is therefore shown for each month, and the maximum overdraft facility needed is shown. In this example, it occurs in March, when the overdraft is projected to reach nearly £33,000. However, by the end of the year, the balance in credit at the bank has recovered to stand at over £70,000. This will be needed to pay the dividends and the tax in the next year. This pattern is common in seasonal businesses, and points to the need for treasury management, by investing surplus cash until it is needed.

	Jan	Feb	Mar	Apr	May	Jun
Income						
Accommodation	13,750	13,750	13,750	16,600	16,600	16,600
Food	4,600	4,600	4,600	5,500	5,500	5,500
Bar sales	2,300	2,300	2,300	2,750	2,750	2,750
Sundry sales	920	920	920	1,100	1,100	1,100
Health club						
Bank loan		15,000		20,000		15,000
TOTAL	21,570	36,570	21,570	45,950	25,950	40,950
Payments						
Food costs	4,750	2,300	2,300	2,300	2,750	2,750
Drinks costs	2,625	1,150	1,150	1,150	1,375	1,375
Sundry purchases	1,375	690	690	690	825	825
Wages	3,500	3,500	3,500	4,200	4,000	4,200
Directors' salaries	6,500	6,500	6,500	6,700	6,700	6,700
Cleaning	800	800	800	800	800	800
Laundry	500	500	500	500	500	500
Rates and water	1,250			1,350	1,350	1,350
Light and heat		2,500			2,800	
Property repairs	500	200	4,000	200	300	
Equipment maintenance	400	450	450	500	550	500
Insurance						9,000
Transport	550	550	550	550	600	3,600
Advertising			3,000	3,000		
Professional fees			4,500			
Sundry expenses	200	200	200	200	200	200
Bank charges			750			750
Finance charges	400	400	400	400	400	400
Capital expenditure		15,000		20,000		15,000
Loan repayments			225	225	525	525
Dividends			20,000			
Tax paid						
	23,350	34,740	49,515	42,765	23,675	48,475
Net inflow/outflow	− 1,780	1,830	− 27,945	3,185	2,275	− 7,525
Opening balance	− 5,000	− 6,780	− 4,950	− 32,895	− 29,710	− 27,435
Closing balance	− 6,780	− 4,950	− 32,895	− 29,710	− 27,435	− 34,960

Figure 9.2 Cash flow forecast – The Supa-Dupa Hotel Ltd,
year ended 31st December 20xx

Figure 9.2 continued

	Jul	Aug	Sep	Oct	Nov	Dec
Income						
Accommodation	40,700	50,600	40,700	31,600	23,750	31,600
Food	13,600	13,600	13,600	10,500	7,900	10,500
Bar sales	6,800	6,800	6,800	5,250	3,950	5,250
Sundry aales	2,720	2,720	2,720	2,100	1,580	2,100
Health club	2,000	2,000	2,000	1,500	1,500	1,000
Bank loan						
TOTAL	65,820	75,720	65,820	50,950	38,680	50,450
Payments						
Food costs	2,750	6,800	6,800	6,800	5,250	3,950
Drinks costs	1,375	3,400	3,200	3,400	2,625	1,975
Sundry purchases	825	2,040	2,040	2,040	1,575	1,185
Wages	6,200	6,900	6,400	5,900	5,500	6,000
Directors' salaries	6,700	6,700	6,700	6,700	6,700	6,700
Cleaning	800	900	900	900	800	800
Laundry	500	500	500	500	500	500
Rates and water	1,650	1,650	1,650	1,650	1,650	1,650
Light and heat		3,200			3,400	
Property repairs						2,500
Equipment maintenance	500	500	500	500	550	500
Insurance						
Transport	600	600	600	600	550	550
Advertising	1,000				2,400	
Professional fees						
Sundry expenses	200	300	200	200	200	200
Bank charges			750			750
Finance charges	400	400	400	400	400	400
Capital expenditure						
Loan repayments	750	750	750	750	750	750
Dividends						
Tax paid			60,000			
	24,250	34,640	91,390	30,340	32,850	28,410
Net inflow/outflow	41,570	41,080	−25,570	20,610	5,830	22,040
Opening balance	−34,960	6,610	47,690	22,120	42,730	48,560
Closing balance	6,610	47,690	22,120	42,730	48,560	70,600

		£
Income		
Accommodation	300,000	
Food	100,000	
Bar sales	50,000	
Sundry sales	20,000	
Health and fitness club	8,000	
		478,000
Expenses		
Food costs	50,000	
Drinks costs	25,000	
Sundry purchases	15,000	
Wages	60,000	
Directors' salaries	80,000	
Cleaning	10,000	
Laundry	6,000	
Rates and water	15,000	
Light and heat	12,000	
Property repairs	8,000	
Equipment maintenance	6,000	
Insurance	8,000	
Transport	10,000	
Advertising	9,000	
Professional fees	5,000	
Sundry expenses	2,500	
Bank charges	3,000	
Loan interest	4,000	
Finance charges	4,800	
Depreciation	20,000	
		353,300
Net profit before tax and dividends		124,700
Tax	60,000	
Dividends	20,000	
		80,000
Retained profit		£44,700

Figure 9.3 Profit projection – The Supa-Dupa Hotel Ltd,
year ended 31st December 20xx

Capital

Loan from bank		£50,000
Draw down	February	£15,000
	April	£20,000
	June	£15,000

Repayments over ten years at 8%

March–April repayments	capital	125	(15,000 over 10 years)
	interest	100	(8% p.a. on 15,000)
		225	
May–June repayments	capital	292	(35,000 over 10 years)
	interest	233	(8% p.a. on 35,000)
		525	
July–Dec repayments	capital	417	(50,000 over 10 years)
	interest	333	(8% p.a. on 50,000)
		750	

Capital expenditure

Conversion work for health and fitness centre

Progress payments	February	£15,000
	April	£20,000
Equipment		£15,000

Income

Accommodation	Number of rooms	Charge per night	Occupancy rate	Number of nights	Projected income
Low season					
Superior double rooms	9	£50.00	36%	120	19,440
Standard double rooms	17	£40.00	42%	120	34,272
Single rooms	2	£30.00	20%	120	1,440
Mid season					
Superior double rooms	9	£60.00	44%	153	36,353
Standard double rooms	17	£50.00	52%	153	67,626
Single rooms	2	£35.00	35%	153	3,749
High season	9	£72.00	84%	92	50,077
Superior double rooms					
Standard double rooms	17	£62.00	85%	92	82,423
Single rooms	2	£45.00	58%	92	4,802
TOTAL					£300,182

Food

Food income is approx 1/3 accommodation income based on previous year.

Bar sales

Bar sales are approx 50% food income based on previous year.

Sundry sales (postcards, books, confectionery etc.)

Sundry sales are approx 40% of bar sales based on previous year.

Health and fitness centre

Income should start in July, after completion of the work. Based on initial offer of annual subscription of £80 per person, or £120 per couple, with single visits at £5 per session.

Figure 9.4　Basis of figures for profit projection and cash flow forecast, year ended 31st December 20xx

Figure 9.4 continued

Expenditure
All regular bills are paid monthly, with one month's credit taken.

Food costs
Food costs are 50% of food income.

Drinks costs
Drinks costs are 50% of bar income.

Sundry purchases
Sundry purchases are 75% of sundry sales.

Wages and salaries
General hotel staff consists of a core number of workers, with additional seasonal workers. One extra person will be taken on when the fitness centre opens.

Cleaning and laundry
These expenses are evenly spread through the year, with a slight increase in laundry during the high season.

Business rates and water
The business rates are due to increase once the fitness centre is built.

Property repairs
The majority of the repairs are done in the least busy times – February and November.

Equipment maintenance
Equipment maintenance is paid monthly on various contracts, plus occasional small repairs.

Insurance
Insurance is paid annually in June. The cover and premium will increase when the fitness centre is built.

Transport
The business owns three vehicles. The tax and insurance are paid in June.

Advertising
Most advertising is done through the tourist board, and is paid in October each year for the following season. Further newspaper advertising is carried out in February and March. There will be additional local advertising for the opening of the new fitness centre.

Professional fees
This consists mainly of the accountancy fees.

Bank charges
These are charged quarterly.

Finance charges
These are payments on an existing hire purchase contract.

Dividends
These will be payable in March.

Tax
This is payable in September on the profits of the previous year.

Accommodation income 300,000
Adjust – deposits received in advance
        at beginning of year   – 30,000
        at end of year   40,000
                       £310,000

Health and fitness centre 8,000
Adjust – income in advance 2,000
                       £10,000

	Per Figure 9.3	Adjust opening creditor	Adjust closing creditor	Adjust opening prepay	Adjust closing prepay	Adjust non-cash item	TOTAL
Expenses							
Food costs	50,000	3,000	– 3,500				49,500
Drinks costs	25,000	1,500	– 1,700				24,800
Sundry purchases	15,000	1,000	– 1,200				14,800
Wages	60,000	1,000	– 1,200				59,800
Directors' salaries	80,000	800	– 1,000				79,800
Cleaning	10,000	500	– 600				9,900
Laundry	6,000	400	– 400				6,000
Rates and water	15,000			– 1,200	1,400		15,200
Light and heat	12,000	1,100	– 1,200				11,900
Property repairs	8,000	500	– 800				7,700
Equipment maintenance	6,000	400	– 500				5,900
Insurance	8,000			– 3,000	4,000		9,000
Transport	10,000			– 1,000	900		9,900
Advertising	9,000			– 1,000	1,400		9,400
Professional fees	5,000	4,500	– 5,000				4,500
Sundry expenses	2,500						2,500
Bank charges	3,000						3,000
Loan interest	4,000					– 4,000	0
Finance charges	4,800						4,800
Depreciation	20,000					– 20,000	0
Tax	60,000						60,000
Dividends	20,000						20,000
TOTALS	433,300	14,700	– 17,100	– 6,200	7,700	– 24,000	408,400

Figure 9.5 Adjustments to profit and loss figures from Figure 9.3

By the end of this chapter, you should be able to:

▶ understand the various terms used in connection with raising loan capital,
▶ have a good grasp of the issues of capital structure and gearing,
▶ appreciate the advantages or disadvantages of each type of finance, and
▶ understand where grants and leasing could be applicable.

Introduction

In this chapter we look at the sources of loan capital and short-term finance available to businesses. We introduce the concept of capital structure, and the effect of the gearing ratio. We examine ways of raising long-term and short-term finance, and also look at two areas closely related to loan finance – grants, and leasing.

Gearing and capital structure

Capital structure refers to the relationship between equity capital and loan capital. Gearing is a key measure of a company's financial structure, referring to the relative proportions of equity capital and loan capital. If the proportion of loan capital to equity capital is high, the company is said to be high geared. Generally, the dividing line between high and low geared companies can be taken as 50%.

EXAMPLE 10.1

XYZ plc

Equity capital	£ 5,000,000
Loan capital	£15,000,000
Total capital	£20,000,000

The gearing is the loan capital (£15,000,000) expressed as a percentage of the total capital (£20,000,000). This works out as 75%, and is high geared. If the figures were reversed, and the loan capital were £5,000,000, the gearing would be 25%.

The significance of high gearing is that if profits increase, the amount of loan interest paid remains the same, and the profit available to the equity shareholders increases. This effect is much more marked in a high geared company than in a low geared company.

EXAMPLE 10.2

High geared company

Profits before interest charges	£5,000,000
Interest charges on loan capital of £15,000,000 at 10%	£1,500,000
Balance of profit for equity shareholders (nominal £5,000,000)	£3,500,000

The return to equity shareholders is 70% on the nominal share capital.

Low geared company

Profits before interest charges	£5,000,000
Interest charges on loan capital of £5,000,000 at 10%	£500,000
Balance of profit for equity shareholders (nominal £15,000,000)	£4,500,000

This time, the return to equity shareholders is 30% on the nominal share capital.

Thus, with high gearing, the risks and rewards are potentially greater for the equity shareholders. This is shown when the profits are lower.

EXAMPLE 10.3

High geared company

Profits before interest charges	£1,000,000
Interest charges on loan capital of £15,000,000 at 10%	£1,500,000
Loss	£500,000

Low geared company

Profits before interest charges	£1,000,000
Interest charges on loan capital of £5,000,000 at 10%	£500,000
Balance of profit for shareholders (nominal £15,000,000)	£500,000

This time the contrast is between a loss, which means no returns for the equity shareholders, and a profit. Although the profit return on equity capital is only 3.3%, it is at least a profit.

The structure of a company's capital is therefore the division between the shareholders, who are the members of the company, and the lenders, who are creditors of the company. Interest paid on loan capital is deductible from the company's profits for tax purposes, whereas dividend payments are not. They have to be paid out of profits.

Term matching

A sound financial principle is that of matching the term of any form of loan or borrowing as far as possible to the expected life of the asset or project which it finances.

EXAMPLES 10.4

- The purchase of freehold property is financed by a mortgage secured on that property.
- Renting premises also remains a viable option in certain circumstances – particularly where a project may require premises of some sort – say, for retail sales – but the project life is uncertain.
- Financing general working capital is best done by bank overdraft facilities.
- Factoring or invoice discounting is the most suitable method of financing book debts.
- Purchase of fixed assets other than freehold property can be done by loans from banks or other sources.
- Hire purchase or finance leases are other ways of financing fixed assets such as equipment or vehicles.

Raising long-term loan capital

Loan capital is provided by lenders who loan money to the company on terms set out in the contract between the company and themselves.

EXERCISE 10.1

What are the principal differences between equity capital and loan capital?

Risk

As we have seen, lenders have a prior claim on the assets of the company, and to that extent, their risk is lower than shareholders' risk. However, there is always a certain degree of risk inherent in investing money in a company, in whatever form.

Independent credit-rating agencies, such as Moody's or Standard and Poor, make assessments of the risk categories of loan capital of companies. Their categorisations follow similar lines to each other – from AAA (Standard and Poor) or Aaa (Moody's) to C (both companies). The triple A rating indicates the lowest risk, and the C rating indicates the greatest risk. In this context, the risk being assessed is the risk of interest payments not being made, and the repayment of the capital being defaulted on. The common name given to the lower risk grades is 'junk bonds'.

In order to compensate for the degree of risk, the interest rate offered on higher risk loans is generally higher than that offered on the least risky loans.

Security

If there is a risk element, it is natural that investors should seek some form of security for the money they have invested. This is frequently achieved by the lenders having a charge over the assets of the company, which means a legal right to use those assets to satisfy their debt.

Charges

There are two types of charge:

- Fixed charge. The lenders have a charge over specific assets of the company.
- Floating charge. The lenders' charge over the assets is not related to any specific assets, but 'floats' over the assets generally. If the company defaults on payment of interest or capital the charge 'crystallises'. When this happens, the lenders have the right to seize any assets and sell them to repay their loans.

Assets over which a charge is held should be easily realisable, non-perishable, and have a high value in relation to their size.

EXERCISE 10.2

What type of assets would best suit these criteria?

Loan covenants

A further form of security is provided by covenants (that is, conditions) written in to the loan contract. These impose certain obligations on the company, giving additional security to the lenders.

EXERCISE 10.3

What covenants might give extra security to lenders?

Personal guarantees

In some circumstances, lenders may seek personal guarantees from directors or owners of the company, or from some third party. This type of security is most applicable to private companies (see the distinction between private and public companies in Chapter 11).

Types of loan capital

A company may raise its loan capital in different forms.

Subordinated loans

- A company may issue different classes of loans or bonds.
- The rights of some classes, while still ranking above shareholders, may be subordinated to a higher class of loans or bonds.
- Subordinated bonds are thus seen to be of a slightly higher risk than the 'senior' loans, and would therefore be expected to carry a higher rate of interest.

Debentures

- Debentures are a form of loan established by a trust deed.
- Debentures normally carry a fixed and/or floating charge over some or all assets of the company.
- For publicly quoted companies, debentures are often quoted on the Stock Market.

Redeemable or irredeemable loans

- Redeemable loans have a fixed date on which they are repayable. The repayment is usually at par (that is, the nominal amount at which they were issued).
- Irredeemable loans have no fixed date for repayment, but can often be traded on the Stock Market.

Bearer bonds

- If a loan is issued on a bearer bond, the holder is not registered with the company. However, the holder of the bond is regarded as the owner, and coupons attached to the bonds give the right to receive the interest, which is often paid annually.

Eurobonds

- This term refers to loan capital issued by large companies that wish to raise their capital on the international market.
- They are often bearer bonds, and usually issued in a different currency from the currency of the home base of the company.
- Eurobonds are often sold to large banks or other financial institutions which either hold them as their own investments or sell them to their own clients.

Deep discount bonds

- This is a form of issuing redeemable loan capital which allows the company to offer a lower rate of interest than usual.
- It compensates for this by offering the bonds at a discount to the nominal value at which they are to be repaid.

EXAMPLE 10.5

> A company may issue a deep discount bond with a fixed life of 15 years, at an initial price of 85% of the redemption value. That is, the bonds are offered at £85 for every £100 nominal value. In simple terms, this means that there is one per cent of added capital value for every year of the life of the bonds, and the interest rate can be one per cent lower to compensate for this.

Investors may often be attracted to this form of bond, because of its tax treatment.

Convertible loans

A convertible loan gives the lender the option to convert the loan to equity shares at a fixed price at specified future dates. The lender remains a creditor of the company until conversion takes place. If the lenders convert the loan into shares, they become members of the company, with the same rights and risks as other shareholders of the same class of shares. Conversion to shares is not compulsory, so the lender only takes advantage of the conversion rights if the share price at the conversion dates are above the conversion price.

From the investor's point of view, this offers a good opportunity to participate in any future increase in the value of the shares of the company.

From the company's point of view, it can:

- economise on the costs of redemption,
- use this method to reduce its gearing, and
- offer lower rates of interest on convertible loans.

As against these benefits, the conversion of a large amount of loan could dilute the control and possibly the future earnings of shareholders.

Warrants

- Warrants are instruments by which the holder has the right (not the obligation) to buy shares in the company at a fixed price at specified future dates.
- The warrants do not give the right to any other benefit from the company, and no interest is paid on them. In a sense, they represent a form of gamble by the investor that the share price will be favourable at the specified future dates.
- This method is one way in which the company can raise capital with no immediate cost (in the form of interest payments). The cost comes later.
- Warrants are sometimes issued in conjunction with loan capital, and sometimes to existing shareholders on the basis of their present holding.

Mortgages

- A mortgage is a loan secured on the security of freehold property.
- Normally, mortgages are provided by large financial institutions, and they have strict conditions applied.
- Mortgages are usually very long-term lending, and raised for the purpose of acquiring or improving the property on which the loan is secured.

Raising short-term finance

Overdrafts

The general rule of term matching dictates that an overdraft facility should not be used for long-term finance, or financing a specific asset. An overdraft is normally used for financing working capital, and this is its traditional use. Bank managers will not often agree to a business overdraft for other purposes.

The cost of an overdraft is usually more than for a loan, in terms of its interest rate, and of the annual review and arrangement fee. However, because of the nature of an overdraft, its overall cost can be less than a loan. The amount of an overdraft varies from day to day, as the balance on the account is used for paying bills and receives money paid in. The interest on an overdraft is calculated on a daily basis on the amount of overdraft that is actually used. Thus, the business may have an overdraft facility for, say, £50,000. However, during the course of its business, its account balance may be anywhere up to that limit (and occasionally beyond it). Its account may even go into the 'black', and have a balance in it rather than being overdrawn.

The interest on an overdraft is calculated on whatever the balance is on a daily basis, not the amount of the facility. Thus, interest is only charged on the amount of the facility which is actually used. A loan is for a fixed term, with fixed repayments, and the interest is charged on the whole amount outstanding, according to the agreement.

Factoring and invoice discounting

Factoring and invoice discounting are two forms of providing finance based on the value of book debts. They work in essentially the same way. The business assigns its book debts to the finance company. The finance company provides a proportion (typically 80%) of the value of all invoices by payment as soon as the invoices are raised and sent to customers. When the customers pay the invoices, the business receives the rest of the value of the invoices, less the finance company's charges.

The essential difference between factoring and invoice discounting is that the factoring company takes over the administration of the sales ledger for the business. Invoice discounters do not do this. For that reason, the charges for factoring are more than for invoice discounting. For the same reason, invoice discounters will generally only take on businesses with a larger turnover, unless they have confidence in the quality of sales ledger administration. Smaller businesses therefore are more likely to find factors to provide finance in this way. Certain businesses, such as builders, are excluded from this form of finance.

Different types of factoring and invoice discounting

Factored finance is provided in two ways:

- *Recourse arrangements*, in which bad debts are recovered against money advanced to the business.

- *Non-recourse arrangements*, in which the finance company agrees to absorb any bad debts. Naturally, this type of arrangement is more expensive than recourse.

Invoice discounting comes in two types:

- *Confidential invoice discounting*. Because the invoice discounter does not take over the administration of the sales ledger, there is no need for the business's customers to know of its existence.
- *Disclosed invoice discounting*. In this case, an 'assignment notice' is printed on the invoices. This is a statement that the debts of the business have been assigned to the invoice discounter. The customers pay the invoice discounting company. If the invoice discounters do not have as much confidence in the business's administration, they may insist on disclosed invoice discounting.

Suitability

Factoring or invoice discounting is particularly suitable for rapidly expanding businesses. As a business expands, the working capital requirement expands, as the gap between current assets and current liabilities becomes greater. In fact, this period of expansion can lead to overtrading. Cash becomes squeezed, and the business cannot pay its debts on time. Many businesses have failed because of this.

This is caused by either insufficient control over the elements of working capital, or lack of planning for this vital growth stage. The lack of control can arise through administrative systems or staff not being able to cope adequately with the greater volume of stock, work in progress, and debtors generated during a period of rapid growth. The lack of planning can happen when management fails to foresee the growth, or does not plan specifically for it. The growth then takes them by surprise. They over-commit the resources of the business and find themselves unable to cope.

This type of finance is also sometimes seen in management buy outs, to provide an additional tranche of finance so that it reduces the reliance on other finance. It can be part of a more flexible financing structure.

Operational details

Factors and invoice discounters will vet client businesses before taking them on, and then check their procedures and administration regularly. As well as the administration, they will be looking for such things as the way in which the business relates to its customers, including the level of customer complaints, and the frequency of issue of credit notes. The larger the business, and when the service is invoice discounting, the finance company will carry out a review, akin to a full audit, of the business. They are also more likely not to take on a client business until it has an established track record, and shows a sound financial position on its balance sheet.

Choosing a finance company to carry out this service need not be onerous. The Factors and Discounters Association is the professional body for this type of finance. Their website at www.factors.org.uk is a good starting point.

Costs and benefits

The cost of the basic service is the finance charge. This is usually a percentage charge tied to the base rate. A typical charge would be 3% over base rate, but this may be negotiated, on the basis of perceived risk. Thus, typically, the rate is higher for factoring, because the businesses are usually smaller, and perceived as higher risk.

The second element of the charge is the administration fee. Because factoring involves administration of the sales ledger, this fee will be higher for factoring. Against this, factoring can be helpful to a smaller business as it frees up management time for more creative and strategic matters.

Benefits
- The main benefit is the immediate cash injection.
- In addition, growing businesses will receive increasing finance as the value of the debtors in their sales ledger increases.
- This finance facility grows with the business.
- There is no restriction of the way the cash generated in this way can be used.

Disadvantages
- Apart from the cost, the major concern of client businesses is the loss of control, particularly with factoring.
- Smaller businesses in particular fear that the finance company may adopt a tougher stance on chasing slow paying customers, with the attendant risk of losing those customers.
- A similar concern is that the finance company will impose lower credit limits on customers' accounts. This is particularly noticeable with non-recourse finance.
- The finance company accepting bad debt risk will enforce credit controls, including setting lower credit limits, much more tightly than one with a recourse agreement.
- External misconception is also sometimes considered as a drawback. A possible perception of factoring and disclosed invoice discounting finance is that it is a source of 'last resort' finance. The business using this type of finance may therefore be suspected of being in financial difficulties. However, this misconception was commoner in the earlier days of this type of financing, and is fast disappearing.

Bills of exchange

A bill of exchange is a written agreement requiring the person to whom it is addressed to pay a specified sum at a future specified date. This form of finance is sometimes used by a customer to pay a supplier of goods. The supplier may keep the bill of exchange until it matures, or discount it. Discounting consists of accepting payment of the amount of the bill, less a discount factor. An institution such as a bank is the discounter, and that institution keeps the bill until it matures, then presents it to the payer.

This method is not commonly used within the UK presently, but is more widespread in overseas trading.

Finance leases and hire purchase

These are alternative methods of financing the purchase of an asset. Although the substance of the transaction is the same, the form is different. Under these schemes, the legal ownership of the asset remains with the finance company, and under the contract, the borrower is only actually hiring or leasing the asset until it is paid for.

We saw in Chapter 3 that one of the fundamental principles of financial reporting is 'substance over form'. Thus, the substance of the transaction of a finance lease is that the buyer is obtaining finance to buy the asset. Therefore, this must be reflected in the financial statements, by showing the asset in the balance sheet, and the borrowing as a liability.

In contrast, the substance of an 'operating lease' is that the lessor actually retains long-term ownership of the asset (usually land or property) and the lessee pays a periodic charge for the temporary use of it. This is shown in the financial statements of the company by a rent or leasing charge as a deduction from profits, as part of the overheads or direct costs.

Finance leases are a popular way of raising finance for specific assets, for several reasons:

- They are flexible. Cancellation clauses can provide for updating the equipment concerned where technology and change is an important factor.
- The finance cost is often reasonable, because the asset itself is the security for the loan.
- The cash outflow is spread over the life of the asset.
- Lease finance can be obtained more readily than other forms of finance – partly because it is usually for lower amounts, and partly because the security means that the leasing company does not have to require such stringent credit checks as other forms of lending.

Sale and leaseback

This involves the company selling an asset to a finance company, and at the same time entering into an agreement to lease the asset back under an operating lease. This is often done with freehold property, since it is the most valuable asset available, and can release a large amount of cash.

As the arrangement is an operating lease, all payments under it will be tax deductible.

Disadvantages of sale and leaseback include the fact that a liability to Capital Gains Tax may arise on the sale of the asset. More significantly, the company has given up any future appreciation in the capital value of the asset.

Grants

Grants may be available from several sources. The obvious advantage of grants is, of course, that they do not have to be repaid. However, there are usually strings of some sort attached. Many of the grants available are aimed at small and medium sized enterprises (SMEs). A summary of grants available is shown on the companion website.

▣ ⍓ **11** Equity capital

LEARNING OUTCOMES

By the end of this chapter, you should be able to:

▶ differentiate between the various types of equity capital,
▶ appreciate the role of venture capitalists, and
▶ understand the arguments relating to the effect of dividend policy.

Introduction

The backbone of any company's finance is its share capital. In this chapter we look at the types of equity capital sources for a company, and the relationship of equity capital to dividend policy. We also look at issues of retaining control in private companies, and repaying capital to shareholders.

Share capital

Ordinary shares

The ordinary share capital of a company is its financial lifeblood. The ordinary shares represent the investment in the business of people who are willing to take commercial risks. The liability of shareholders for company debts is limited to the amount they have invested in the company. Historically, limited liability provided the boost needed for investment in businesses, and provided the growth potential for the industrial revolution.

Ordinary shareholders form the bulk of the membership of the company, and they control the company by their votes. The management of the company is delegated to directors, who are answerable to the shareholders.

Ordinary shareholders can only receive dividends out of any profits left after the prior claims of other investors including loan creditors and preference shareholders.

Preference shares

As the name suggests, preference shares have a prior claim on the profits and assets of the company. They rank before ordinary shares in paying dividends, and in the distribution of assets in the case of the winding up of the company.

They therefore present a lower risk profile, and the returns are correspondingly lower. Typically, preference shares carry the right to a fixed dividend, which is usually cumulative. Thus, if the company is unable to pay the preference dividend in any year, it is rolled over to the following year.

There are different types of preference shares.

Participating preference shares

These shares give preference shareholders the right to participate in the variable dividend paid to ordinary shareholders after their fixed dividend has been paid.

Redeemable preference shares

These shares have a fixed repayment date. Because of this factor, they are seen as a lower risk investment and therefore carry a lower rate of fixed dividend.

Convertible preference shares

These shares carry the right to convert into ordinary shares at a fixed price at specified future dates. They work in a similar way to convertible loan stocks seen in the previous chapter.

Deferred shares

Some companies issue deferred shares, which rank after ordinary shares in the 'pecking order'. Because of this, the risk profile is higher, and investors in deferred shares would expect a greater reward.

Capital markets

In order for a company to be able to raise money from the general public, it must first be a public limited company (plc), rather than a private company (ltd). However, there must also be a mechanism to enable the company to raise the new capital it needs, and for shareholders to sell or buy shares. In this section we will look at these markets, and consider the efficiency of capital markets in fulfilling this function.

In the UK, the markets which exist to fulfil this requirement are the London Stock Exchange, the Alternative Investments Market (AIM), and the Unlisted Securities Market (USM). Although similar principles apply to the other two markets, we will concentrate our studies on the Stock Exchange. Its functions are:

1. To provide a *primary* market for companies to raise new capital. This is done by companies using the market to make new share issues (see further details below), or issues of new debenture or loan stocks.
2. To provide a *secondary* market for investors to buy or sell their shares to other investors.

In order for a company's shares to be traded on the Stock Exchange, it must first meet fairly stringent requirements relating to the size of the company, its past profit history, disclosure of information and so on. In addition, there are continuing requirements to issue regular information, and the disclosure requirements are more strict than those of the Companies Act and accounting standards.

Once a company is listed, analysts employed by stockbrokers, and financial journalists, will closely monitor its activities. The degree of scrutiny it suffers may not always be welcome, but is an inevitable consequence of a listing.

Capital market efficiency

The term 'efficiency' in relation to capital markets does not mean the administrative organisation of the Stock Exchange or any other market. It indicates whether the share price quoted on that market accurately reflects the true value of those shares, taking into account all relevant information.

To be perfectly efficient, a capital market would exhibit the following features:

- There would be no cost involved in issuing or trading shares,
- There would be no difference in the ability to raise capital no matter what quantities were involved.
- Investors would have complete and perfect knowledge of all the company's future prospects.
- Investors would only invest in companies for financial motives. (Think of football fans investing in their local football club.)
- All relevant information about a company would be immediately available to and acted upon by investors.

There have been studies on stock market behaviour, which pinpoint some ways in which the behaviour of share prices does not seem to operate in a perfectly logical way. Why, for example, do Mondays show an above average fall in share prices? Why is it more possible to profit by buying shares at the beginning of April, then sell them at the end of April? Why do smaller companies tend to produce a higher yield on shares than larger companies? Why do shares with a lower price–earnings ratio tend to outperform shares with a higher price–earnings ratio (the opposite of what might logically be expected)?

These studies indicate that markets are driven by human beings, liable to non-rational behaviour. This reinforces the fact that there can never be a perfectly efficient market. However, the Stock Exchange provides as near as we can humanly get to that.

Issuing shares

A company may raise equity capital in different ways, dependent on whether it is a public company or a private company. A private company may raise equity capital by the participators in the company – often a small number of people, perhaps members of the same family – buying shares privately. Public companies have ways to make public offers (see below).

Issue price and share premiums

Shares may be issued at their face value, which is known as the nominal value of the shares. Thus, shares are designated by their class and their nominal value, for example, 'Ordinary shares of 25p'.

However, shares may be issued at a premium. That is to say, the shareholder pays more than the nominal value of the shares. The company must account for this premium, and hold it in a special account, which may only be used for certain restricted purposes.

EXERCISE 11.2

A company offers 1 million shares for sale, with a nominal value of £1 each, at a price of £1.50 each. What will be its total receipts if it sells all the shares offered, and how will it account for those proceeds?

A public company may make a public offer of its shares.

Public offers

The mechanism is that the company makes an offer of sale of its shares by advertisement in newspapers, and publication of a prospectus. This sets out details of the shares on offer, and various other relevant details of the company's finances, including, crucially, the reason for the issue of shares to raise money. The company itself sets the price, and takes the risks of the issue.

EXERCISE 11.3

What risk do you think there is in making a public offer for sale?

Underwriting

In making an issue of shares, a company will often have the issue underwritten, to minimise the risk.

This means that an exterior organisation, either stockbrokers or merchant bankers, act as the 'issuing house', which publishes the prospectus, and arranges for institutional investors, such as pension funds or insurance companies, to guarantee to buy any shares not taken up by the general public or the existing shareholders. This incurs a fee, payable to the underwriting institution. In practice, the institution passes on a proportion of this fee to the institutional or private investors who have agreed to take the risk of buying the shares.

Issue by tender

This is another way of making a public issue of shares. The public is invited to make bids to offer to buy a specified number of shares at a price which the buyer offers. When the deadline for bids has passed, the company works out the right price, known as the striking price, to raise the money it requires from all the bids received, taking into account the quantities and prices bid for. All offers received below the striking price will be rejected, and all offers at or above the striking price accepted at the striking price.

Rights and scrip issues

Rights issues

Rights issues are made to raise additional capital, as described in Appendix 2. This method provides a relatively cheap way for a company to raise more equity capital. The risk is less than in making a public issue because the existing shareholders are more likely to take up the rights issue offer. The rights certificate may be sold, and the value of this can be calculated by reference to the existing share price and the offer price of the new shares.

EXERCISE 11.4

> Shares in XYZ plc are currently valued at £2 each. The company makes a rights issue offer to existing shareholders of 1 new share for every 1 share owned, at a price of £1.80 each. Calculate the value of the rights certificate if the shareholder does not wish to take up the rights.

There is a risk involved in making a rights issue, however. The risk is based on the fact that, for a rights issue to be successful, the offer price cannot be higher than the currently-quoted share price. Otherwise, the shareholder would have no incentive to take up the rights issue. The company therefore has to make the offer sufficiently attractive, by offering the shares at a discount. The risk is that during the inevitable time gap between the offer price being decided, and the final date for acceptance of the offer, the share price might have fallen below the offer price.

Scrip issues

Scrip issues (also known as bonus issues) are issues of free new shares to existing shareholders, and are often useful in expanding companies when the company wishes to make its shares more marketable.

A scrip issue simply increases the number of shares in issue, so the market price will fall correspondingly. Thus, if the scrip issue was 1 for 1, the number of shares in issue will double, and the price would be expected to halve. However, the reason for the issue is often that the share price is becoming too high. Thus, for example, one share priced at £10 is harder to sell than two shares priced at £5 each. Therefore, although in theory, the market capitalisation should not change, the company's shares often become more marketable.

However, it often happens that scrip issues are made by expanding companies, and are accompanied by dividend increases. The share price after a scrip issue therefore often performs better than before.

From the company's viewpoint, making a scrip issue transfers money out of reserves into paid-up share capital of the company. This means that reserves that were previously distributable are now not distributable. Although this may not seem to be a positive signal, in fact it tends to generate confidence amongst potential investors, and lenders see this as a boost to the confidence in the company, because the larger the equity base of the company, the less risk exposure there is to lenders.

Classes of shares and retaining control

We have touched on the difference between private and public companies. As long as a company remains a private company, the owners of the shares (often members of a family) can exercise effective control. Once it 'goes public', however, that control is diluted or lost. In between there is often a stage where the original owners wish to retain control, but need to raise more capital than they can afford privately.

Issues of different classes of shares can often accomplish this. Restricted or non-voting shares can be issued. Thus, there could be 'A' shares, 'B' shares, and so on, with theoretically no limit to the number of classes of shares.

This way, dividends can be declared at different rates for each class of share. This method is often used when a patriarchal figure who started a company wishes his children to take over the company. He can issue different classes of shares to his children, with restricted voting rights, so that he retains control of the decisions, and decides what dividends to pay on each class of shares. When he judges the time is right, he can sell some of his shares to his children, to give them some of the control and voting rights.

Repaying capital to shareholders

There may be occasions when a company has surplus cash which it wishes to return to its shareholders. There are several ways of doing this.

1. Buying its own shares on the stock market. This involves paying the going rate for the shares.

2. Buying shares from its shareholders by private agreement. This can involve repurchasing the shares from the shareholders as a whole, or from certain classes or groups.
3. Making a tender offer to all shareholders. This involves offering to buy the shares at a specified price within a certain period.

Repurchasing shares involves their cancellation after they have been repurchased.

EXERCISE 11.5

What consequences might there be for the company and for shareholders of repurchase of its shares?

Special dividends

An alternative method of returning cash to shareholders is by way of a special dividend.

EXERCISE 11.6

What consequences may there be of paying a special dividend, especially if the dividend is much more than the normal dividend?

Venture capital

This form of finance consists of funding provided, by a bank or other type of institutional investor, in return for a stake in the business. In this way, it becomes a partner in the business, taking risks and reaping rewards. The venture capitalist does not usually take an active part in managing the business, although it can often provide advice through long experience of this sort of financing. It also often provides valuable contacts and inside knowledge.

Who are venture capitalists?

The main providers of venture capital in the UK are firms funded by institutions such as pension funds, insurance companies or banks. They invest primarily in private or unquoted companies. The British Venture Capitalist Association represents the vast majority of the firms in this field.

Types of venture capital

Venture capitalists identify different stages of business development for which they would be prepared to consider providing finance. Because of the differing needs of each stage, their approach varies according to the stage. The stages of business life were seen in Chapter 8, and the varying types of finance required.

Criteria

Venture capitalists put significant amounts of money into what could potentially be a business risk. They therefore wish to satisfy themselves of several things before they invest their money.

- *Market potential.* The potential of the project for which capital is required will be investigated thoroughly. If there is no prospect of the project becoming marketable and a commercial success, they will not risk their money. If they see the opportunity to create a new market by an innovative new product or service, they are more likely to support that project, than one which aims at penetrating an existing market where there are competitors.
- *Management* Venture capitalists will examine thoroughly the management team, its experience and skills. They must decide whether they think the management can carry through the project to achieve the objective.

The business seeking venture capital must make out a strong, convincing case, with business plans, for the project. We saw in Chapter 9 the contents of a business plan, and the following essential elements should be covered:

- The ideals and strategy of the business.
- The management skills and experience of the personnel involved.
- The management structure, and how the project may modify this.
- The market in which the business operates, with strengths and weaknesses of the competitors.
- The commercial viability of the product or service, with details of market research carried out.
- The prospects of growth of demand for the product or service.
- The nature and amount of the funding required.

Venture capitalists' involvement

Once the money has been invested, the venture capitalist will monitor the business regularly, but not become involved in the day-to-day management of the business. Their involvement means that management will be much more answerable to them. Besides sharing in profits, the venture capitalist will be interested in the methods and accountability of the management team.

The business obtaining venture capital must submit regular management accounts to the venture capitalist, and be subject to monitoring visits. This involvement should not be seen as a disadvantage. The venture capitalist, in seeking to protect his investment, will also be working for the benefit of the business, and any advice should be viewed in a constructive light.

Incentives

There are certain tax incentives to venture capital, and these are detailed on the companion website.

Dividend policy

Equity capital has a cost, and this cost is the dividends paid on the shares. However, dividends do not generally distribute the whole of the profit. Management of companies has to decide a policy on dividend distribution.

The dividend policy pursued by a company can have a radical effect on the value of shares – whether the company is quoted on the Stock Exchange or not. This at least is the traditional view, but it has been challenged in academic circles. The conflicting views are examined here, but the first important point to make is that the prime aim of management is to increase shareholders' wealth. We saw this principle in Chapter 7, in the section on total shareholder value. The evidence is that managers of companies *perceive* that a company's dividend policy is important in improving the wealth of shareholders.

The nature of dividends

Before we look at the arguments, let us recap on the nature of dividends. They represent the return on shareholders' investment in the company's business. As such, shareholders expect a reward for taking risks.

Company law imposes limits on the amount of money that can be distributed as dividends.

- *Private companies* may only distribute *realised* profits.
- *Public companies* may distribute profits, whether they have been realised or not. However, these profits must be calculated in accordance with generally accepted accounting principles.

Dividend cover

Let us recap on the subject of dividend cover. This term refers to the difference between the amount of profits made and the amount distributed as dividends. The 'cover' is expressed as a multiple of the dividends distributed.

EXERCISE 11.7

> XYZ Ltd makes a profit of £500,000. Its issued share capital is £1 million. It declares a dividend for the year of 20p for each share. Calculate the dividend cover.

Companies usually strive to maintain a good level of dividend cover – that is, they do not usually distribute all of their profit.

EXERCISE 11.8

> Why do you think this is?

Let us look at an example of how a greater level of dividend cover affects the ability of companies to continue to pay dividends.

> Two companies, ABC Ltd and XYZ Ltd, both make a profit in their first year of trading of £500,000. They both have issued share capital of £1 million. Company ABC Ltd declares a dividend of 50p per share, and company XYZ Ltd declares a dividend of 20p per share.
>
> The following year, they both make profits of £350,000. What will be the effect of this on the ability to pay dividends?

The form of dividends

The usual expectation is that dividends will be distributed in the form of cash. In theory, however, they could be distributed in any form. A chain of supermarkets, for example, could distribute profits in the form of groceries to its shareholders. However, this is not seen in practice, and would be impracticable.

Sometimes, however, profits are distributed in a different form to cash. The most common form of alternative payment is extra shares in the company, known as a scrip dividend.

Conflicting views on dividend policy

The traditional view

The traditional view on dividend policy is that shareholders invest to increase their wealth. This is done in two ways – by regular payments of dividends, and by increase in the value of the shares.

Further, the value of shares is seen to be dependent to a large extent on the payment of dividends. The dividends influence the share value in two ways:

1. The actual amounts paid as dividends, in absolute terms, have an obvious effect. Thus, if one company pays a dividend of 6p per share, and another pays a dividend of 5p per share, in circumstances that were in all other respects the same, the share which had the higher dividend would be of more value.
2. Perhaps more importantly, the share value is influenced by the pattern of dividends. The shares of a company with a history of steadily increasing dividends, even if that increase is unspectacular, will have a greater value than the shares of a company whose dividends fluctuate, and are seen to be unreliable.

The traditional view (seen in Chapter 8, when considering the valuation of shares in takeovers or mergers) is that dividend policy has an effect on share value. This should perhaps be qualified by the observation that unwarranted increases in dividend payouts lead to insufficient retained profit, in turn leading to an adverse effect on future profits. Analysts of businesses would therefore take this into account, and the share value correspondingly discounted.

This traditional view could be summarised by the saying:

▶ A bird in the hand is worth two in the bush.

In other words, an investor prefers to receive a certain £1 now, as dividend, rather than £2 at some time in the future. The future always involves a degree of uncertainty. Thus, greater dividends now should increase the value of the shares.

The consequence for management

This view leads inevitably to the conclusion that, as future dividends will be discounted in relation to present dividends, the task of management is to maximise shareholders' worth, and therefore dividend payouts as far as consistent with prudent retention of profits for investment in the business.

The alternative view

The traditional view has been challenged by certain modern theorists in the field of economic and management theory. This view is most associated with the work of two academics, Modigliani and Miller.

The alternative theory states that, *in conditions of a perfectly efficient market*, the value of a share will not be affected by the company's dividend policy. This is because the value of shares is solely affected by the result of the investment projects which a company undertakes. This value will remain constant, regardless of the relative levels of dividends paid and profits retained. Under this theory, the lowering of the share value produced by the lowering of dividend payout is compensated by the increase in the value of the company as a whole resulting from the investment of the retained profits in profitable projects. Research has demonstrated that there is no significant correlation between dividends and share values.

Under this alternative view, shareholders could adjust the monies they receive in two ways:

1. If the dividend payout is low, the value of the shares should increase in value. Therefore the shareholder can cash in part of the shareholding to compensate for the low dividend, and be left with the same value in the remaining shares.
2. If the dividend payout is high, and the shareholders do not need all of it, they can plough back the excess dividend by buying more shares.

In either case, the shareholder's total value remains the same.

The consequence for management

If the task of management under the traditional view was to maximise the dividend payout, what is the consequence under this alternative view?

If the dividend policy has no effect on total shareholder wealth, management should be indifferent to the level of dividend payout. Their task should be to discover and actively to manage the most profitable investment projects.

Caveats

The alternative view, based on economic theory, is now widely accepted. However, there are two important caveats.

1. As highlighted above, it depends on a perfectly efficient capital market. In practice, capital markets are not perfectly efficient, due in part to the costs of issuing and trading in shares. Therefore, to that extent, the theory does not describe the real world.
2. There is the effect of taxation. The alternative theory assumes a world with no taxation. In practice, tax rules have a significant effect on the preferences and behaviour of shareholders. For example, it is generally preferable to have increases in wealth taxed under Capital Gains Tax rules rather than Income Tax rules. Therefore, it is seen as preferable to a certain extent to take profits in the form of increases in share values rather than in the form of dividends. The position is further complicated, however, by tax incentives, including such things as Enterprise Investment Schemes (EIS), Venture Capital Trusts (VCT), and Individual Savings Accounts (ISA).

◼ ▾ Appendix I Useful websites

The companion website

The companion website for this book is at **www.palgrave.com/masterseries/whiteley**
It contains much additional practical and useful information, in particular about the following subjects:

- Rewarding employees and share scheme incentives
- Reporting requirements of the Companies Act 1985
- Accounting Standards
- Types of business insurance
- Tax compliance and planning
- Individual and partnership self assessment
- Corporation tax self assessment
- PAYE – a summary
- VAT danger areas
- Stamp Duty – a summary
- Bankruptcy and liquidation principles, and small claims in the County Court
- Credit card trading
- Self diagnosis credit control health check
- Incentives for venture capital

Government bodies

Business Link   **www.businesslink.org**

This is an official government body, but the website is packed full of useful tips, information, links, and advice. It is one of the most useful of all government sites for the self-employed.

Companies House   **www.companieshouse.gov.uk**

This is the central registration agency for all limited companies.

Customs and Excise   **www.hmce.gov.uk**

This is the site of Customs and Excise, which administers VAT. A whole section of the site is devoted to VAT matters.

Department of Trade and Industry   www.dti.gov.uk

This is the government department dealing with all matters relating to trade and industry. It is more relevant to bigger businesses, but you may find some parts of the site useful.

Department for Work and Pensions   www.dwp.gov.uk

This is the name of the new department, since June 2001, dealing with work, family and pensions. Contributions for Social Security are now dealt with by the Inland Revenue.

Inland Revenue   www.inlandrevenue.gov.uk

This site is very useful, and gives a lot of helpful advice for the self-employed, as well as general tax advice.

Insolvency Service   www.insolvency.gov.uk

Easy-to-use site from the government's official insolvency service.

Office of Fair Trading   www.oft.gov.uk

This is the site of the Office of Fair Trading, dealing with all aspects of consumer regulation and law. Its slogan is 'Protecting customers; encouraging competition'.

Serious Fraud Office   www.sfo.gov.uk

The Serious Fraud Office is the government body dealing with fraud and has links to international fraud prevention organisations.

Other official and semi-official bodies

Advertising Standards Authority   www.asa.org.uk

This body is the watchdog for advertising complaints.

Association of British Insurers   www.abi.org.uk

This is the body representing British insurance companies.

Association of Chartered Certified Accountants   www.acca.co.uk

This is the site of the body governing Certified Accountants, and can put you in touch with them.

British Bankers' Association   www.bba.org.uk

This site provides information which will help you understand the various banking considerations a business might encounter at various stages of its business cycle, from starting up to selling or closing down.

British Chambers of Commerce
(Chamber Online)   www.chamberonline.co.uk

This body co-ordinates the work of the many local chambers of commerce and trade, which bring together businesses in local areas, to represent them in matters of local importance – such as rating problems, and fighting business crime.

British Franchise Association www.british-franchise.org.uk

This is the body for franchising operations of all sorts.

British Venture Capitalist Association www.bvca.co.uk

This is the national body representing venture capitalists.

Factors and Discounters Association www.factors.org.uk

This is the body for factoring and invoice discounting finance companies.

Federation of Small Businesses www.fsb.org.uk

This independent body champions the cause of small businesses. It is the UK's largest small business lobby group. The site gives advice and help on all sorts of matters, including things like dealing with late payers.

Institutes of Chartered Accountants www.chartered-accountants.co.uk

This site covers the Institutes in England and Wales, Scotland, and Ireland. It can put you in touch with Chartered Accountants anywhere in these regions.

National Federation of Enterprise Agencies www.nfea.com

This is the national organisation of Enterprise Agencies.

Telework Association www.tca.org.uk

This is Europe's largest network association for teleworkers. The website gives information about all aspects of teleworking, including items about telecottages.

Banks

All the major banks have either dedicated website addresses or dedicated pages of their main website for businesses. The addresses of most of the major banks are listed here.

Alliance and Leicester	www.alliance-leicestercommercialbank.co.uk
Bank of Scotland	www.bankofscotland.co.uk/business
Barclays Bank	www.business.barclays.co.uk
Co-operative Bank	www.co-operativebank.co.uk/business
Halifax	www.halifax.co.uk/businessbanking
HSBC	www.ukbusiness.hsbc.com
Lloyds TSB	www.success4business.co.uk
NatWest	www.natwest.com/smallbusiness
Royal Bank of Scotland	
Small businesses	www.rbs.co.uk/small_business
Corporate banking and financial markets	www.rbs.co.uk/CBFM

Business angels, mentors and incubators

AngelBourse   **www.angelbourse.com**

This organisation facilitates investors buying and selling shares in unquoted companies.

Business Incubation Network   **www.ukbi.co.uk**

An association of 'incubators' giving mentoring and other help to new businesses.

National Business Angels Network   **www.nban.com**

The national organisation for business angels.

The Venture Site Ltd   **www.venturesite.co.uk**

This site links businesses requiring capital with business angels wanting to invest.

Credit management and insurance

Better Payment Practice Group   **www.payontime.co.uk**

This site provides free information and advice on credit management, including a 'business doctor'. This is an organisation set up by the British Chambers of Commerce to encourage businesses to pay debts on time and to advise businesses on better credit management practices.

Bizhelp24   **www.bizhelp24.com**

This site gives advice on cash flow management and many other general business topics.

GerlingNCM   **www.gerlingncm.com**

An insurance company providing credit insurance and credit management advice.

LloydsTSB Commercial Finance   **www.ltsbcf.co.uk**

This is the commercial finance arm of LloydsTSB, offering credit insurance against customer insolvency and late payment.

Fighting fraud

Betesh Fox & Co   **www.fraud.co.uk**

This site gives information on fraud over a wide range of sectors including accounting, banking and insurance.

Control Risks Group   www.crg.com

'Solutions for risks at every stage of business' including sections on IT security and investigation services.

Kroll   www.krollworldwide.com

This site provides up to date business intelligence.

Public Concern at Work   www.pcaw.co.uk

This organisation is a registered charity aimed at 'making whistle-blowing work'.

ScamBusters   www.scambusters.com

This site provides plenty of examples of Internet scams, and the latest news.

US National Fraud Information Centre   www.fraud.org

This site provides information about the latest scams, particularly those on the web.

Independent commercial organisations

Better Business   www.better-business.co.uk

This site is the website of the business magazine of the same name. It gives information on many areas, including producing business plans.

Beyond Bricks   www.beyondbricks.ecademy.com

This is part of the DTI's mentoring initiative. It is particularly slanted towards Internet entrepreneurs.

Bizwise   www.bizwise.co.uk

This site offers a wide range of business advice, at a subscription. You can also use this site to market your business on their register.

Business Finance   www.businessfinance.uk.net

Deskdemon   www.deskdemon.co.uk

This site provides many free office tools, and a Royal Mail postcode search and telephone directory search.

Enterprise Advisory Service International   www.govgrants.com

This organisation provides a service to businesses searching for government grants. It operates on a commercial basis, charging a modest fee to members.

Exchange and Mart   www.exchangeandmart.co.uk

This is the famous source of second hand goods. It has a business section for all kinds of business equipment and services.

Just for Business
www.j4b.co.uk

This site gives access to a database of grants available to businesses. Registered users will also receive regular updates on new developments which may affect them.

Markets Unlocked
www.marketsunlocked.com

This is a UK-based market place for buying and selling. It claims to deal with everything your company buys, everything your company sells, in every industry sector, in every country.

Marylebone Warwick Balfour Group
www.mwb.co.uk

This company specialises in investment in the property sector, looking specifically at underdeveloped property. Sectors such as hotels, leisure parks, retail stores could find help here. It also operates serviced offices.

MTI
www.mtifirms.com

This is a venture capital manager, providing funds in the form of equity capital to high technology businesses.

Pipex Websell
www.websell.pipex.net

This company is a Payment Service Provider, which handles the requirements of accepting credit card and debit card transactions over the Internet.

SPSS
www.spss.com

This company produces software packages of statistical techniques which can be used in financial management, amongst others. Their picturesque name for their product is 'data mining technology'.

Startups
www.startups.co.uk

This site gives advice over a wide range of subjects, from starting up, franchising, through to business structure, the law, business equipment, working at home, and much more.

Virginbiz
www.virginbiz.net

This site helps companies build their own websites.

WJB Chiltern
www.wjbchiltern.com

This firm provides tax and wealth management solutions.

Working From Home
www.wfh.co.uk

This is a British Telecom site, for those working from home. It gives a link to other people working from home. It provides a forum, links to useful sites, and business tips.

■ ⚥ Appendix 2 Investment terms

Classes of shares

The share capital of a company may not consist entirely of shares which carry equal rights. Different classes of shares may exist, which give different rights to their holders. In theory, there could be an infinite number of different types of shares. However, the following are the most common.

Ordinary shares. These give the shareholders the right to participate in the profits of the company by way of a variable dividend declared from time to time. In most cases, dividends are declared twice a year. An interim dividend is declared – usually when the half-yearly results are known. Then, a final dividend is declared after the full year's results are known. Ordinary shares usually carry the greatest degree of risk, compensated by the greatest degree of reward in the company's profits.

Preference shares. These shares have preference in the event of the winding up of a company. However, the reward is potentially not so great as for ordinary shares. It is usually a fixed rate, expressed as a percentage. The preference dividend is paid before any dividend on the ordinary shares. The interest rate paid on these shares is, however, still a dividend. That means that it is dependent on the company making a profit. This is in contrast to loan capital which does not confer ownership of the company, and the interest on which is a charge on the profits of the company, and is paid whether or not the company makes a profit.

However, most preference shares are cumulative in nature. Therefore, if the company cannot pay a preference dividend one year, that means that there is also no dividend on the ordinary shares. However, if sufficient profit is made the following year, the arrears of the preference dividend are made up as well as paying the current preference dividend.

Convertible preference shares. Preference shares may be convertible. This means that they may be converted into ordinary shares at specified dates, and for a pre-determined price. Investors look to this form of share for a relatively high dividend yield with good prospects of capital growth.

Deferred shares. Occasionally a company may issue deferred shares, which have rights deferred below those of ordinary shares.

Redeemable shares. Shares of any class may be redeemable. This means that the company has the right to buy back those shares at specified dates, and at a price which is either pre-determined or the method of calculation of which is pre-determined. The memorandum and articles of the company must have special provisions allowing the company to redeem its shares. Unless specifically stated, shares are not redeemable.

Nominal value of shares

All shares have a nominal value. This is the nominal amount which each share contributes to the capital of the company. Thus, the shares of XYZ plc may be described as Ordinary shares of £1 each. This means that their nominal value is £1. The original issue of the shares by the company is usually for this nominal amount. However, shares may often be issued by the company at a premium (see main text).

Just as the nominal value of a share is not necessarily the amount paid for it, it is also not necessarily the amount that would be received if the company wound up. In the event of a winding up of a company, there is a definite order in which various creditors of the company are paid out. All creditors must be paid out before the shareholders (that is, the owners of the company) can be paid anything. Then, if there are any preference shares, they are paid out before any ordinary shares. Thus, ordinary shares rank last in the queue (unless there are deferred shares). If there is insufficient money left, ordinary shareholders could get back less than the nominal value of the shares.

By the same token, however, if there were more money left over after all others were paid off, the ordinary shareholders would get back more than the nominal value of the shares.

Warrants

Warrants are referred to as instruments. They give the owner of the warrants the right to buy a certain quantity of shares in the company which issues them at a fixed price at some future date. The warrants themselves can be bought and sold through a stockbroker. If they confer the right to buy the shares at a significantly lower price than the market price, then they are obviously valuable, and the price of the warrants would be roughly equivalent to the discount which the warrants represent.

Warrants are generally issued by companies to shareholders in proportion to the number of shares currently held. Because they are treated differently for tax purposes they can be more valuable to shareholders, and therefore can be seen as of greater value than a straightforward dividend. They can be used by the company as a way of raising additional equity capital.

Rights issue

This is a way for a company to raise more equity capital. Existing shareholders are given the right to buy additional shares in the company at a specified price. This price is usually at a discount to the current market price of the shares. If the shareholder does not wish to or have the money to take up the rights – that is, to buy the new shares – the rights certificate may be sold through a stockbroker.

Rights issues are generally expressed in terms of the proportion of new shares offered to existing shareholders, and in terms of the price at which the new shares may be bought. For example, a rights issue could be one new share for every four existing shares at a price of 80p per share.

Scrip issue (or bonus issue)

This is an issue of free new shares by a company. It is expressed in terms of the proportion of new shares issued to the existing holding. Thus, a scrip issue could be, say, three new shares for every ten existing shares.

Debenture stocks

A debenture is a loan which is secured on particular assets of the company issuing it. It is usually redeemable at a specified future date, and bears a fixed rate of interest. Because it is secured on specific assets, there is greater security, and the risk is not so high. The yield on debentures would therefore not be expected to be as great as for unsecured borrowing.

Unsecured loans

Unsecured loans obviously do not have as much security as debentures. They usually carry a fixed interest rate, and a specified redemption date. However, because of their slightly higher risk factor, they would be expected to yield slightly higher than a debenture.

Floating rate loans

These loans can have the same characteristics as debentures or unsecured loans, but the one difference is that the interest rate is not fixed. It is a variable rate, which moves in accordance with market rates of interest.

Convertible loans

These loans carry the option to convert the loans into ordinary shares of the company at specified dates and at a predetermined price. To this extent they are similar to convertible preference shares.

Market sector

In share price listings in newspapers, the companies are divided into different sectors. These represent the type of business carried on by the companies. Thus, typical headings might include banks, electricity, real estate, pharmaceuticals, investment trusts, water, and so on.

This classification enables investors and analysts to compare like with like when making a judgement about a company.

Market capitalisation

This is the measure of the size of the capital invested in the company. It consists of the total number of shares issued by the company multiplied by the share price.

EXAMPLE

> XYZ plc has 10 million shares in issue. The market price of the shares is £5 per share. Therefore the market capitalisation of the company is £50,000,000.

It is obvious that, since the price of the shares can fluctuate from day to day – even from hour to hour – the market capitalisation of the company fluctuates in the same way.

Earnings per share

This is a measure of the profits of the company attributable to each share. The formula is the net after tax profit divided by the number of shares in issue.

EXAMPLE

> The after tax profit of XYZ plc for the year ended 31st December 2003 is £5 million. The company has 10 million shares in issue, so the earnings per share are £0.50.

This measure is invariably judged on the trend over a number of years. The increase or decline in earnings per share will be used by investors to make a judgement on the value of the shares.

Earnings growth

This is a simple measure of how the company's performance has improved or otherwise over the recent past. If the company is able to produce regular, even if unspectacular, growth of its earnings per share year after year, it is a good prospect for investors. If there is a dip in one year only, there may well be a valid reason. Investors will however not be keen to invest in a company of which the earnings per share regularly decrease.

Price–earnings ratio

This is the relationship between the price of a share and the earnings of the company. The earnings are the profits after tax, and attributed to each share, as described above. The measure is the number of times the earnings per share must be multiplied to arrive at the share price.

> The earnings per share of XYZ plc are £0.50. The share price is £5. Therefore, the price–earnings ratio is 10. The share price represents ten years' after tax profits.

This ratio can be compared with the market as a whole, or with other companies in the same industry sector.

Quality of earnings

The price–earnings ratio described above is based on historic figures. For an investor, this information is not as relevant as future figures. However, historic figures are a known quantity, but future earnings are unknown and uncertain.

The price–earnings ratio when based on future forecasts is known as the prospective price–earnings ratio. The quality of earnings is based largely on 'market sentiment'. This stands for what analysts employed by stockbrokers think of the company and its future prospects. If they have doubts about the company, and in particular its ability to maintain the profit levels, then the quality of earnings is said to be low.

Dividend yield

The dividend paid by a company is expressed as an amount per share. To arrive at the dividend yield, the amount of the dividend is expressed as a percentage of the share price.

EXAMPLE

> The dividend for the year ended 31st December 2003 paid by XYZ plc is 20p per share. The market price of the shares is £5 per share, so the dividend yield is 4%.

The yield is calculated on the market price of the shares, not the nominal value of the shares. For example, if the nominal value of the shares is £1, the yield of the 20p dividend would appear to be 20%. However, the market price gives a truer reflection of the value of the shares, and therefore of the real yield.

Dividends are often declared twice a year, as an interim dividend and a final dividend. The dividend yield is calculated on the whole year's dividend, not just the last one to be declared. The comparison of dividend yield is most commonly made with other companies in the same business sector.

Dividend cover

This measure relates to the amount of 'cover' given to the dividends by the earnings of the company.

> The earnings of XYZ plc for the year ended 31st December 2003 are 50p per share. The dividend declared is 20p per share. The dividend cover is therefore 2.5 times.

The lower the dividend cover, the more vulnerable the dividends would be. If the company's profit decreased, there would be more chance of it not being able to pay a dividend in future.

Interest yield

This is a measure of the actual interest rate an investor would achieve on fixed interest stocks and bonds, including government stocks. It is calculated in a similar way to the dividend yield.

EXAMPLE

> XYZ plc has a loan (or debenture) stock. The nominal rate of interest is 12%, but the price of the stock is £150 for every £100 of nominal stock. Thus, by simple division of the interest rate by the price, the interest yield is seen to be 8%.

Interest yields are affected by the prevailing rates of interest, and by the standing of the company which issued the stock or bond. Thus, loan stocks or bonds issued by 'blue chip' companies are said to be 'investment grade' issues. The yield on these is less than the yield on lower grade issues – that is, issues by companies with a slightly lower reputation. The increased yield on lower grade bonds is a reflection of the increased risk attaching to these issues.

Redemption yield

This term relates to the comparison of yields from fixed interest stocks or bonds, including government stocks. The comparison goes one step further than the interest yield calculation. It does this by taking into account the premium or discount in the price of the stock or bond. In effect, what it measures is the total return on the investment if it were held until the redemption date.

EXAMPLE

> The XYZ plc stock in the example above shows an interest yield of 8%. However, the redemption yield would be quite different if the stock had, say, six years to redemption compared to twenty years to redemption. The redemption yield with six years to redemption would be 2.4%, but the redemption yield with twenty years to redemption would be 6.3%.

The redemption yield calculation gives a truer comparison of the real yield on interest bearing stocks or bonds.

Net asset value

This is simply the total assets of the company less all of the liabilities – be they short-term liabilities, long-term liabilities, provisions for losses, and so on.

Net asset value per share

This is the net asset value of the company divided by the number of ordinary shares in issue. This gives a theoretical value of the assets represented by each share. The comparison of this value with the share price gives a discount or premium. This measure is particularly important in property companies and investment trust companies.

◤ Answers to exercises

CHAPTER 2

EXERCISE 2.1

ANSWERS

	Current year	Previous year
(a)	£500 million	£450 million
(b)	£505 million	£452 million
(c)	£70 million	£65 million

EXERCISE 2.2

ANSWERS

	Current year	Previous year
(a)	£65 million	£55 million
(b)	£530 million	£464 million
(c)	£385 million	£320 million

EXERCISE 2.3

ANSWER

(a) The share capital has increased, so there has been an issue of new shares.

(b) The nominal value of the new shares issued was £30 million (that is, £150 million less £120 million).

(c) The shares were issued at a premium of 33.3% (that is, the nominal value of the new share issue was £30 million, and the share premium is shown as £10 million).

(d) The total raised by the new share issue was £40 million (that is, £30 million plus £10 million).

(e) The company has paid off £5 million of its long-term debt (that is, £85 million less £80 million).

(f) The company has invested £50 million in new fixed assets (that is, £400 million less £350 million).

(g) The actual gross profit in money terms has remained the same as the previous year, but the gross profit percentage has decreased by 4.4%

(h) The total income of the company from all sources has increased by £53 million (that is, £505 million less £452 million).

(i) The net profit in money terms has decreased by £3 million, and in percentage terms by 2.8%.

(j) The overheads have increased in money terms by £6 million, but they have decreased as a percentage of turnover by 2.1%.

(k) The working capital has increased by £10 million.

(l) The total capital of the company has increased by £65 million.

EXERCISE 2.4

SOME ANSWERS

- Why was the overall gross profit lower in percentage terms and in absolute terms than both the previous year and the budget?
- Why was the gross profit on fuel sales so much lower than budgeted? Is there a possibility of a leak in the pumps or tanks?
- Why were new car sales not up to the budgeted figure, and why is the gross profit percentage less than both the budgeted figure and the previous year's figure? Does the dealership agreement with the car company need revision?
- Why did the second hand car sales underperform in sales volume, and profit rate? Does this underperformance reflect the abilities of the salespeople?
- Why did the servicing and spares department underperform in sales volume and profit rate compared to the budget? Could there be any inaccuracies in recording things like transfers of materials between departments?
- Is it worth continuing the fuel sales, given that they produce so little gross profit? Could the space taken up be better used for something else?

These are just some of the questions that a closer look at the analysis figures might produce.

EXERCISE 2.5

ANSWER

There are many more variables – in addition to all the variables which affect the gross profit rate there are also the overhead expenses – all of these affect the net profit percentage.

EXERCISE 2.6

SUGGESTIONS

- Many NPOs (such as local government departments and other public bodies) receive grants, and are responsible for spending the money. Their performance measures would relate to the effectiveness of their spending, and comparisons with budgets would be important.
- Charities commonly monitor the amounts spent on core projects, to advance their aims, as against administration and fund raising expenses.
- Some organisations exist to carry out certain functions, to make an impact of some sort in a particular place, or in a particular environment. They need to develop some performance measures to indicate the effectiveness of their activities in achieving the aims.

CHAPTER 3

DISCUSSION QUESTION 3.1

SUGGESTION

Non-financial managers and directors are often over-optimistic about future prospects, particularly when the project is one they have instigated. They might be tempted to put reliance on their most optimistic assumptions. The same thing can often colour their view of the presentation of reports of past transactions – perhaps to boost the share price, or to influence the bank manager when applying for a loan. They can therefore find the concept of prudence hard to understand, or to be reconciled to. Nevertheless, prudence is a generally expected principle in external accounts.

EXERCISE 3.1

- *Retail shop*   Goods are bought and resold at a profit. The variable costs are the costs of the goods bought in for resale. The fixed costs are the establishment costs of the shop and all overheads thereof, including salaries of the shop staff (who must be in the shop whether any sales are made or not).
- *Manufacturing business*   The variable costs include the raw materials which are manufactured into the finished product, and also the wages cost of the production workers, since these are needed to convert the raw materials into the finished product. Certain factory costs (such as maintenance of machinery, power costs, and so on) are also variable costs, since they are needed to keep the factory running, and would not be incurred if the factory was not producing the finished goods. Fixed costs would include the overheads of the business, including sales costs, administration, administrative office costs, and so on.

CHAPTER 5

QUESTION 5.1

This is the order of their liquidity. This means the order in which they can be turned into cash. Thus, stocks of raw materials have to go through all the processes before they are finished goods. While they are going through this process, they are called 'work in progress'. When they are ready to be sold, they are finished goods. When they are sold to customers, they become converted into debtors. Only when the customer pays, is the money actually ready for the business to use.

EXERCISE 5.1

SUGGESTIONS

The obvious cost is the cost of the money tied up in stock being carried on the business's shelves. Other indirect costs include the increased administrative cost of carrying stocks. Storage space is needed for stock, and the cost of space can be extremely high. Handling costs increase as the volume of stock increases. In addition, there are the possibilities of pilferage, damage and obsolescence. Therefore, if excess stock is being carried, these costs and risks are correspondingly higher.

If a business carries twice as much stock as necessary, it may need extra staff to record and control the excess stock, and the risk of pilferage and obsolescence is doubled.

EXERCISE 5.2

In a manufacturing business, too little stock could mean the whole production process grinding to a halt. This could mean many production workers becoming idle, and there are further knock-on effects down the line. The 'worst case scenario' is of a manufacturer not being able to complete production of an order, and failing to meet the contract terms. The sale, and possibly the customer, is lost, and the business is left with a lot of worthless part-finished work in progress.

For a retail or wholesale business, not having adequate stock for customers is the kiss of death. They will simply go elsewhere if they can get the item straight away, rather than having to order something and wait for its arrival. Too little stock means a lost sale, and possibly a lost customer.

In whatever business type, being short of stock could mean ordering a special delivery at short notice, possibly incurring extra transport costs, and having to buy at a dearer price than the normal terms.

EXERCISE 5.3

Annual usage is 156,000. Therefore weekly usage is 156,000/52 = 3,000 items. The lead time is four weeks, so the re-order level should be four weeks of the usage, plus the minimum level. This works out to 13,000 items.
This can be expressed as a formula as follows:

$$(L \times U) + M$$

where:

U = usage (in weeks, or days)
L = lead time (in weeks, or days)
M = minimum quantity

EXERCISE 5.4

To utilise the normal terms of payment gives an extra 46 days of credit. The cost of this extra credit is 2%. This can be annualised by calculating:

$$365/46 \times 2\% = 15.87\%$$

This is slightly more than the company's present cost of finance. It represents the cost of using the full payment terms. Over one year, this would cost the company £1,870 (i.e. 1.87% – the difference between the company's existing finance cost and the cost of not taking the discount.)

EXERCISE 5.5

The cost of extending credit to customers includes the following elements:

- *The finance cost.* When a business extends credit to customers it is in effect giving them an interest free short-term loan. This must be financed, and the direct cost to the business is the rate of interest charged by the bank on overdrafts.
- *Opportunity cost.* Even if the business does not need to borrow from the bank on overdraft, there is a lost opportunity cost of the money sitting in its customers' bank accounts which could be in their own account, and earning interest. Another, perhaps more important opportunity cost is that the money could have been used in some more important way inside the business itself, for example, by investment in some form of business opportunity.
- *Administration cost.* The cost of administering credit control includes salaries of the staff needed (or in a small business the lost opportunity of management time involved), the stationery and postage involved, the telephone calls, and so on
- *Bad debt* cost. All the above costs are incurred for all debts, and when a debt is written off as bad, that is a further cost.

EXERCISE 5.6

Present situation:

Credit given	$60/365 \times £1,000,000 = £164,383$	
Finance cost –	$£164,383 \times 14\% = £23,014$	
Bad debts		£ 5,000
Total cost		£28,114

Situation if discount system in force:

Credit given	$60/365 \times £1,000,000/2 = £82,192$	
Finance cost	$£82,192 \times 14\% = £11,507$	
Cash discount	$£1000,000/2 \times 2\% = £10,000$	
Bad debts		£ 2,500
Total cost		£24,007

The benefit in offering the cash discount, if all the assumptions were correct, is £4,107. The credit control costs could also show savings, as bad debts reduce, and fewer customers take the full credit.

EXERCISE 5.7

Processes that hold up an invoice could include:

- Physical checking of quantities, weights or measures
- Checking quality
- Checking against original order and stores requisition
- Checking calculations on the invoice
- Passage through the accounts department purchase ledger
- Authorisation for payment.

EXERCISE 5.8

There should be specific wordings for accounts that are overdue by specific times:

- A general reminder if the account is not settled within the normal credit period.
- A stronger letter if it is still not settled within the next month.
- A final letter threatening action for recovery.

EXERCISE 5.9

Factors include the following:

- The nature of the business,
- The cost and availability of borrowing,
- The general economic climate,
- The cyclical nature of trade,
- Seasonal variations,
- Relationships with suppliers,
- The opportunity cost of investing cash.

EXERCISE 5.10

ANSWER

Stockholding period

$$\frac{((b) + (e))/2}{(f)} \times 365 = \quad 83 \text{ days}$$

Debtor days

$$\frac{(i)}{(a)} \times 365 = \quad \underline{76 \text{ days}}$$

Subtotal 159 days

Less Creditor days

$$\frac{(l)}{(c)} \times 365 = \quad \underline{73 \text{ days}}$$

Operating cash cycle $\underline{86 \text{ days}}$

CHAPTER 6

EXERCISE 6.1

Some of the techniques which can be used to make pricing decisions are as follows:

- Customer research – face-to-face or telephone interviews,
- Analysis of competitors' pricing,
- Activity based costing,
- Break-even analysis,
- Measurement of price sensitivity,
- Research based on surveys,
- Trade-off analysis,
- Economic value analysis.

EXERCISE 6.2

SUGGESTION

Businesses sometimes use the principle of 'loss leaders' – selling an item at or below cost to attract customers. For example, supermarkets often sell items such as bread or specially promoted items cheaply to get customers into the store. The loss leader items are placed strategically so that customers must visit nearly all parts of the store to get to the loss leader items. This encourages extra sales of items with a normal profit margin.

EXERCISE 6.3

SUGGESTION

The following questions might be asked, amongst others:

- Why was more rubber and less steel used?
- Does it point to some malfunction in the process?
- Was the original estimate wrong?
- Is there any wastage which can be rectified?
- If the quantity of steel used is less than the standard amount, will it cause any defect in the quality of the finished product? Is the customer likely to reject the finished article?

EXERCISE 6.4

The main taxes are:

Income Tax
Capital Gains Tax
Inheritance Tax
Corporation Tax
Value Added Tax
National Insurance
Stamp Duty
Customs Duty
Excise Duties (for example on petrol, tobacco products, alcoholic beverages)
Business Rates
Road Tax

EXERCISE 6.5

First, the goods must be requisitioned, normally by the stores department, using the criteria seen in Chapter 5, concerning re-order levels. The receipt of goods would be checked against the delivery note. That would then be checked against the order sent out. The invoice when received would be checked against the delivery note, and order. The accuracy would be checked, and the invoice then passed to the purchase ledger department for recording. The monthly balancing of the ledgers then triggers the writing of the cheque, which would then be signed by an authorised person.

EXERCISE 6.6

SUGGESTIONS

- Tax authorities, such as the Inland Revenue and Customs and Excise.
- Banks and other lenders.
- Prospective purchasers of the business, in a takeover.
- Suppliers to the company, wishing to establish credit terms.
- Customers of the company.

EXERCISE 6.7

The consequences of a qualified report depend on the exact nature of the qualification. A relatively minor qualification may not cause too many ripples. However, a serious qualification would first of all cause concern to the shareholders. The auditor's report is their assurance that their company is being run well on their behalf by the directors and managers.

A serious qualification could lead to a fall in the value of the company's shares, and therefore be of major concern to the shareholders. This in turn could lead to calls for the removal of some or all of the directors or managers.

CHAPTER 7

EXERCISE 7.1

Investors put their money into businesses for a variety of reasons. Some may want maximum income immediately. Some may look for an income that has a reasonable chance of increasing from year to year, to try to keep up with inflation, or to beat it. Others may look for capital growth in the value of the investment. Yet others may look for a balanced approach of an increasing income and some capital growth.

EXERCISE 7.2

SUGGESTIONS

- Reasonable market capitalisation.
- As low a price/earnings ratio as possible.
- Steady growth of earnings – organic growth, not just from acquisitions.
- Reliable quality of earnings.
- Good dividend yield.
- Adequate dividend cover.

EXERCISE 7.3

The payback time for this project is 50 months (£10,000/£200). This assumes that the additional costs of retaining the old van remain constant.

EXERCISE 7.4

The payback time for this project is 20 months. Note however that this calculation assumes that the profit per unit will stay constant. It also introduces constraints of resources: can the business produce an extra 5,000 units per month on existing capacity of employees, factory space, machinery and equipment, and administrative staff?

EXERCISE 7.5

The total profit from the project is £25,000. Over 5 years, this averages £5,000 per year. The cost of the project is averaged at £10,000 per year, and the average return is therefore 50%.

EXERCISE 7.6

Here, the total figures are the same, and this method yields the same overall result of 50%. However, the difference is that the income starts to build up over the years, and most of the income is received in the later years.

EXERCISE 7.7

The present value is £100. The figures are the same as used in Example 7.1.

EXERCISE 7.8

The cash flow (not discounted) is:

	Cash outflow	Cash inflow
Now	£1,000,000	
Year 1		£300,000
Year 2		£300,000
Year 3		£350,000
Year 4		£350,000
Year 5		£350,000

Now, the discount factors are added:

	Cash outflow	Cash inflow	Factor	NPV	
Now	£1,000,000		1	£1,000,000	
Year 1		£300,000	0.9091		£272,730
Year 2		£300,000	0.8264		£247,920
Year 3		£350,000	0.7513		£262,955
Year 4		£350,000	0.6830		£239,050
Year 5		£350,000	0.6209		£217,315
				£1,000,000	£1,239,970

Deducting the final columns shows a net present value to the business of £239,970.

EXERCISE 7.9

The variables are:

- Initial outlay
- Project life span
- Sales income from project:
  - Sales volume
  - Sales price
- Costs of the project:
  - Direct, variable costs
  - Overhead costs
  - Finance costs

EXERCISE 7.10

(a) £1,239,970 – this is simply the same value as shown in the credit column of the NPV calculations
(b) 84,175 units (to the nearest 5 units)
(c) £8.42 (to the nearest penny)
(d) 33.67%
(e) £113,300
(f) £188,270 (to the nearest £10)

These answers have been calculated using a spreadsheet.

EXERCISE 7.11

ANSWER – (MOST SENSITIVE FIRST)

1st equal	Sales volume (15.2% below)
	Sales price (15.2% below)
	Gross profit (15.2% below)
4th	Cost of investment (24% above)
5th	Normal overheads (126.6% above)
6th	Marketing and promotion (276.5% above)

The most sensitive variables are those which have the lowest percentage variance between the expected figure and the figure which would reduce the NPV to zero. In general terms, these variances do not indicate a high risk level.

EXERCISE 7.12

SUGGESTIONS

- The investment of £1,000,000 could be broken down into cost of machinery, vehicles, other assets, installation costs, downtime, disruption to existing production, and so on.

- The additional sales forecast could be broken down into home sales and export sales, and in each of these categories, further analysis could be done on the size of the total market, and the expected market share. This has an obvious inter-relationship with the marketing and promotion costs.
- The sales price could be further analysed to test market elasticity of demand, and the possibility of price increases (or decreases) during the life of the project.
- The direct costs could be broken down into the different elements – materials costs, labour costs, factory costs, research and development costs, direct overheads, and so on. These will have an effect on the gross profit margin.
- The overheads could be broken down to their constituent elements, and particular attention paid to finance costs.
- The additional marketing and promotion costs in years 1 and 2 could be tested for the different possibilities of marketing and promotion activities, advertising campaigns and so on.

CHAPTER 8

EXERCISE 8.1

It is easy to see the difficulties of measuring future cash flows. Future events are highly uncertain, as we saw in Chapter 7. In addition, preparing any sort of forecast of future cash flows requires certain assumptions to be made. If a company is looking at forecasts of another company's future cash flows, how much reliance can it place on the figures?

But why should the valuation of assets be difficult? The answer can be seen in the various methods which might be used to place a value on the assets, and the existence of assets which are not shown on the balance sheet.

EXERCISE 8.2

Think about the values used in the balance sheet figures. The notes to the accounts will show the basis of valuation of assets and depreciation if they vary materially from normal accounting standards.

Fixed assets are usually shown at historic cost less depreciation. If the assets were bought a long time ago, their cost will have been relatively low compared to current values, and there will have been many years' depreciation written off. They will therefore stand in the balance sheet at a very low value. Even assets bought fairly recently will have a balance sheet figure which is probably nothing like their current value or replacement cost.

Current assets are not usually so problematic, but even those figures can vary significantly from current values or replacement costs. Stock, for example, is valued for balance sheet purposes at the lower of cost or realisable market value. Work in progress is valued on a similar basis, but the valuation may vary considerably depending on the stage of completion of the work. Debtors are usually stated at their book figures, with some provision for bad and doubtful debts. Once again, these figures may not have much relevance to a value for merger or takeover purposes.

EXERCISE 8.3

The main drawback is that this method is not based on any evidence that the company is a going concern. The values used are what the company might expect on a forced sale of the assets sold piecemeal, not the total assets of the business as a whole. The value of the assets therefore would be considerably less than the value on a going concern basis.

EXERCISE 8.4

It may be fairly easy to obtain replacement values for some items such as machinery, vehicles, and so on. However, other items, particularly intangible assets such as goodwill, patents, and brand names can be difficult to value realistically, and the process can be very expensive.

EXERCISE 8.5

Sometimes, non-economic factors may affect share prices. Football club shares, for example, may be in demand by supporters of the club, not for the hope of future returns, but out of loyalty, or for the expectation of privileged rights to obtain match tickets.

Market prices are relevant to relatively small purchases and sales of shares. A large public company, for example may have millions of shares, but it would be unusual for a purchase or sale of its shares on the Stock Exchange to be of such a quantity as to represent a material proportion of its capital. Therefore, the quoted share price is only appropriate for share dealings of non-material amounts. For a purchase or sale of a significant proportion of the capital of a particular company, the normal share price would not be relevant.

Predator companies wish to gain control of the target company, so the number of shares involved will necessarily make up a material proportion of the total capital. The predator company would expect to have to pay a premium to existing share holders over and above the quoted share price in order to gain control.

EXERCISE 8.6

First of all, the company must be in the same business sector and industry. Thus, it is no good comparing the value of shares in a banking company with those of a motor manufacturer.

For a fair comparison, the company should be as similar as possible to the company to be valued. For example, its risk profile should be similar, and this is to some extent tied in with the management style. It is very difficult to find two companies run in exactly the same way. Similarly, the companies compared should have a similar track record, in regard to past growth and dividend policy. It is also probable that the unquoted company will have a different policy in relation to director's remuneration from the quoted company. There are therefore many adjustments to make to the bare figures before attempting a comparative valuation.

It is unlikely that the companies to be compared will be of similar size. If a quoted company is being compared to an unquoted company, the quoted company will usually, but not necessarily, be much larger in terms of business activity, and of market capitalisation.

Finally, if all the other factors were matched perfectly, it could not be said that the values of the shares of the two companies are identical. The very fact of the shares being quoted on a recognised market means that those shares are more marketable than non-quoted shares. The degree of marketability is a further factor influencing the value of the shares, and the unquoted company's shares will always be at a discount to the quoted company's shares.

EXERCISE 8.7

Many factors in the generation of profit are uncertain, and others are the result of management policy. Other items, including particularly the dividend policy and the amounts invested in new assets, or realised from the sale of assets, are even more at the mercy of the management's policies.

EXERCISE 8.8

We have already seen above that this could be done as a defence against an unwelcome takeover bid. The company may sell off its 'crown jewels' to make it less attractive to a predator company, and improve its cash reserves.

Demerger may also be a response to problems of one sort or another, such as improving the company's gearing, or resolving a cash shortage. Another problem that could be solved by divestment is the higher risk profile of a particular part of a company's business, which could be adversely affecting market sentiment towards the company as a whole. Divestment means that the high risk element is taken out of the company's profile, and market sentiment improved.

Conglomerate companies often find that the difficulties of managing diverse businesses mean that the market undervalues the assets of a particular division, and divestment may be the answer.

However, demerger may also be carried out for a more positive reason. Management may decide, on reviewing its strategy, that a particular division or operation is no longer compatible with its objectives, or it may decide on a new set of objectives and a new strategy, and a particular part of its business no longer suits the new objectives. For example, management may decide that in the past, it has diversified too much, and now wishes to focus on its core activities. The peripheral activities may therefore be sold off. The management of the company may also decide that selling off a part of the business will allow a better, and more profitable, use of available resources.

EXERCISE 8.9

Some solutions are:

- Persuading employees to accept revised working and pay conditions. This can be successful if it is seen to be a temporary measure.
- Outsourcing. Some of the tasks done by employees could be done by external sources – sub-contractors, and so on
- Seasonal working could be a solution in some businesses.

CHAPTER 10

EXERCISE 10.1

The main differences are:

- Providers of loan capital (lenders) are not members of the company.
- Lenders have no further claim on the assets of the company other than as provided by the terms of their contract with the company.
- Lenders have a prior claim on the company, and their demands must be met before any proceeds can be paid to shareholders.
- Interest paid on loan capital is tax deductible.

EXERCISE 10.2

The most readily realisable and suitable asset is land or property. Its value is easy to measure, and does not tend to decline in normal circumstances.

EXERCISE 10.3

SUGGESTIONS

- The company must send the lenders financial reports.
- The company must not issue any additional loan capital without the permission of the existing lenders.
- If any assets are subject to a charge, those assets have to be specifically insured.
- The company must not dispose of certain assets without the permission of the lenders.
- Certain payments, such as dividends to ordinary shareholders, or payments to directors, should be subject to restrictions.
- Minimum and maximum levels must exist for certain key ratios such as liquidity or gearing.

CHAPTER 11

EXERCISE 11.1

SUGGESTION

If investors are assured of a market to sell their shares or buy extra ones, they are more likely to invest in a company.

EXERCISE 11.2

ANSWER

It sells 1 million shares at £1.50 each, and therefore receives £1,500,000 from the issue of the shares.

The £1 million will be credited to share capital in its accounts, and the £500,000 will be credited to the share premium account, which must be shown separately in the company's financial statements.

EXERCISE 11.3

SUGGESTION

The company has to set the number and price of the shares offered for sale. If the public perceive the price of the shares to be too high, the issue may be undersubscribed, and the company will not raise enough money. If the price is perceived to be too low, the offer will be oversubscribed, and the company will have to turn away many potential investors, and not raise as much as it could have done.

EXERCISE 11.4

ANSWER

Existing holding	100 shares – value	£200
Additional offer	100 shares – cost	£180
Total new holding	200 shares	£380

The value of each share is now therefore £1.90 each.

The offer price is	£1.80 each
The value of the rights is therefore	10p each

EXERCISE 11.5

For the shareholders, the transaction means that they have more cash, but fewer or no shares in the company. There could be Capital Gains Tax consequences, since the repurchase by the company counts as a disposal for Capital Gains Tax purposes.

For the company, the capital structure of the company could be radically different after a repurchase. The gearing would be changed, because once the shares have been repurchased and cancelled, the share capital of the company will have been reduced, while the borrowings remain unchanged. The lender or lenders may be concerned to see this disruption of the gearing, and consequent increase in their risk exposure.

EXERCISE 11.6

The shareholders may incur tax consequences, particularly if the dividend puts their income into a higher tax rate. Market sentiment may not react well to special dividends, since this interrupts the normal pattern of dividends, and may create expectations of a similar level of ordinary dividends in future. If those extra future dividends are not forthcoming, the share price may suffer.

On the other hand, the shareholders do not lose their holding of shares in the company, in whole or in part.

EXERCISE 11.7

ANSWER

The dividends paid will be £200,000. The profits are £500,000. Therefore the dividend is covered 2.5 times.

EXERCISE 11.8

SUGGESTION

There are two main reasons why this is considered prudent practice.

1. Retaining profits, sometimes referred to as 'ploughing the profits back' into the business, is a good source of internal finance.
2. A good level of dividend cover means that dividends are not liable to fluctuate severely – particularly when profits vary.

EXERCISE 11.9

Company ABC Ltd distributed all of its profits in the first year. This means that the dividend was covered once. Company XYZ's dividend was covered 2.5 times.

In the second year, company ABC Ltd does not have any accumulated profits brought forward, because it has paid them all out in the first year. Therefore it can only declare a maximum dividend of 35p on its shares for the second year, which is less than the first year's dividend.

Company XYZ Ltd retained £300,000 of its profits from the first year, and with the profits from the second year, it now has £650,000 accumulated profits in the second year. It could, in theory, declare a dividend of up to 65p per share. In practice it can easily maintain its dividend of 20p per share, even increase it slightly, and still have profits retained in the business.

Glossary

Accounting conventions	Conventions taken as normal in the drawing up of financial statements
Asset turnover	A measure of the usage of fixed assets in generating turnover
Audit	Independent examination of accounts
Bill of exchange	Instrument giving credit to purchaser of goods or services
Break-even point	The level of turnover at which the income and expenses will be equal
Budget	Method of controlling costs and income by comparison with forecasts
Business angels	Individuals offering finance and assistance
Cost accounting	Methods of arriving at costs of items produced
Credit control	Control of monies owing from debtors
Current assets	Short-term assets which change from day to day in the course of business
Current liabilities	Short-term liabilities
Current ratio	The relationship between current assets and current liabilities
Discount	Reduction in price given as incentive
Discounted cash flow	Method of appraising projects
Equity	The share capital of a company
Factoring	Method of raising finance on book debts
Finance lease	Means of financing the purchase of an asset
Gearing	The relationship between loan capital and share capital
Hire purchase	Means of financing the purchase of an asset
Internal controls	Systems of administrative checks on aspects of operations
Internal rate of return	Method of appraising projects

Invoice discounting	Method of raising finance on book debts
Loan covenants	Conditions in a loan agreement to ensure security for the lender
Merger	Combination of two similar sized businesses
Organic growth	Business growth from internal sources – not from acquisitions of other businesses
Overdraft	Arrangement with bank to permit the customer to draw in excess of the deposited funds
Overtrading	Lack of cash resources often encountered in growing businesses
Project appraisal	Methods of appraising the economic viability of future projects
Quick ratio	The relationship between all current assets except stock and work in progress to current liabilities
Return on capital employed	Profitability ratio showing the relationship between profit (before interest and taxation) and all long-term capital employed.
Rights issue	Issue of shares to existing shareholders at preferential rates
Sale and leaseback	Method of fund raising by selling assets and then leasing them back
Scrip issue	Issue of free shares to existing shareholders
Statistical analysis	Method of using ratios between key figures in financial statements
Stock turnover	A measure of how quickly stock is used in the business
SWOT analysis	Analysis of strengths, weaknesses, opportunities and threats
Takeover	Acquisition of one business by another
Term matching	The process of matching finance provided with the object for which it is provided
Treasury management	The management of surplus cash resources
Venture capital	Equity finance offered by institutional investors
Warrants	Instruments giving the right to buy shares at a fixed price at a specified date
Working capital	Current assets less current liabilities

■ ▼ Further reading

AIRMIC, ALARM, and IRM, A Risk Management Standard, 2002.

Arnold, G., *Corporate Financial Management*, Financial Times/Pitman, 1998

Atrill, P., *Financial Management for Non-Specialists*, Financial Times/Prentice Hall, 2000

Bass, R., *Credit Management*, Nelson Thornes, 1994

Brigham, E. *et al.*, *Intermediate Financial Management*, Thomson Learning, 1999

Broadbent, M. and Cullen, J., *Managing Financial Resources*, Butterworth-Heinemann, 1997

Cox, D. and Fardon, M., *Management of Finance*, Osborne Books, 1997

Davies, D., *The Art of Managing Finance*, McGraw Hill, 1997

Kind, J., *Accounting and Finance for Managers*, Kogan Page, 1999

Lumby, S. and Jones, C., *Investment Appraisal and Financial Decisions*, Chapman & Hall, 1999

McKeon, P. and Gough, L., *The Finance Manual for Non-Financial Managers*, Prentice Hall, 2000

McLaney, E., *Business Finance*, Financial Times/Prentice Hall, 2000

McLaney, E., *Business Finance: Theory and Practice*, Pitman, 1997

Palepu, K., 'Predicting takeover targets, a methodological and empirical analysis', *Journal of Accounting and Economics*, 8, 1986, pp. 3–55

Rees, B., *Financial Analysis*, Prentice Hall, 1995

Samuels, J. *et al.*, *Financial Management and Decision Making*, International Thomson Business Press, 1998

UK 200 Group, *The Financial Controls Handbook*, The Daily Telegraph, 1997

Van Horne, J. and Wachwicz, J., *Fundamentals of Financial Management*, Prentice Hall, 1995

Whiteley, J., *Going for Self Employment*, How To Books, 2003

Whiteley, J., *Small Business Tax Guide*, How To Books, 2003

▼ Index